S0-ADI-949

AGAPE, EROS, GENDER

Issues of gender and sexuality have recently come to the fore in all humanities disciplines, and this book reflects this broad interdisciplinary situation, although its own standpoint is a theological one. In contrast to many contemporary feminist theologies, gender and sexuality (*eros*) are here understood within a distinctively Christian context characterized by the reality of *agape* – the New Testament's term for the comprehensive divine-human love that includes the relationship of man and woman within its scope. The central problem is addressed by way of key Pauline texts relating to gender and sexuality (1 Corinthians 11, Romans 7, Ephesians 5), texts whose influence on western theology and culture has been enduring and pervasive. They are read here in conjunction with later theological and non-theological texts that reflect that influence – ranging from Augustine and Barth to Virginia Woolf, Freud and Irigaray. As in the author's previous books, the intention is to practise a less restrictive approach to biblical interpretation which locates the texts within broad theological and intellectual horizons.

FRANCIS WATSON is Professor of New Testament Exegesis at the University of Aberdeen. He took his D.Phil. at Oxford and from 1984 to 1999 was Lecturer in New Testament Studies and Reader in Biblical Theology at King's College London. Professor Watson's previous books are *Paul, Judaism and the Gentiles* (1986), *Text, Church and World* (1994), and *Text and Truth* (1997).

AGAPE, EROS, GENDER

Towards a Pauline sexual ethic

FRANCIS WATSON

CABRINI COLLEGE LIBRARY
610 KING OF PRUSSIA ROAD
RADNOR, PA 19087

CAMBRIDGE
UNIVERSITY PRESS

BT
708
.W38
2000

#42580073

PUBLISHED BY THE PRESS SYNDICATE OF THE UNIVERSITY OF CAMBRIDGE
The Pitt Building, Trumpington Street, Cambridge United Kindgom

CAMBRIDGE UNIVERSITY PRESS
The Edinburgh Building, Cambridge CB2 2RU, UK   http://www.cup.cam.ac.uk
40 West 20th Street, New York, NY 10011–4211, USA   http://www.cup.org
10 Stamford Road, Oakleigh, Melbourne 3166, Australia

© Francis Watson 2000

The book is in copyright. Subject to statutory exception and to the provisions of
relevant collective licensing agreements, no reproduction of any part may take place
without the written permission of Cambridge University Press.

First published 2000

Printed in the United Kingdom at the University Press, Cambridge

Typeset in Baskerville 11/12.5pt   [CE]

A catalogue record for this book is available from the British Library

ISBN 0 521 66263 x hardback

610 KING OF PRUSSIA ROAD
RADNOR, PA 19087

Contents

Preface

Disciplinary boundaries within the theological curriculum are a necessary concession to the complexity of the subject matter and the inevitable limitations of the individual scholar. It makes good pragmatic sense that one person should be a New Testament scholar, another a systematic theologian, and another an ethicist – so long as the boundaries remain open, ensuring freedom of movement between the disciplines. But where boundaries are closed, they define a subject matter which is now held to be the exclusive preserve of a single group of scholars. Communication between the disciplines is subject to severe restrictions. Thus, the New Testament scholar becomes incapable of serious theological reflection on the New Testament texts. The systematic theologian makes only cursory forays into the fields of the biblical scholar or ethicist, and may even believe that an apology is due for trespassing in someone else's professional domain. The ethicist may seek to develop a Christian ethical reflection that shows scant regard for any theological or biblical foundations. In this way, 'theology' becomes a flag of convenience for a number of related but basically autonomous disciplines. All sense that Christian theology is ultimately concerned with a single, simple subject matter disappears.

This book represents my third attempt to develop an interdisciplinary approach to biblical interpretation that refuses to be deterred by the warning notices that biblical scholars have posted at regular intervals along the boundaries of their discipline: notices that warn against allowing contemporary concerns to undermine the integrity of pure scholarship, and that prohibit all serious theological engagement with the biblical texts – on the grounds that such an engagement is inevitably partisan, confessional and divisive. Insofar as they identify a number of possible dangers, these warnings are certainly not groundless. But they should never have been regarded as absolute laws, defining the limits of the discipline and closing it in on itself. They are at best no more than guidelines for interdisciplinary dialogue, and they may or may not be relevant in any given instance.

This particular exercise in interdisciplinary dialogue takes the form of a study in Christian sexual ethics which proceeds by way of a series of readings of three selected Pauline texts. The intention is not to offer an exegesis of the Pauline texts to which is appended, secondarily, some consideration of their 'contemporary relevance'. Ascertaining what the texts say is indeed a necessary first step, and at this point standard exegetical methods are indispensable. But in the last resort, to interpret is *to use the texts to think with*. To confine interpretation to the ever more precise reproduction or retracing of what the texts say is to neglect their canonical function, which is to *generate* thought, not to restrict it. Their genre as canonical texts demands that they be set *within broad horizons*, and not merely returned to an 'original historical situation' in the first century.

The Pauline texts relating to sexuality and gender are few, brief and cryptic. They often fail to say what we think they should say, and we sometimes wish they had left unsaid what they actually do say. They are a problem for us. Yet they have been extraordinarily influential. Along with the texts of Genesis 1–3 which they themselves have mediated to subsequent Christian tradition, these Pauline texts are deeply embedded in Christian ethical reflection, from Tertullian and Augustine to Barth, and beyond. A rich heritage, a living tradition for us to enter into? Or does the extent of these texts' influence simply increase our unease? If these texts do not say what they ought to say, and say what they ought not to say, then their blindnesses and errors will be writ large across the entire tradition they have helped to shape. In these circumstances, a contemporary Christian sexual ethics might do better simply to *abandon* Paul (after subjecting him to the necessary critique). A movement '*towards* a Pauline sexual ethic' is surely unthinkable? 'Away from', perhaps, or (preferably) 'beyond', but not 'towards'?

In this book, I shall not be reading the selected Pauline texts uncritically. But my readings are governed by the assumption that the appropriate criteria for judging them are available to us only in and through the texts themselves, in their testimony to the reality of the divine agape. If agape – the inner-trinitarian love opened up to human participation in Jesus and his Spirit – is the beginning and end of Christian faith and living, then it is agape that must provide the final criteria for Christian reflection on sexuality and gender. But this agape is not present to us in unmediated form, and can only be articulated through engagement with the canonical texts. What these texts say or do not say about sexuality and gender must be read in the light of their unique and irreplaceable testimony to the divine agape that has taken the form of a corresponding human agape, in Jesus and, through his Spirit, in a community in which there are both men and women, together and not apart from one another. These men and women are no strangers to the reality of eros. But they practise together a qualitatively different love, whose origin and pattern is the divine love to which they are constantly redirected, in worship, preaching and sacrament, and in their mutual presence to one another. 'We love, because he first loved us' (1 Jn. 4.19): whatever is said about sexuality and gender must conform to that confession.

Yet there must be engagement not only with the text but also with the world – the 'secular' world which, especially in recent times, has had much to say on the topics of sexuality and gender that is directly relevant to the interpretation of the canonical texts. In each of the three parts of this book, a verse-by-verse theological interpretation of a selected Pauline text is therefore preceded by a reading of a modern text that deals with closely related issues in the conceptuality and idiom of our own times. Although ostensibly 'secular' in orientation, these modern texts belong – consciously or unconsciously – within the *Wirkungsgeschichte* of the Pauline texts with which they are here linked. Texts by Woolf, Freud and Irigaray will naturally not say the same thing as the Pauline texts with which they are paired (1 Cor. 11, Rom. 7 and Eph. 5). But not saying the same thing is simply a precondition of fruitful dialogue. Readings of these modern texts open up interpretative possibilities that would never have come to light if we confined ourselves to the safety of the canonical text, refusing the risk of engagement with the secular. A further dimension is added when the Pauline texts are read in conjunction with the readings of Christian interpreters such as Augustine and Barth. Throughout, the intention is to articulate the distinctive logic (or theo-logic) of a *Christian* sexual ethics that necessarily takes the form of a *biblical* sexual ethics – if the term 'biblical' can be freed from its biblicistic connotations.

I am deeply indebted to Michael Banner, Richard Hays and Douglas Campbell, for many insights into (respectively) theological ethics, New Testament ethics and Pauline interpretation. Although – the conventional disclaimer – they are not to be held responsible for the views I here develop, I do not think that this book would have been written without them. I am also grateful to Grace Jantzen, Emma Tristram and Nicholas Watson, who read the first chapter in draft and helped me to clarify my thinking about the book as a whole.

PART I

Velamen: 1 Corinthians 11

Whatever the later and earlier material that must also be taken into account, and in spite of the difficulties, the aim here is a 'Pauline sexual ethic' – an ethic grounded in the Pauline texts and already partially embodied in the ongoing life of the Christian community, yet requiring to be articulated anew in a situation in which it is exposed to previously unheard-of pressures and challenges. The 'ethic' that is to be articulated does not consist primarily in a set of prescriptions for sexual conduct. Not that it omits to prescribe, or consigns the whole area to individual freedom of choice so long as this is exercised in a manner respectful of the freedom of the other. It does prescribe – yet not in a vacuum, but out of an ethos which provides the underlying rationale for its prescriptions and makes persuasive and compelling what might otherwise seem arbitrary and repressive.

This Pauline ethos is that of a community in which men and women together participate in the grace of the Lord Jesus Christ, the love of God, and the common life (*koinōnia*) of the Holy Spirit. Here, the love of God is poured into our hearts by the Holy Spirit given to us – a divine love that issues in a responsive human love towards God and the neighbour. It is on the basis of this ethos of love that it can be said that woman is not apart from man nor man from woman, in the Lord and within the Christian community. Here, the agape that binds women and men together is not that of eros. Unless eros is assigned to its proper limits, it is the corruption of love and not its fulfilment. The admittedly ambivalent symbol of the veil or head-covering is to be understood in this light, as a barrier intended to ward off the male erotic look that would prevent woman's voice from being heard, as, in prophecy and prayer, she utters the word of God to the congregation and the responsive word of the congregation to God (1 Cor. 11). Far from being a sign of her subordination, the veil is her authority to speak in this way. Since this divine–human dialogue is the articulation of agape, it can also be said that the veil signifies the necessary distinction between eros and agape, excluding the one so as to preserve the space of the other.

Yet the veil remains an ambivalent symbol. It makes woman invisible, and can all too easily be seen as the first step towards the silencing of women that occurs a few chapters later, at least in the final form of the Pauline text. The veil can also be seen as signifying not the exclusion of eros for the sake of agape but the exclusion of women for the sake of an all-male church leadership. Statements subordinating women to male 'headship' are, after all, found in this very passage, which can indeed be read as a series of proof-texts demonstrating the need for a 'post-Christian feminism' that separates itself from what it perceives as an irredeemably patriarchal church. Because this reading must be taken seriously, both as a reading of the text and as a reading of church and society in and through the text, we preface a reading of the Pauline text in terms of the problematic of agape, eros and gender (chapter 2) with a reading of a modern text that is itself – in part – a critical feminist reading of the Pauline text: Virginia Woolf's *Three Guineas* (chapter 1). Its author advocated a 'separatist' feminism according to which women must learn to embrace and exploit the role of 'Outsider' that has been assigned to them; she lacked any formal theological training, and had no intention of arguing theologically. Yet, despite her manifest intentions, her text can still be read as a critical affirmation – and on Christian theological grounds – of the Pauline claim that man and woman belong together.

CHAPTER ONE

Belonging together

'Neither is woman apart from man nor man apart from woman, in the Lord' (1 Cor. 11.11). In the Lord, woman and man are not independent of one another but interdependent. They face each other and must constantly reckon with the being of the other. They do not face away from one another; they do not find their true being by taking a path that diverges from the path of the other, crossing it only occasionally and accidentally. In the Lord, they belong together. That is so within the Christian community, in which Jesus is acknowledged as Lord, and also outside it; for, whether or not Jesus is acknowledged, it remains the case that God 'has put all things [*panta*] in subjection under him' (1 Cor. 15.27). The sphere in which man and woman belong together is coextensive with the sphere of this universal lordship. This 'belonging-together', to which all humans are called, is not a mere neutral coexistence. It is the belonging-together of agape, a pattern of living with others that this same Pauline text will later articulate and celebrate (1 Cor. 13).

   Belonging-together does not exclude difference. If difference were dissolved into homogeneity, it would no longer be 'man' and 'woman' who belonged together; they would belong together not *as* man and woman but only as sharing in an undifferentiated humanity. In the Lord, humanity is not undifferentiated. But neither is the difference an absolute heterogeneity, which would make it hard to speak of a 'humanity' in which woman and man both share. Belonging-together acknowledges difference, but this is the difference of those who belong together, not the difference of those who are

3

separated. The possibility of separation – 'woman apart from man', 'man apart from woman' – is raised only in the form of its negation. Possibilities are not negated at random, however, and the negation concedes that a self-definition that excludes the other might at least be attempted. Man might define himself as apart from woman; woman might define herself as apart from man.

What it means for man to define himself apart from woman is clear enough. Speaking only of himself, he either fails to notice her existence or construes it as the mirror-image of his own. His identity is supposed to represent a universal human norm. Her identity is submerged in his; it is taken for granted that what is true of him must also be true, although secondarily and to a lesser extent, of her. Man defines himself 'apart from woman' in the sense that the difference represented by 'woman' is subsumed into a universal male identity. This self-definition is inscribed within language itself: 'man' both included woman and suppressed her difference by assimilating it to a male norm. As the universally human, 'man' is apart from woman. Within this schema of solitary universality, woman's difference may indeed be acknowledged as a subordinate reality – but only in order that the distinctive male self-image might be reflected back in the mirror of the other. In the mirror, the disclosure of the image is achieved only by way of a reversal, in which right is seen to be right only in the image that displays it as left, as its opposite. The image of the other may be subject to praise or blame, but in either case the appearance of otherness is an illusion: for the image of the other serves the image of the narcissistic self and has no identity of its own outside that necessary service. Even in speaking of woman as the image of the other, man continues to speak of himself.

It is this project of male self-definition apart from woman to which the term 'patriarchy' polemically refers. Can this term do justice to the *total* reality of the male–female relationship, throughout history? 'Patriarchy' might represent a *metanarrative*, adapted perhaps from the claim of Marx and Engels that 'the history of all hitherto existing society is the history of class struggles'.[1] But it might also represent a *model*: a framework within which to view reality, disclosing a truth that is neither the truth of the whole nor a mere effect of the model itself; not the whole truth, but truth nevertheless. Understood as a model, 'patriarchy' would not occlude or compete with concepts such as 'class' and 'race' as means of articulating the reality of human sociopolitical life in its irreducible complexity. Within its limitations, 'patriarchy' identifies a project of male self-definition, 'apart from woman', whose effects are all too real. The critical use of this concept in historical or theological analysis is itself always subject to critical evaluation; the concept can never guarantee in advance the truth of the analysis. Conversely, the possible deficiencies of the analysis need not detract from the value of the concept.[2]

In reaction against masculine self-definitions 'apart from woman', woman may define herself as 'apart from man'; and this project of resistance may present certain formal resemblances to the masculine self-definitions it strives to counter. Thus, the male may now serve as the image of the other in which the self-image – now the self-image of woman – is disclosed. But the formal symmetry – man defines himself apart from woman, woman defines herself apart from man – should not be allowed to mask the underlying asymmetry. The two projects of self-definition cannot be seen as twin expressions of a perennial, perhaps not very serious conflict of two equal and opposite principles. In one project, self-assertion is the dominant element; in the other, the resistance of the victim of that self-assertion. The asymmetry of thesis and antithesis means that no cheap and easy synthesis is available. Belonging-together does not represent a *via media* between two equal and opposite extremes, 'patriarchy' and 'feminism'. The two terms

---

[1] 'The Communist Manifesto' (1848), in David McLellan (ed.), *Karl Marx: Selected Writings*, Oxford: Oxford University Press, 1977, 221–47; 222.

[2] Michèle Barrett is critical of the term 'patriarchy' in current usage, arguing that to use it 'is frequently to invoke a generality of male domination without being able to specify historical limits, changes or differences' (*Women's Oppression Today: The Marxist/Feminist Encounter*, London and New York: Verso, 2nd edn 1988, 14). This problem is resolved if the concept of 'patriarchy' is understood as a model and not as an implied metanarrative.

are incommensurable – not only because of their historical asymmetry but also because of the semantic indeterminacy of 'feminism'. If the term 'patriarchy' refers to the project of male self-definition apart from woman, it is not clear that 'feminism' refers univocally to the project of female self-definition apart from man. 'Feminism' is a contested term; there are many feminisms, overlapping and diverging. 'Feminist' reflection on the belonging-together of woman and man is quite conceivable. The concept of belonging-together opposes not 'feminism' but those strands of feminism and feminist theology which either advocate or (more likely) simply presuppose a self-definition apart from man.

The Pauline text that speaks of the belonging-together of man and woman also speaks, problematically, of the veiling or covering of woman's head. The image of the veil is taken up by one of the text's woman readers, Virginia Woolf, in the course of a polemical plea for woman's separate identity.[3] Her own text is not simply a reading of the Pauline text; it is an account of the relation of man and woman that resists compromise and premature synthesis, and that pushes the project of self-definition apart from man in the direction of a separatist account of woman as Outsider. Woman is defined as Outsider in relation to the patriarchal institutions that administer society and that lead it inexorably towards war. She is Outsider in relation to patriarchal institutions in general, but more particularly in relation to the Church, whose all-male priesthood represents patriarchy's innermost shrine and secret. The enormity of this

---

[3] My primary text in this chapter is Virginia Woolf's *Three Guineas*; page references are to the Penguin edition, edited by Michèle Barrett, where it is published together with *A Room of One's Own* (London: Penguin Books, 1993). Barrett underlines the importance of this text for contemporary feminism, describing it in her introduction as 'a book that has now found its time' (ix), and contrasting its current timeliness with the hostility it encountered when it was first published; on this see Hermione Lee, *Virginia Woolf*, London: Vintage, 1997, 691–4. The impact on recent feminist literary criticism of Woolf's work as a whole is well illustrated by Jane Marcus's hyperbolic comment: 'She seems hardly to have lived among her contemporaries but to speak directly to the future, to our generation' ('Thinking Back through our Mothers', in *New Feminist Essays on Virginia Woolf*, ed. Jane Marcus, London: Macmillan, 1981, 1–30; 4). Recent criticism has rejected the charge that Woolf failed to carry through her feminism into her novels (as argued by Patricia Stubbs, *Women and Fiction: Feminism and the Novel, 1880–1920*, London: Methuen, 1979, 231).

situation, so cunningly concealed and so hard to grasp, makes it impossible for the Outsider to co-operate with men even in the cause of justice and peace of which she approves. Man has defined himself apart from woman, and the catastrophic social consequences of his decision continue to hem us in. In defining herself apart from man, woman is fighting for life itself, and the notion of an ultimate belonging-together of man and woman is no more than a faint utopian glow on the horizon.

This text is an expression of what is now called a 'post-Christian feminism', in which separation from the Christian church is paradigmatic of separation from patriarchal institutions in general. What is to be gained by engaging it in a close reading? What will come to light is the extent to which Christian agape as the basis of the belonging-together of man and woman is acknowledged *in this text itself*, despite its manifest intentions. To bring this situation to light is to expose the gulf between the transcendental basis of the Christian community and its empirical reality; but it is also to detect symptoms of the transcendental basis within empirical reality. Only through the appearance of truth can idols and ideologies be exposed. If feminist critique claims to be grounded in truth, it is at least conceivable that this truth-claim is in the end positively related to the transcendental truth-claim that a post-Christian, secularizing culture has sought to repress. That there is this positive relationship has yet to be shown; to assume it *a priori* would be theological wishful thinking. But if this relationship does not exist, the nature and basis of the truth on which a feminist ideology-critique might take its stand remains an open question; or rather, within the relativizing ethos of postmodernity, an ineffable mystery.[4]

---

[4] The issue of the relation of feminism to truth is raised by Sabina Lovibond, in dialogue with Richard Rorty: 'Should we say that there is ("ultimately") *nothing but* an evaluatively neutral *ensemble* of social constructs or "discourses" to which different groups assign different values in accordance with their own preferences? Or can these evaluations be seen as answerable to a universal or quasi-universal standard that would identify some discursive regimes, but not others, as tolerable?' ('Feminism and Pragmatism: A Reply to Richard Rorty', *New Left Review* 193 (1992), 56–74; 67).

THROUGH THE SHADOW OF THE VEIL

As she prepared to write the work eventually published as *Three Guineas* (1938), Virginia Woolf wrote in her diary for Tuesday 16 February 1932: 'I'm quivering & itching to write my – whats it to be called? – "Men are like that?" – no thats too patently feminist: the sequel then, for which I have collected enough powder to blow up St Pauls' (*Diaries*, IV.77).[5] As the preceding lines show, her impatience has been exacerbated by the petty annoyances of the day: there are problems with Nelly and Lottie (the servants), Miss McAfee has turned down an article, and dinner tonight with Ethel Sands means that much valuable time will be lost. But it is characteristic of the intellectual to be able to draw a clear dividing-line between ephemeral matters and the long-term project – in this case, a writing that will blow up St Paul's.

Why does she want to blow up St Paul's? This building is identified in *Three Guineas* as one of a number of central London landmarks that together symbolize the dominant masculine order – along with the Bank of England, the Mansion House, the Law Courts, Westminster Abbey and the Houses of Parliament (133). But is that a good enough reason for wanting to blow it up? St Paul's differs from the other buildings in explicitly placing itself under the aegis of a male patron. The same is true, however, of another domed building in central London. In *Jacob's Room* (1922), it is noted that 'not so long ago the workmen had gilt the final "y" in Lord Macaulay's name, and the names stretched in unbroken file round the dome of the British Museum' (143). One of the readers (for the reference is to the British Library, within the Museum) is 'Miss Julia Hedge, the feminist', who was waiting for her books to arrive: 'Her eye

---

[5] In addition to *Three Guineas* and *A Room of One's Own*, other works by Woolf cited here are: *Jacob's Room*, Oxford: Oxford University Press, 1992; *To the Lighthouse*, London: Penguin Books, 1992; *Orlando: A Biography*, London: Penguin Books, 1963; *The Waves*, London: Grafton Books, 1977; *The Years*, London: Penguin Books, 1968; *Moments of Being*, ed. Jeanne Schulkind, London: The Hogarth Press, 2nd edn 1985; and *The Diary of Virginia Woolf*, vol. IV: 1931–1935, ed. Anne Olivier Bell and Andrew McNeillie, London: The Hogarth Press, 1982.

was caught by the final letters in Lord Macaulay's name. And she read them all round the dome – the names of great men, which remind us – "Oh damn", said Julia Hedge, "why didn't they leave room for an Eliot or Brontë?"' (144–5). But Julia Hedge has no intention of blowing up the British Museum. As the narrator of *A Room of One's Own* (1929), Virginia Woolf herself visits the British Museum in order to research her forthcoming paper on 'Women and Fiction'. Entering through the swing-doors, 'one stood under the vast dome, as if one were a thought in the huge bald forehead which is so splendidly encircled by a band of famous names' (24). She has, as it were, strayed into a male brain, and the thoughts about women that she finds there are all the thoughts of men. However, although irritated by what she finds, and especially by Professor von X.'s monumental *The Mental, Moral, and Physical Inferiority of the Female Sex*, she never betrays any inclination to blow up the British Museum. Why, then, is St Paul's chosen instead as the target of her incendiarism?

In *The Years* (1937), Martin Pargiter, on his way to visit his stockbroker, passes St Paul's, part of the stream of 'little men in bowler hats and round coats', of 'women carrying attaché cases', of vans, lorries, and buses: 'Now and then single figures broke off from the rest and went up the steps into the church. The doors of the Cathedral kept opening and shutting. Now and again a blast of faint organ music was blown out into the air. The pigeons waddled; the sparrows fluttered' (183). Admiring the building from the outside, Martin suddenly recognizes his cousin Sara, who has been attending the service. He invites her to lunch in a nearby restaurant, where the following dialogue takes place:

'I didn't know you went to services', he said, looking at her prayer-book.
　　She did not answer. She kept looking round her, watching the people come in and go out. She sipped her wine . . . They ate in silence for a moment.
　　He wanted to make her talk.
　　'And what, Sal,' he said, touching the little book, 'd'you make of it?'
　　She opened the prayer-book at random and began to read:

'The father incomprehensible; the son incomprehensible – ' she spoke in her ordinary voice.

'Hush!' he stopped her. 'Somebody's listening'.

In deference to him she assumed the manner of a lady lunching with a gentleman in a City restaurant. (185)

To attend a service at St Paul's is to behave abnormally. Individuals may break off from the passing crowd to do so, but they thereby identify themselves precisely as individuals, who may justly be interrogated about their conduct. Sara's answer is drawn from the *Quicunque vult*, which, as her prayer-book would inform her, is 'commonly called the Creed of Saint Athanasius' and is appointed to be sung or said at Morning Prayer on certain feast days in preference to the Apostles' Creed. The words of this text belong only to the ecclesiastical interior of St Paul's and are quite inappropriate on the secular exterior. To utter these words, in a restaurant, where there are many to overhear it, and in one's ordinary voice, is to commit a solecism. Sara is therefore silenced, even though Martin had previously 'wanted to make her talk'. More to the point, the words she quotes are no answer to the question that has been put to her. They merely confirm the abnormality of the interior and of those who worship there. What concern can Sara possibly have with the incomprehensible father and the incomprehensible son to whom the worship is addressed? A woman may reasonably enter the 'huge bald forehead' of the British Library and become for a while a thought in a vast male brain; for, although all the thoughts about women there are men's thoughts, their progenitors are *only* men. They are not God. The woman reader who has infiltrated the brain can sit there drawing her caricature of Professor von X. with impunity. But what if she enters the huge bald forehead of St Paul? (An ancient source assures us that St Paul was indeed bald.)[6] She can hardly sit there drawing caricatures of the incomprehensible father and son; for they are not human, they are divine. The all-male

---

[6] In the apocryphal *Acts of Paul and Thecla* (ii.3), Paul is described as 'a man of little stature, thin-haired upon the head, crooked in the legs, of good state of body, with eyebrows joining, and nose somewhat hooked, full of grace' (translation from M. R. James (ed.), *The Apocryphal New Testament*, Oxford: Clarendon Press, 1924, 273).

relationship that lies at the heart of the deity is underlined by Sara's mention only of the father incomprehensible and the son incomprehensible, without proceeding with the Creed to the Holy Ghost incomprehensible. Sara's conduct in worshipping at St Paul's is as incomprehensible as the father and the son. It participates in their incomprehensibility, and her response tacitly acknowledges this. Woolf's narrator therefore remains resolutely on the outside, along with Martin, approaching closely enough to hear snatches of organ music and of the 'faint ecclesiastical murmur' from within (184), but declining to enter.[7]

Here then is the reason for the planned incendiarism: St Paul's represents the deification of the male. At the British Museum, the male is still recognizably human, and even the names around the dome – Macaulay and the others – are at best only half-way to deification. At St Paul's, the situation is otherwise. St Paul himself is human, but the father and the son whose names circulate in his brain are not. They are divine, and they therefore appear to represent an exclusively masculine symbolic order in which God is the male and the male is God. The unique function of St Paul's is therefore to project into transcendence the male-dominated social order represented by the other great buildings of central London. The material that will blow up St Paul's will also bring down the whole of that social order with it.[8]

Incendiary imagery is still employed in the final form of the text that Woolf envisages in 1932; but it plays a subordinate role, as befits a pacifist manifesto, and it is not now directed against St Paul's cathedral. In *Three Guineas* the building escapes attack, but the man whose name it commemorates does not.

[7] When, in *The Waves*, a character (Bernard) gives his impressions of the interior of St Paul's, the tone is sceptical and contemptuous (222–3).
[8] In chapter 12 of *Text, Church and World: Biblical Interpretation in Theological Perspective* (Edinburgh: T. & T. Clark, Grand Rapids: Eerdmans, 1994), I have argued that biblical father/son language should be understood in an anti-patriarchal sense. This language originates in Jesus' naming of God as *Abba* and God's corresponding naming of Jesus as 'son', and a patriarchal misinterpretation can occur only where this origin is forgotten. Where this occurs, the unreality of the resultant patriarchal deity will eventually become obvious, as Sara Pargiter's ironic, mocking quotation – 'the father incomprehensible; the son incomprehensible' – indicates.

St Paul, we learn here, 'was of the virile or dominant type, so familiar at present in Germany, for whose gratification a subject race or sex is essential' (300). St Paul is assimilated to Hitler.

Three Guineas is a substantial work, comparable in scale to a medium-length novel and divided into three parts that correspond to the 'three guineas' of the title. Its setting is fictional. A male correspondent wrote, three years ago, asking Woolf or her fictional *alter ego* how she thinks war can be prevented. Now at last she writes her reply. Although she has long been deterred by the difficulty of the question, 'one does not like to leave so remarkable a letter as yours – a letter unique in the history of human correspondence, since when before has an educated man asked a woman how in her opinion war can be prevented? – unanswered' (117). Embedded in her response are replies to two further letters, one from the treasurer of a women's college, the other from the secretary of a society for promoting the interests of professional women. After due reflection and with considerable ambivalence, a cheque is sent to each (parts 1 and 2), and to the initial correspondent, who is the secretary of a society devoted to the prevention of war (part 3). In the end, however, the emphasis falls on the need for women to resist assimilation to male institutions – the academy, the professions, even the anti-war society whose pacifist convictions Woolf shares. Declining the invitation to join, Woolf announces the formation of an unstructured 'Society of Outsiders', in which women dedicate themselves to analysis and critique of the patriarchal order.

The Pauline injunction that women should be veiled serves initially as an image of women's unjust, oppressive confinement to the private sphere. At this point, St Paul incarnates the figure of the dictator. He is Creon, who shut Antigone up in a rocky tomb; he is Hitler, and the obscure authors of letters to the newspapers demanding that women be banished from the workplace. In the passage on veiling, Paul invokes 'the familiar but always suspect trinity of accomplices, Angels, nature and law, to support his personal opinion', arriving a few chapters later at 'the conclusion that has been looming unmistakably ahead of us' – that women are to be silent outside the confines of their own homes (299). St Paul presided grimly over the whole Victorian concept of 'chastity', which affected every aspect of female behaviour; and 'even today it is probable that a woman has to fight a psychological battle of some severity with the ghost of St Paul' (301). The way forward, it seems, is to do away with the Pauline veil which – ever-present although almost invisible – divided the private sphere of women from the public sphere of men. The veil must be consigned to the past; only reactionaries want to reimpose it.

And yet the marginal position represented by the veil is *also* a prerequisite for the critique of the patriarchal order undertaken by the 'Society of Outsiders', in word and deed. The veil – or the shadow still cast by this now-outmoded garment – gives women a curious and critical perspective on the professional world of men. This masculine world must be seen 'through the shadow of the veil that St Paul still lays before our eyes', and from this angle it is undoubtedly a strange place:

At first sight it is enormously impressive. Within quite a small space are crowded together St Paul's, the Bank of England, the Mansion House, the massive if funereal battlements of the Law Courts; and on the other side, Westminster Abbey and the Houses of Parliament. There, we say to ourselves . . . our fathers and brothers have spent their lives. All these hundreds of years they have been mounting those steps, passing in and out of those doors, ascending those pulpits, preaching, money-making, administering justice. It is from this world that the private house . . . has derived its creeds, its laws, its clothes and carpets, its beef and mutton. (133)

But as women look more closely, they are astonished at what they find. Who would have thought that men took such pleasure in dressing up?

Now you dress in violet; a jewelled crucifix swings on your breast; now your shoulders are covered with lace; now furred with ermine; now slung with many linked chains set with precious stones. Now you wear wigs on your heads; rows of graduated curls descend to your necks. Now your hats are boat-shaped, or cocked; now they are made of brass and scuttle shaped; now plumes of red, now of blue hair surmount them . . . Ribbons of all colours – blue, purple, crimson – cross from shoulder to shoulder. After the comparative simplicity of your dress at home, the splendour of your public attire is dazzling. (134)

This clothing not only looks striking, it also speaks. Every item has symbolic meaning, and every detail serves to communicate the wearer's status, achievements, and moral and intellectual worth. This comprehensive professional dress code is illustrated by a series of photographs of 'a general', 'heralds', 'a university procession', 'a judge' and 'an archbishop', which serve to locate the text as a piece of anthropological research into an exotic tribe whose offices and institutions will be quite unfamiliar to readers.

Yet, seen from the perspective of the Outsider, 'through the shadow of the veil', this dress code is *sinister* as well as exotic. Within it there lurks a culture of *war*. The connection is obvious: 'Your finest clothes are those you wear as soldiers' (138). The professional dress code is a seamless garment, and at its centre lies the seductiveness of military uniform – which, even now, clothes the reality of immanent war in the false colours of an essentially masculine patriotic fervour. In rejecting the dress code and its attendant honours, Outsiders can make a small but definite contribution to the cause of peace. They will maintain an attitude of complete indifference to their brothers' fevered preparations for war, refusing to participate in the accompanying rhetoric. They will purge themselves of the destructive illusions of patriotism. The Society of Outsiders would work in parallel with other societies dedicated to the prevention of war, but it would hold itself aloof in order not to lose the distinctive perspective of women. Women alone can observe the world from the perspective of 'the shadow of the veil that St Paul still lays upon our eyes' – a perspective which discloses that the ultimate truth underlying the male world's dazzling appearance is the culture of violence and war. A woman may be intimidated in the workplace, a country may be annexed with bombs and poison gas – and the same forces are at work in both cases. The veil, still signifying separation, although this time within the public sphere itself, has now become the necessary condition for perceiving the truth and for venturing whatever acts of small-scale resistance are appropriate and possible. The veil is women's prerogative. Only women can belong to the Society of Outsiders; only women look at the world 'through the shadow of the veil'.

The feminism of this text is shaped by a particular historical situation, marked by the movement for women's emancipation on the one hand and the rise of Fascism on the other; and its construal of this situation is limited by the perspective of one for whom political power is held by 'fathers and brothers' – that is, by close relatives with whom she has much in common. 'When we meet in the flesh we speak with the same accent; use knives and forks in the same way; expect maids to cook dinner and wash up after dinner; and can talk during dinner without much difficulty about politics and people; war and peace; barbarism and civilisation . . .' (118). Throughout the book, Woolf's concern is with 'the daughters of educated men', that is, with professional women, the hardships they have endured in the recent past and the dilemmas they continue to face in the present. Nothing is said of the hardships and dilemmas of those women who are expected to cook and to wash up. Yet Woolf is conscious that she is speaking from the limited perspective of a particular class, and makes no pretence to universality. In this respect, she is perhaps more self-aware and self-critical than some more recent feminisms, in which 'women's experience' is understood as a trans-cultural universal. In addition, in her overriding preoccupation with the problem of war she addresses an issue that impinges on all social classes alike.

More important than the limitations of her feminist perspective is her vacillation between the feminist projects of 'equal rights' and 'separate identity', with a constant bias towards the latter.[9] This vacillation is dramatized in the ambivalent symbol of the veil, drawn from 1 Corinthians 11.2–16 as traditionally understood. The veil signifies the division of the public sphere inhabited by men from the private sphere inhabited by women. As such, the veil is rejected, and its instigator is denounced as

[9] Alex Zwerdling gives an illuminating account of the historical background to this tension between feminisms of equality and of difference (*Virginia Woolf and the Real World*, Berkeley, Los Angeles, London: University of California Press, 1986, 210–42). Woolf's 'separatist thinking was a radical departure from the assumptions of the women's movement' (237), and was occasioned by her sense that 'the movement had not sufficiently divorced itself from the world created by men; it had been largely uncritical of the existing institutions of society and anxious merely to enter them' (238). The Suffrage movement's enthusiastic support for the First World War exemplifies this lack of critical distance.

the archetypal male oppressor. The entire nineteenth- and twentieth-century movement for women's emancipation – and especially for admission to higher education and to the professions – is presented as a struggle against the veil and everything it represents. Despite real progress, the struggle continues; the voice of the oppressor, demanding that women leave the workplace to men and return to the home that is their natural habitat, is as loud in democratic England as it is in fascist Germany. On the other hand, the danger is that precisely as women succeed within the male world of the professions, they will assimilate its culture – which is a culture of war. The possibility of a voice of independent critique and resistance will have been eliminated. Women, existing at the margins of higher education and the professions, should not resent their marginality; they should treasure it. They must continue to stand within the shadow of the dividing veil, identifying themselves as Outsiders who can criticize the war-oriented world of the patriarchal institutions from a privileged perspective. The veil of difference is to be rejected, but it is simultaneously to be preserved. Having rejected it, women must now ensure that the priceless treasure it offers – the Outsider's privilege of critical insight – is not lost. As the Outsider watches 'the procession of educated men', moving onwards 'like a caravanserie crossing a desert' (183), it is vitally important to ask the critical question: 'Where is it leading us?' (184).

The text dramatizes the dilemma posed by different feminisms – one a feminism of equal opportunity, the other a feminism of separation; one optimistic about the possibility of reforming male-dominated institutions as women gain access to them, the other pessimistic about this possibility and about the value of this access. The claim that 'woman is not apart from man nor man from woman, in the Lord', contained in a Pauline passage that Woolf discusses at some length, is ostensibly rejected in favour of a feminism in which woman must define herself as apart from man. Her 'Outsiders' are vehemently opposed to the church as the archetypal patriarchal institution, and the idea that men and women relate appropriately to one another 'in the Lord', in the ecclesial context of agape, would have been instantly dismissed had Woolf bothered to mention it at all. And yet, contrary to its author's intentions, it is precisely this idea that this 'separatist' text permits and encourages us to think. Woolf's own text shows that this initial 'apart from man' is actually the precondition for a situation in which 'neither is woman apart from man nor man apart from woman, in the Lord'. Despite itself, her text gives grounds for the theological conclusion that, in the Lord, women and men are inter-dependent.

THE THREAT OF PEACE

In *Three Guineas*, Woolf sets her discussion of women's place in a male-dominated society in the context of the issue of war and peace. However widely the argument ranges, the correspon-dent's initial question – how can we prevent war? – is never forgotten.[10] The author and her correspondent are agreed that war is an unmitigated evil and that it cannot be justified. They maintain their pacifist conviction even in the face of Fascism, at a historical juncture – 1938 – when the tide of public opinion is turning decisively against them. They do not advocate a policy of 'appeasement' that involves turning a blind eye to the evils of Fascism. They agree that the essence of Fascism is its violence, and that to oppose it with violence is to allow oneself to be corrupted by it. Satan cannot be cast out by Satan. If the essence of Fascism is disclosed in the violence that destroys Guernica or Coventry, what is it that is disclosed when the target is Cologne or Dresden? The 'horror and disgust' evoked by images of war are shared. 'War, you say, is an abomination; a barbarity; war must be stopped at whatever cost. And we echo your words. War is an abomination; a barbarity; war must be stopped' (125).

---

[10] According to Elizabeth Abel, 'Woolf's political agenda in *Three Guineas* is less to articulate a pacifist response to the fascist threat, her stated goal, than to bring the impending war home, to resituate the battlefield in the British family and workplace' (*Virginia Woolf and the Fictions of Psychoanalysis*, Chicago: Chicago University Press, 1989, 91). This seems a misstatement. Woolf's aim is to show how the feminist analysis and agenda is relevant to the pacifist one. The pacifist issue is not the scaffolding for the argument, it lies at its heart.

The author's correspondent is a man – a barrister, very much part of the masculine order that the outsiders observe from their peculiar vantage point 'through the shadow of the veil'. Yet – to the author's astonishment – he has broken ranks by asking her advice about what might seem a purely masculine concern: war and the prevention of war. He has also asked her for a donation for the pacifist society of which he is honorary treasurer, thereby acknowledging the new economic autonomy which (for the author) is a necessary condition for the independence of mind presupposed by his question. On the basis of this apparently rather hopeful situation, the author enthusiastically sends the anti-war society her guinea – 'would that it were a million!' (226). And yet, asked to join that society, she declines; for her rejection of war, ostensibly shared with her correspondent, is located within a larger argument whose premises he may be expected to reject. The problem of war is consistently interpreted as a *gendered* problem. War is a *male* activity:

For though many instincts are held more or less in common by both sexes, to fight has always been the man's habit, not the woman's. Law and practice have developed that difference, whether innate or accidental. Scarcely a human being in the course of history has fallen to a woman's rifle; the vast majority of birds and beasts have been killed by you, not by us . . . (120–1)

Interpreted in this light, the problem of war cannot be isolated from the wider problem of men's treatment of women. The same male violence of which war is the supreme epiphany is also manifested in the fathers' continuing attempts to subjugate their daughters, locking them up in the private world of the home, or, if this proves impossible, ensuring that their participation in the public world of the professions remains as marginal as possible.

It is Fascism that discloses the connection. Fascism glorifies the male warrior and the wife and mother who heals his wounds and bears his children. It requires the separation of the two worlds of men and women, the reversal of women's hard-won freedoms, and it can call upon a long legacy of hostility to those freedoms: the hostility of men who feel threatened by them, and the hostility of women who, lacking economic or

intellectual independence from their husbands, have internalized the patriarchal delimitation of their role. Far from being a
pathological phenomenon of certain societies remote from our
own, Fascism actually discloses the dynamics of 'normal' social
life in capitalist countries that pride themselves on their democratic traditions and their capacity for social progress. There is
no perceptible difference between English and German expressions of the view that paid work is a male prerogative and that
'homes are the real places of the women who are now compelling men to be idle' (174):

> Are they not both saying the same thing? Are they not both the voices
> of Dictators, whether they speak English or German, and are we not
> all agreed that the dictator when we meet him abroad is a very
> dangerous as well as a very ugly animal? And he is here among us,
> raising his ugly head, spitting his poison, small still, curled up like a
> caterpillar on a leaf, but in the heart of England. (175)

As in Freud's account of sexuality, the distinction between the
aberrant and the normal cannot be maintained. The aberration
discloses and grounds the reality of the normal, as the excluded
term of a binary opposition revenges itself on the privileged
term by recurring at its very heart.

In disclosing the connections between war, maleness and the
subjugation of women, Fascism thus serves as a mirror in which
a supposedly democratic society can see, even if in heightened
and exaggerated form, its own lineaments. But it is the female
author who holds this mirror up and invites her male correspondent to look into it. Will he accept that what he sees there
is in any sense a true reflection of the society to which he
belongs? Or will he argue, as many of Woolf's first readers did,
that women's emancipation, however important and desirable,
must now be subordinated to the far more urgent and quite
different concerns that arise from the threat of Fascism? Will he
claim that it is one thing to confine women to the home, quite
another to subject that same home and its inhabitants to the
terrors of aerial bombardment? Even if he appears to endorse
the claim that Fascism is a mirror in which we see our own
reflection, will he be capable of retaining this insight by placing
the oppression of women at the centre of his political vision and

holding it there? If he fails to do so (as is all too probable), will it not be because – as a beneficiary of the dominant patriarchal order who takes its privileges for granted – he regards the cause of women as much less important than the cause that he himself espouses? The optimism that welcomes the new reality of 'men and women working together for the same cause' (227) is tempered by the pessimistic conclusion that – as one of the working titles for this text puts it – 'men are like that'. Because even the honorary treasurer of the anti-war society has been shaped by the same social forces that have issued in the hyper-masculinity of Fascism, he too must be kept at a certain distance even as the integrity of his work is acknowledged and honoured. The Outsiders share an experience of being outside that he lacks, and this experience is a necessary although not a sufficient condition of the integrity of their political vision.[11]

But is it necessarily the case that 'men are like that', incapable of grasping that the issue of gender is of *fundamental* political significance? Woolf's own text gives grounds for doubting it. The question hinges on the issue of *experience*. Is the respective experience of those whom Woolf coyly calls 'the sons and daughters of educated men' so radically different that the sons are constitutionally incapable of understanding what the daughters are saying?

The honorary secretary of the anti-war society is introduced in the following terms:

You . . . are a little grey on the temples; the hair is no longer thick on the top of your head. You have reached the middle years of life not without effort, at the Bar; but on the whole your journey has been prosperous. There is nothing parched, mean or dissatisfied in your

---

[11] Woolf's aloofness towards the anti-war society may be compared to Mary Daly's criticism of organizations that 'fix all their attention upon some deformity *within* patriarchy – for example, racism, war, poverty – rather than patriarchy itself, without recognizing sexism as root and paradigm of the various forms of oppression they seek to eradicate' (*Beyond God the Father: Towards a Philosophy of Women's Liberation* [1973], London: The Women's Press Limited, 1986, 56). As Woolf proposes a Society of Outsiders that will preserve women's distinctive identity and experience, so Daly advocates a 'sisterhood of women', that is, of those women who 'decide that independent "bonding" with each other and cooperation on this basis with male-governed groups is the better choice' (59). Like Woolf, Daly finds intimate connections between masculinity and war, and sees in Fascism the full disclosure of a 'masculine metaphysical madness' that is still alive and well today (120).

expression. And without wishing to flatter you, your prosperity – wife, children, house – has been deserved. You have never sunk into the contented apathy of middle life, for, as your letter from an office in the heart of London shows, instead of turning on your pillow and prodding your pigs, pruning your pear trees – you have a few acres in Norfolk – you are writing letters, attending meetings, presiding over this and that, asking questions, with the sound of the guns in your ears. For the rest, you began your education at one of the great public schools and finished it at the university. (117–18)

The description appears to make the correspondent a typical representative of the male-dominated establishment, marching confidently near the front of the strangely attired procession of fathers and brothers, an unknowing participant in the culture of violence that it secretly represents. The division between the sexes seems at this point to be absolute: 'Obviously there is for *you* some glory, some necessity, some satisfaction in fighting which *we* have never felt or enjoyed' (121; italics added). But if that description fitted the correspondent, he would never have written asking how war could be prevented; and he would never have become honorary treasurer of a society that holds that 'war must be stopped at whatever cost' (125). If he has written 'with the sound of guns in [his] ears', that sound is presumably not music to his ears but an unspeakable cacophony. But that means that he has seen through the illusions of a particular masculine self-image, which Woolf illustrates from a biography of a certain Viscount Knebworth: 'The difficulty' – his biographer writes – 'to which he could find no answer was that if permanent peace were ever achieved, and armies and navies ceased to exist, there would be no outlet for the manly qualities which fighting developed, and that human physique and human character would deteriorate' (122). Woolf acknowledges, however, that this ideology of masculinity is by no means universal by quoting the testimony of the poet Wilfred Owen:

Already I have comprehended a light which will never filter into the dogma of any national church: namely, that one of Christ's essential commands was: Passivity at any price! Suffer dishonour and disgrace, but never resort to arms. Be bullied, be outraged, be killed; but do not kill . . . Thus you see how pure Christianity will not fit in with pure patriotism. (122)

According to Woolf, this is very much a minority view among men. The vast majority 'are of opinion that Wilfred Owen was wrong; that it is better to kill than to be killed' (123). Yet her correspondent remains, as late as 1938, a committed advocate of the minority position. Middle-aged now, he belongs to the generation of Wilfred Owen – the generation that was decimated in the years from 1914 to 1918. The sound of guns in his ears is the sound not only of the next war but also of the last war; the gunfire sounds loudly and persistently in his own memory. His pacifism is almost certainly the result of a similar revelation to the one described by Owen. As a member of the ruling classes, he will have been a member of the 'national church' and assimilated the prevailing ideology of manliness and military glory. Judging from his background, he is unlikely to have been a conscientious objector. Like Owen, he will have learned his pacifism not second-hand but as the result of first-hand experience of risking being killed, of killing, and of seeing others killed.

His pacifism stems from a first-hand experience of war that his sister lacks. According to Woolf, 'the daughters of educated men' responded with enthusiasm to the events of August 1914 because military hospitals, fields and arms factories offered them an alternative to the intolerable confinement of the private house. 'Consciously she desired "our splendid Empire"; unconsciously she desired our splendid war' (161). It is as a nurse that the correspondent's sister comes closest to the reality of war. Her experience of the immediate impact of war on human bodies is, of course, first-hand; but she still lacks her brother's experience of risking being killed, of killing, and of seeing others killed. She is at relatively little risk of being killed. She has never directed machine-gun or bayonet against her fellow human beings. She has no direct experience of the sudden deaths of others, since her concern is with those who die lingering deaths or who may recover from their wounds. Since war has always been men's work and alien to her, her pacifism will not fundamentally jeopardize her identity as a woman. Her brother's situation is different. As a convert to pacifism, he has experienced what Woolf calls an 'emancipation from the old conception of virility' (322); but, if he lives in a society where the old conception is still the majority view, his identity as a man will be called into question. He is the intended target of the distinction between 'a nation of pacifists and a nation of men' (322): as it happens, the words are Hitler's, but the correspondent will be familiar enough with this disjunction between pacifism and masculinity from his own first-hand experience. As a pacifist who refuses to bear arms, he is not a 'real man'. As an advocate of 'passivity at any price', he involuntarily takes upon himself the symbolic identification of passivity with femininity. He becomes 'effeminate'. He also exposes himself to the accusation of 'cowardice', which may be voiced by women as well as by other men. Experience shows, according to Woolf, 'that a man still feels it a peculiar insult to be taunted with cowardice by a woman in much the same way that a woman feels it a peculiar insult to be taunted with unchastity by a man' (316). The male's susceptibility to such taunts indicates 'that courage and pugnacity are still among the prime attributes of manliness' (317); it is also a sign that, for men and women alike, pacifism is incompatible with sexual prowess. War is a spectacle intended to evoke feminine admiration, and to decline war is to forfeit the admiration. To the slurs of effeminacy, cowardice and impotence we must add another: treachery, the betrayal of one's native land. It is 'patriotism' that leads men to go to war, in the conviction that – in the words of the Lord Chief Justice of England – our country is 'a castle that will be defended to the last' (123). Within an ideology such as this, what is to be said of the man who – supposedly on moral grounds – does nothing and allows the castle to be overrun? What does a man like that deserve? The stirring rhetoric of patriotism is of a piece with the glamour of military uniform, whose 'splendour is invented partly in order to impress the beholder with the majesty of the military office, partly in order through their vanity to induce young men to become soldiers' (138). Women, 'who are forbidden to wear such clothes ourselves, can express the opinion that the wearer is not to us a pleasing or an impressive spectacle' (138); women can refuse to participate in the violent sexual game that uniform signifies. Men may do likewise. But if they do so, what is signified by the rhetoric and the spectacle will be their own castration.

The rhetoric and the uniform change over the years; but, although aware that 1938 is not 1914, Woolf is chiefly struck by the continuities.[12] Underlying the changes the same gendered dynamics are at work, apparently untouched even by the widespread revulsion evoked by 'the Great War'. In that case, however, a man's decision to be a pacifist – advocating passivity at any price, holding that war must be stopped at whatever cost – still jeopardizes his masculinity. This results not only in a certain social stigma but also in *insight*: the 'light' that Owen claims to have 'comprehended' entails a new awareness of the social construction of gender. By the light of this disclosure, a masculinity that has previously seemed entirely natural, a non-negotiable bestowal of nature herself, is seen to be no more than a set of cultural assumptions which can and must be changed. Despite his apparent impotence, the pacifist is a challenge to the gender stereotype, and the stigma that he experiences is an indication of the threat that he poses. Since stereotypical views of masculinity and femininity are always co-ordinated, the pacifist's insight will encompass not only masculine stereotypes but gender stereotypes in general. Gender ideologies do not focus on a single sex alone. They are concerned with the duality, and a quality or role assigned to one will be co-ordinated with a complementary quality or role assigned to the other. A modification at one point will have effects throughout the system as a whole. If, through the light of revelation, a particular construal of masculinity becomes visible as such and is rejected, this cannot but affect the corresponding construals of femininity. Of all men, the pacifist should be

---

[12] Woolf's insistence on the continuities between early- and mid-twentieth century warfare challenges the post-war consensus that although the First World War was an unnecessary waste the Second World War was just in principle, justified in the manner it was conducted, and highly satisfactory in its outcome. The disastrous effects of this consensus are pointed out by Stanley Hauerwas, writing from an American perspective: 'World War II continues to set a terrible precedent for American thinking. For that war is what most Americans think a just war is about – namely, a war you can fight to win using any means necessary because your cause is entirely just' (*Dispatches from the Front: Theological Engagements with the Secular*, Durham and London: Duke University Press, 1994, 143).

peculiarly open to the feminist's insight into the relation between war, gender and the subordination of women. He cannot be regarded as just another representative of an undifferentiated patriarchy.

The 'patriarchy' against which the Society of Outsiders defines itself is, in fact, not the seamless robe that it takes itself to be. It is full of holes. Its project is to cover the whole of reality, so that reality itself will appear as patriarchal. Yet, at point after point, the gaps and tears in the garment allow a reality to show through that is other than patriarchy and contrary to it. It is these gaps and tears that make the existence of a Society of Outsiders possible in the first place, for otherwise the seamless robe would enfold all men and women alike and no one would be in a position to see through it. Even in the case of the church (for Woolf, the Church of England), the patriarchal project encounters serious difficulties. If we ask, Is war right or wrong?, the church gives us no clear answer:

> The bishops themselves are at loggerheads. The Bishop of London maintained that 'the real danger to the peace of the world to-day were the pacifists. Bad as war was, dishonour was far worse'. On the other hand, the Bishop of Birmingham described himself as an 'extreme pacifist . . . I cannot see myself that war can be regarded as consonant with the spirit of Christ'. So the Church itself gives us divided counsel – in some circumstances it is right to fight; in no circumstances is it right to fight. (124)

This division among the bishops has come to light in the *Daily Telegraph*, 5 February 1937, and is said, with heavy irony, to be 'distressing, baffling, confusing'. But it might better be seen as a faint sign of hope. We must look more closely at this division and what it signifies.

In the figure of the Bishop of London, the church fulfils its calling, bestowed on it by patriarchy itself, to be patriarchy's transcendental guarantor. 'London' is a fit symbol of the male-dominated world of public life: for there (as we already know) 'within quite a small space are crowded together St Paul's, the Bank of England, the Mansion House, the massive if funereal battlements of the Law Courts; and on the other side, Westminster Abbey and the Houses of Parliament'. There 'our fathers and brothers have spent their lives' (133). It is entirely proper that the Bishop who presides over this world should speak for it. He knows that war is 'bad'. He has noticed that people get hurt by it. But it is not as bad as all that; it is not so bad that it 'must be stopped at whatever cost'. War, in fact, is good as well as bad. (The Bishop may perhaps have pointed out here that war develops manly qualities, and that human physique and character would deteriorate without it. Or he may have demonstrated that the proposed war meets the criteria for a 'just war' that are decreed by tradition.) It is not war but 'dishonour' – loss of self-esteem – that must be stopped at whatever cost. The Bishop does not pause to consider whether the crucified Christ shares his views on war and dishonour, for he speaks here not in Christ's name but on the much more impressive authority of patriarchy itself. Having braced himself for war and reassured himself with the thought of its relative goodness, he not only dissents from 'the pacifists' but actually sees in them 'the real danger to the peace of the world'. The pacifists are wolves in sheep's clothing, and are exposed as such by the sharp eyes of the Bishop – conscious as ever of his solemn duty to protect the genuine sheep from predators.

In spite of these almost unanswerable arguments, the Bishop suffers the severe embarrassment of being contradicted by a brother bishop in the very same issue of the *Daily Telegraph*. Birmingham lacks the prestige of London. The Outsider would probably not have conceded that 'at first sight it is enormously impressive' (133) if she had taken Birmingham rather than London as her symbol of the public world. In London, St Paul's and Westminster Abbey stand for the Church's presence at the heart of the nation's life. 'Birmingham, on the other hand, had not much interest in the Church . . . Its temper was . . . predominantly Nonconformist.'[13] London establishes the norm, Birmingham represents dissent from the norm; London is the inside, Birmingham the outside. The Bishop of Birmingham is therefore an Outsider, and as such, unlike his counterpart in London, he is not ashamed to ask whether war is

---

[13] G. L. Prestige, *The Life of Charles Gore*, London: Heinemann, 1935, 249.

'consonant with the spirit of Christ' and to answer in the negative. He sees through the posturing of his brother, for whom it is ultimately Christ's command and practice of non-resistance that is 'the real danger to the peace of the world'.[14]

In doing so, he exposes an embarrassing hole in the patri-archal fabric. Patriarchy must pay lip-service to Christ if it is to have the transcendental guarantee that it covets. But Christ proves himself to be unreliable. He shows a marked tendency to evade the role that patriarchy would thrust upon him. One hopes and expects to see him in the procession of fathers and brothers, but he seems to be absent. He is an Outsider. Through 'the spirit of Christ', he is at work still to shape a mode of being in the world that is fundamentally at odds with the metropolitan norm.[15]

Two men (a Poet, a Bishop) trace back to a third (Christ) a disclosure that forces them to rethink the very nature of 'manhood'. But to rethink masculinity is not to rethink maleness

---

[14] An account of the bishop's pacifism is given in John Barnes, *Ahead of his Age: Bishop Barnes of Birmingham*, London: Collins, 1979, 344–64. For the broader context, see Alan Wilkinson, *Dissent or Conform? War, Peace and the English Churches 1900–1945*, London: SCM Press, 1986.

[15] With the possible exception of Mary Daly, recent feminist theology does not appear to endorse Woolf's option for pacifism. Feminist theology has often sought con-vergence with Latin American liberation theology, which does not deny that there can be a legitimate violence of the victim directed against the violence of the oppressor (see, for example, Sharon D. Welch's *Communities of Resistance and Solidarity: A Feminist Theology of Liberation*, Maryknoll: Orbis, 1985, 15–31, where the con-vergence between feminist and liberation theologies makes the question of the violence of the victim a non-issue). Ched Myers acutely analyses liberation theolo-gians' unease with Jesus' practice of nonviolence, arguing that 'the ambivalent relationship between Marxist political hermeneutics and the cross suggests that it has already been decided, on other grounds, that the strategy of nonviolence does not represent genuinely revolutionary politics' (*Binding the Strong Man: A Political Reading of Mark's Story of Jesus*, Maryknoll: Orbis, 1991, 471). The nonviolence at the heart of Jesus' gospel 'has been betrayed not only by interpreters of the right but of the left as well. For in identifying his movement as a necessarily subversive one, the fact remains that he calls his followers to take up the cross, not the sword. The way of nonviolence reckons with execution, not dreams of Maccabean heroism and revolu-tionary conquest . . . It is a deliberate revolutionary strategy, embraced in the conviction that only nonviolence can break the most primal structures of power and domination in the world, and create the possibility for a new order to dawn in the world' (286). The theological issue here is trenchantly expressed by John Howard Yoder: 'Theologians have long been asking how Jerusalem can relate to Athens; here the claim is that Bethlehem has something to say about Rome – or Masada' (*The Politics of Jesus*, Grand Rapids: Eerdmans, 1972, 13).

alone, in isolation. To be man is not to be man alone but to be man together with woman, just as to be woman is to be woman together with man. The recognition that Christ forbids the violence that is the traditional prerogative of the male is a sign of hope for men and women alike.

THE ARCHBISHOP AND THE MANX CAT

Woolf provides a set of photographs to illustrate her image of the procession of fathers and brothers. The photographs confirm her claims about the fathers' and brothers' peculiar dress sense, and several of them also demonstrate their fondness for processing. One is entitled 'A University Procession'; and processions are also under way in the photographs entitled 'A Judge' and 'An Archbishop'. The title, 'An Archbishop', indicates that the author intends to draw attention to the type and not to the individual office-holder, whose name is not given. Like the other fathers and brothers, he is, by modern standards, oddly dressed. His mitre, with its peaks at front and back and its dip in the middle, flaunts its difference from all other known headwear. His stole is broad and richly embroidered, and is made of such thick and heavy material that will-power alone keeps him from sinking under its weight. His left hand grasps a thick wooden staff, surmounted by an elaborate silver structure vaguely reminiscent of ecclesiastical architecture and presumably representing the Church, which would fall to the ground were he to relax his grip. Against the dazzling white background of his cassock there hangs a silver and jewelled crucifix, signifying perhaps the indissoluble union of faith and temporal power. But most striking of all is not his attire but his face. It is the lined, hollow-cheeked face of an old man whose eyes, nose, mouth and jaw are resolutely and grimly set as if to defy any who would challenge his right to rule. Behind him, the downturned eyes and folded hands of an altar-boy express an almost feminine submissiveness.

In Virginia Woolf's *Orlando: A Biography* (1928), there is a curious scene during which the hero changes sex. Orlando is a young aristocrat, elevated to a high position at court by the favour of Queen Elizabeth I and dispatched by King Charles II as ambassador to Constantinople. Returning home as a woman, she becomes the confidante of literary luminaries such as Dryden, Pope, Swift and Addison, marries and fulfils her own literary ambitions during the Victorian period, and marks her arrival at the present day (11 October 1928) by paying a visit to Marshall and Snelgrove's, the department store. At the turning-point of the book, the ambassador falls into a trance, and his biographer finds herself at a loss as to how to proceed. Should she heed the counsel of the Ladies Purity, Chastity and Modesty, who advise her to conceal the truth about what happened next? But events overtook her as she deliberated. Trumpet blasts appealed for the truth to be uncovered, and the virgin sisters fled in disarray. Orlando awoke:

He stretched himself. He rose. He stood upright in complete naked-ness before us, and while the trumpets pealed Truth! Truth! Truth! we have no choice but to confess – he was a woman . . . No human being, since the world began, has ever looked more ravishing. His form combined in one the strength of a man with a woman's grace. As he stood there, the silver trumpets prolonged their note, as if reluctant to leave the lovely sight which their blast had called forth; and Chastity, Purity, and Modesty, inspired, no doubt, by Curiosity, peeped in at the door and threw a garment like a towel at the naked form which, unfortunately, fell short by several inches. Orlando looked himself up and down in a long looking-glass, without any signs of discomposure, and went, presumably, to his bath. (97)

This biographical account of a magical sex-change may appear to be frivolous, but the question it raises is not at all frivolous. The question is this: if it could happen to an Ambassador, could it also happen (*mutatis mutandis*) to an Archbishop?

Woolf values the church chiefly as an image of patriarchy in its purest and most transcendental form. The God of whom it speaks 'is now very generally held to be a conception, of patriarchal origin, valid only for certain races, at certain stages and times' (319).[16] Although God is dead, however, the church

---

[16] In place of 'God', Woolf proposes a 'philosophy': 'that behind the cotton wool is hidden a pattern; that we – I mean all human beings – are connected with this; that the whole world is a work of art; that we are parts of the work of art. *Hamlet* or a Beethoven quartet is the truth about this vast mass that we call the world. But there

retains an exemplary significance. Like Fascism, it can be held up as a mirror to society at large. In particular, its refusal to allow women to minister in the sanctuary aptly symbolizes women's marginalization in public life. Because the ordination of women would undermine the symbolic function she has assigned to the church, Woolf is as resolutely opposed to it as is the Archbishop himself. Yet she is genuinely interested in the report prepared by the Archbishops' Commission (1935), in response to the request of 'daughters of educated men' to be admitted to the priesthood. She reports at some length the theological and exegetical arguments to which, as the Commission concedes, the daughters of educated men can legitimately appeal, and she also quotes its guarded conclusion: 'While the Commission as a whole would not give their positive assent to the view that a woman is inherently incapable of receiving the grace of Order . . . we believe that the general mind of the Church is still in accord with the continuous tradition of a male priesthood' (252). But Woolf underplays the admission that it is only tradition that bars women from the ordained ministry, despite the theological arguments in its favour. She does not see that, in conceding the weakness of its own case and the strength of the opposing one, the Commission is in effect casting doubt on the permanent masculinity of the Archbishop himself. The Commission as a whole would not give positive assent to the view that the Archbishop is inherently incapable of becoming a woman, although it believes that this would create some difficulties for the general mind of the Church.

Woolf fails to exploit this point partly because she does not wish women to be ordained and partly because she is more interested in the report's psychological account of male resis-

---

is no Shakespeare, there is no Beethoven; certainly and emphatically there is no God; we are the words; we are the music; we are the thing itself' ('A Sketch of the Past' [1939–40], in *Moments of Being*, 72). This philosophy derives from the revelatory moment, as experienced by Mrs Ramsay in *To the Lighthouse*: the moment when one becomes aware that 'there is a coherence in things; something, she meant, is immune from change, and shines out (she glanced at the window with its ripple of reflected lights) in the face of the flowing, the fleeting, the spectral, like a ruby . . . Of such moments, she thought, the thing is made that remains for ever after. This would remain' (114).

tance to women's ordination. In declining to admit women to the priesthood, it seemed advisable to the Commission 'to give psychological and not merely historical reasons for their refusal' (253). Professor Grensted of Oxford was therefore commissioned 'to summarize the relevant psychological and physiological material' (253), and, following the conventional disclaimers about the limits of psychological knowledge and the controversial nature of psychological theories, he offered an analysis of male resistance to women priests, as expressed in the predominantly hostile evidence presented to the Commission. This resistance, he argues, is the product of an 'infantile fixation' – an unconscious fear of women grounded in repressed memories of infantile sexuality. It is, to say the least, a novelty for a church report to appeal to Freudian speculations about a 'castration complex', and to trace the general mind of the church back to an 'infantile fixation'. Grensted writes:

This strength of feeling, conjoined with a wide variety of rational explanations, is clear evidence of the presence of powerful and wide-spread subconscious motives. In the absence of detailed analytical material . . . it nevertheless remains clear that infantile fixation plays a predominant part in determining the strong emotion with which this whole subject is commonly approached . . . Whatever be the exact value and interpretation of the material upon which theories of the 'oedipus complex' and the 'castration complex' have been founded, it is clear that the general acceptance of male dominance, and still more of feminine inferiority, resting upon subconscious ideas of woman as 'man manqué', has its background in infantile conceptions of this type. These commonly, and even usually, survive in the adult, despite their irrationality, and betray their presence, below the level of conscious thought, by the strength of the emotions to which they give rise. It is strongly in support of this view that the admission of women to Holy Orders, and especially to the ministry of the sanctuary, is so commonly regarded as something shameful. This sense of shame cannot be regarded in any other light than as a non-rational sex taboo. (254)

Underlying this aetiology of resistance to women's ministry is a Freudian tale that is judiciously left untold, although it is hinted at. Hostile emotions well up into the conscious mind when the issue of women's ordination is raised, and these can be traced back to a traumatic and long-repressed event in the sexual development of the small boy. One day, the boy notices for the first time that his sister lacks a penis. She is 'man manqué': man who lacks, is deficient and falls short. The effect of this discovery is shattering. In the course of the Oedipal relationship with his mother, the boy has already discovered that he possesses a penis and that stimulating it is pleasurable. He also discovers that adults disapprove of his pleasurable activities and threaten him with castration, but he pays no heed to their threats – until the day when he discovers, through observation of his sister, that the threats are meant seriously. In his sister he encounters one who is otherwise like him, but who is manifestly the victim of castration. If it happened to her, might it not also happen to him? His sexuality will need to be reorganized. He must abandon his sexual relationship with his mother and his self-stimulation, and he must identify himself instead with his father, to whom he has previously been hostile and whose threat of castration he has previously ignored. Since 'normal' development into adult sexuality is achieved only very rarely, the 'castration complex' that succeeds the 'oedipus complex' can leave him with an enduring although unconscious fear of the being whose lack exposed the secret of his guilty love. He revenges himself on her by excluding her from his sanctuaries. That is why the 'general mind of the Church' resists women's ordination.

This translation of the general mind of the Church into Oedipal and castration complexes appears to offer the strongest possible support for those 'daughters of educated men' who wish to be admitted to the ordained ministry. Once the secret of male resistance is out, who would any longer dare to expose his complexes to public view? In the face of this devastating argument, the Archbishop himself will stifle his objections. Unfortunately, there is a lifeline which must, in all fairness, be offered to him. The Freudian tale can also be told from the standpoint of the sister.[17]

[17] The double narrative, distinguishing the perspective of the sister from that of her brother, is to be found in Sigmund Freud, 'The Dissolution of the Oedipus Complex' (1924), and 'Some Psychical Consequences of the Anatomical Distinction between

One day, while playing with her brother, the small girl notices that he has something that she lacks. This too is a shattering discovery, and she directs her anger against her mother. Why has her mother not equipped her with a penis? Turning away from her mother, she now enters the Oedipal relationship with her father, hoping to obtain from him the child which would constitute an acceptable penis-substitute. The transfer of her affections from father to potential husband may in due course be accomplished fairly smoothly. But, as in her brother's case, there is considerable scope for error. The girl may refuse to accept her lack of a penis; she may continue to behave as if she possesses one. The tables may therefore be turned on the 'daughters of educated men' who wish to enter the church or the other professions. Are they not secretly motivated by a penis-envy that is no more creditable than their brothers' fear of castration? The 'man manqué' argument can be played both ways. The result is a stalemate in which the Archbishop and the status quo are bound to be the winners.

Woolf is fully aware of the ambivalence of the 'man manqué' view. In *A Room of One's Own* (1929), she gives a celebrated account of two meals, the first a sumptuous lunch-party at an Oxbridge men's college, the second a frugal dinner at Fernham, an impoverished women's college.[18] As she reclines in a window-seat after lunch, she notices a tailless cat padding across the quadrangle. The Manx cat

did look a little absurd, poor beast, without a tail, in the middle of the lawn. Was he really born so, or had he lost his tail in an accident? The tailless cat, though some are said to exist in the Isle of Man, is rarer than one thinks. It is a queer animal, quaint rather than beautiful. It is strange what a difference a tail makes – you know the sort of things one says as a lunch party breaks up and people are finding their coats and hats. (12)

the Sexes' (1925), in *The Penguin Freud Library* 7, ed. Angela Richards, London: Penguin Books, 1991, 315–22, 331–43.

18 The lunch-party is 'distinguished not only by its bounty and excellence but by the magical nature of its provenance, the sense of a return to some originary plenitude now produced under the aegis of the father. Gratification is known before desire is felt. With no command uttered, and agency scarcely revealed, course follows course in a prelinguistic economy of desire' (E. Abel, *Virginia Woolf*, 99).

The Manx cat from the Isle of Man is obviously an image of woman: Man/Manx = man manqué. Woman is the Man(x) who lacks a tail; the Latin *penis* originally meant 'tail'. The more difficult interpretative question is who it is who resorts to the infantile definition of woman as Manx, as man manqué. The Manx cat is noticed by the female narrator, and her amusement is without doubt a defensive strategy intended to ward off the terrible knowledge that the Manx cat communicates. But that knowledge is ambiguous. The narrator's point may be: this is how I am perceived within this all-male college – as tailless, a Manx cat, man manqué. Or her point may be: this is how I perceive myself within this affluent, all-male college – as man manqué, my physical lack corresponding to the material and intellectual lack that I suffer through exclusion from its resources. Is she the object of fear, or the subject of envy? Perhaps she is making both points simultaneously, while pretending to make neither. The Manx cat is woman, but who knows whether it represents her in terms of man's castration complex or her own penis-envy? The cat remains inscrutable, enjoying its power over the Archbishop, the Professor, the general mind of the Church, and the daughters of educated men alike. In other words, more prosaically expressed, the Manx cat confirms that psychology is of only limited value in discussion of women's roles within the church. If the Freudian tale is plausible or fantastic in one of its versions, it is equally plausible or fantastic in the other. In practice, the two versions of the story cancel each other out and result in stalemate and victory for the status quo.

If anything is to be done about the Archbishop's eternal masculinity, we must turn to the Commission's theological arguments. Theology will show, perhaps, that 'neither is woman apart from man nor man apart from woman, in the Lord'. And, granted the ambiguities of this statement, it will show how the phrase 'in the Lord' resolves them. Whatever light psychology may or may not shed upon the relationship between man and woman, it knows nothing of how that relationship appears 'in the Lord'. This is a matter for theology, which is able to show that the patriarchal church – the church as ruled by fathers and brothers, the Archbishop's church – has feet of clay. It does not rest on eternal foundations. Theology does so primarily not by denouncing and negating but by pointing to the church's true foundation and by asking how far the Archbishop's church still rests on that foundation. Theology does all this even in the hands of a Commission which, although it will not venture a dogmatic denial of woman's capacity for ordained ministry, is convinced that any change to the status quo would be quite inappropriate now or in the foreseeable future.

'In the Lord' refers us not to a patriarchal ruler but to Jesus.[19] Compelled to turn to the New Testament in order to address the question put to them, the Commission found that 'the Gospels show us that our Lord regarded men and women alike as members of the same spiritual kingdom, as children of God's family, and as possessors of the same spiritual capacities . . . ' (quoted in *Three Guineas*, 249–50). 'It would seem then that the founder of Christianity believed that neither training nor sex was needed for this profession', and that his belief was rightly interpreted and summarized in the affirmation that 'there is neither male nor female: for ye are all one in Christ Jesus' (250). The divine gift was bestowed upon carpenters, fishermen, but also on women:

As the Commission points out there can be no doubt that in those early days there were prophetesses – women upon whom the divine gift had descended. Also they were allowed to preach. St Paul, for example, lays it down that women, when praying in public, should be veiled. 'The implication is that if veiled a woman might prophesy [i.e. preach] and lead in prayer.' How then can they be excluded from the priesthood since they were once thought fit by the founder of the religion and by one of his apostles to preach? That was the question, and the Commission solved it by appealing not to the mind of the founder, but to the mind of the Church. That, of course, involved a distinction. For the mind of the Church had to be interpreted by another mind, and that mind was St Paul's mind; and St Paul, in interpreting that mind, changed his mind. (250)

---

[19] The identification of the *kyrios* as patriarchal ruler is reinforced by Elisabeth Schüssler Fiorenza's neologism 'kyriarchy', which refers to 'the rule of the emperor/master/lord/father/husband over his subordinates' (*Jesus Miriam's Child, Sophia's Prophet: Critical Issues in Feminist Christology*, London: SCM Press, 1994, 14). The neologism does not allow *kyrios* to be redefined along the lines of Mk. 10.42–5.

The Pauline veil is no longer an ambivalent symbol of division, as it is elsewhere in Woolf's text; it represents woman's authority to proclaim, in accordance with the mind of Christ. However, the authorization was quickly revoked. The Commission appealed to the prohibition of 1 Timothy 2.12 – whether the author be 'St Paul or another' – to justify their claim that the church has changed its mind. (They might also have appealed to 1 Cor. 14.34–35, with the same qualification.) Woolf comments:

> That, it may frankly be said, is not so satisfactory as it might be; for we cannot altogether reconcile the ruling of St Paul, or another, with the ruling of Christ himself who 'regarded men and women alike as members of the same spiritual kingdom . . . and as possessors of the same spiritual capacities'. But it is futile to quibble over the meaning of words, when we are so soon in the presence of facts. Whatever Christ meant, or St Paul meant, the fact was that in the fourth or fifth century the profession of religion had become so highly organized that . . . the prophet or prophetess whose message was voluntary and untaught became extinct; and their places were taken by the three orders of bishops, priests and deacons, who are invariably men . . . (250–1)

If we turn from exegetical debates to facts, we find (for example) that whereas an archbishop currently receives a salary of £15,000 and a bishop £10,000, a deaconess or a parish worker receives no more than £150 a year in recognition of her labours (252). In the church as elsewhere, salary differentials must be taken as a measure of the value ascribed to different types of paid work, and it is therefore hard to avoid the conclusion that the church values the work of men much more highly than the work of women. That is the material fact, and the Commission had no intention of allowing theology or the founder of Christianity to interfere with it.[20]

Because the church must serve as a symbol of patriarchy in transcendental clothing, Woolf is content to allow the Commis-

[20] The Commission's theological and exegetical arguments anticipate the more recent debate about the ordination of women in the Church of England (see Mary Hayter, *The New Eve in Christ: The Use and Abuse of the Bible in the Debate about Women in the Church*, London: SPCK, 1987, 118–43; Ruth B. Edwards, *The Case for Women's Ministry*, London: SPCK, 1989, 39–85).

sion to acquiesce in the status quo. The Church of England has refused to admit women to the ordained ministry – and 'long may she exclude us!' (207). The Outsider is the mirror-image of the Archbishop. They complement one another and are necessary to one another, so that even here woman is not apart from man nor man from woman – precisely at the point where man's self-definition excludes woman and woman's retaliatory and defensive self-definition excludes men. But instead of defining herself over against the patriarchal monolith, the Outsider might have chosen to exploit the admission that – however impressive it may appear – the monolith is in fact a mere facade that knowingly conceals the reality it is supposed to represent. The mind of the church must conform to the mind of Christ. The admission that the church has changed its mind, and that the mind that it has changed is the mind of Christ, is an admission of error far more damning than the 'infantile fixation' theory.

It is the mind of Christ that exposes the perversity of the mind of the church, and not the Freudian aetiology. The strong and hostile feelings that the issue of women's ministry arouses are indeed symptomatic of a repressed originary experience. But this experience is not an infantile theory about bodily differentiation but the original encounter with Christ, in whom there is neither male nor female, and in whom – in the absence of hierarchical and essentialist definitions of maleness and femaleness – man and woman are defined not as apart from one another but in relation to one another. The fact of repression indicates that this encounter too could be experienced as a traumatic threat of castration: and this repression is the origin of the Archbishop's eternal masculinity. Yet if there is – to return to the testimony of the Bishop of Birmingham – a 'spirit of Christ' that even now shapes a mode of being in the world that conforms to the mind of Christ, there is no reason to think that the Archbishop's position is secure. On the contrary, his masculinity is in jeopardy.

According to the Commission, 'the Gospels show us that our Lord regarded men and women alike as members of the same spiritual kingdom, as children of God's family, and as possessors of the same spiritual capacities . . . ' In this deceptively bland statement, we may find the repressed moment of trauma that the spirit of Christ seeks to expose and heal. The phrase 'children of God's family' is not simply pious rhetoric. It alludes to the words of Jesus: 'Truly I say to you, unless you turn and become like children, you will never enter the kingdom of heaven' (Matt. 18.3). It is here that the original, repressed threat is to be found. The point of the saying is not to idealize childhood or to offer a refuge from adult reality in infantile fantasy. Instead, Jesus articulates the possibility and the promise that the long historical process in which adult gendered identity is constructed and fixed may be unravelled and undone, so that identity may be recreated. The parabolic figure of the child represents here the human whose identity is fluid and malleable, potential rather than actual, not yet solidified and fixed. According to the parable, an old history of identity-formation is to be undone and superseded by a new history in which the product of the old history is radically reshaped. To submit oneself to that new history is to enter the kingdom of heaven. The fixed identity that emerges from the primary history is, of course, a gendered identity, and it now becomes clear how it is that Jesus' utterance may be heard as a threat of castration. Indeed, the old identity is bound to perceive it as such, and from its own standpoint it is not wrong to do so. Jesus commands that the bodily member that leads one into sin be cut off (5.29–30). He commends those who have made themselves eunuchs for the sake of the kingdom of heaven (19.12). Indeed, he himself wields the knife: he has come not to bring peace but a sword (10.34).[21]

---

[21] These additional sayings indicate that an interpretation of Matt. 18.3 in terms of gender and identity can be defended even on the basis of standard exegetical criteria. The conventional apolitical view that the saying encourages readers 'to realize their dependence on God, to entrust their entire lives to him and to expect everything from him' (E. Schweizer, *Good News according to Matthew*, ET London: SPCK, 1976, 363) does not reflect a greater fidelity to the dictates of the historical-critical method. Exegesis such as this recalls Albert Schweitzer's complaint that, in modern scholarly works, 'Many of [Jesus'] greatest sayings are found lying in a corner like explosive shells from which the charges have been removed' (*The Quest of the Historical Jesus*, ET London: A. & C. Black, 2nd edn 1911, 398). Elisabeth Schüssler Fiorenza's more political interpretation is moving in the right direction: for her, the point of the

Jesus poses a threat to the gendered identities that history has laboriously constructed and passed off as nature. He calls for men and women to turn from them and to become again like children so that their identities may be recreated. In particular, Jesus is a threat to *masculine* gendered identity, the social construct arbitrarily erected on the basis of the inalienable maleness and femaleness given in creation. He challenges the belief that masculine identity entails the exclusion of women from the public sphere, just as he challenges the related belief that masculine identity ('manliness', 'virility') is constituted by the violence of war and its surrogates. He comes to disturb the peace of masculine complacency and feminine acquiescence, not because his goal is destruction for his own sake but in order to clear the ground for new, more flexible constructs in which men and women learn to relate to one another 'in the Lord' and in the light of the kingdom of heaven that is creation's goal.

saying (in its Marcan form, Mk. 10.15) is that 'the child/slave who occupies the lowest place within patriarchal structures becomes the primary paradigm for true discipleship . . . This saying is not an invitation to childlike innocence and naiveté but a challenge to relinquish all claims of power and domination over others' (*In Memory of Her: A Feminist Theological Reconstruction of Christian Origins*, London: SCM Press, 1983, 148).

CHAPTER TWO

Eros veiled

The veil may be a symbol of division. It can represent a gendered distribution of space, demarcating the public and the private realms in which man and woman respectively have their being. It can be resented because of the restrictions it enforces, and cherished as the source of wisdom and insight. Certain Pauline or deutero-Pauline texts, enjoining silence and docility as the conditions of woman's marginal participation in the public sphere, make this a plausible interpretation of the Pauline image. On closer reading of the Pauline text, however, it appears that the veil is the symbol not of woman's enforced silence but of her authority to speak – to speak, indeed, to and from God on behalf of the congregation, to declare in her own voice the word of the Lord and the answering human word. 'Every woman praying or prophesying with uncovered head dishonours her head' (1 Cor. 11.5). Granted that woman speaks and must speak to and from God, the veil is the mark of her right to do so. Woman 'must have authority on the head . . .' (v. 10), and the veil is that authority – assuming what must later be demonstrated, that the veil is indeed the issue here. The speech that the veil authorizes is not a marginal speech that occurs behind closed doors but a speech that belongs at the heart of the public life of the worshipping congregation. But why is this speech subjected to the condition of the veil? And how is it that the veil that authorizes speech can also be seen – with some plausibility – to deny speech and to enjoin silence?

In the face of this paradox, it is inappropriate to protest the text's innocence and to lay the blame on its 'male interpreters' and on the deutero-Pauline gloss in 1 Corinthians 14.34–5 that has led them astray. It is equally inappropriate to welcome the veil and the exclusion as negative conditions for a space 'apart from man' in which woman subjects man's works to silent yet critical scrutiny. In the Lord, woman is not apart from man nor man from woman, and that togetherness is distorted and undermined if her voice is not heard at the heart of the public space of worship. To anticipate: the veil is the condition of woman's speech in that it intercepts and prohibits the male gaze that would convert her into an object and prevent her recognition as a speaking subject. It is agape and not eros that must rule in the public sphere of the congregation, and for that reason the veil is interposed as the condition of woman's speech and of man's listening to woman's speech – the speech not of an abstract 'autonomous subject' but of one who has been freed by the gospel to declare in her own language the mighty works of God. The veil is a symbol directed at man. In its blankness it admonishes him to hear the word of the Lord in the medium of a woman's voice and to make her response to this word his own. In order that he may listen and not look, it imposes on him the humiliation of a blindfold. For the sake of the agape that is the condition of true speaking and hearing within the body of Christ, eros – or woman as construed by the erotic male gaze – must be veiled.

Paul's attempt to interpose the veil was questionable not only culturally and politically but also theologically – as he himself later tacitly acknowledges. In the new covenant, he will argue, it is proper that women and men should behold the glory of the Lord with unveiled face; it is only the Law that speaks from behind a veil, and the Law has now reached its limit (2 Cor. 3.12–18). Yet, beneath the surface of the awkward, assertive and embarrassed Pauline discourse, genuine theological concerns are still recognizable.[1]

---

[1] Theological reflection on gender here takes the form of a close reading of a particular passage – in contrast to a more historically oriented approach which, taking its cue from the explicit reference to women prophets in 1 Cor. 11.5, reads the whole of 1 Corinthians as a drama in which Pauline patriarchalism struggles to suppress the incipient feminist theology of the Corinthian church (Elisabeth Schüssler Fiorenza, 'Rhetorical Situation and Historical Reconstruction in 1 Corinthians', *NTS* 33 (1987), 386–403; Antoinette Clark Wire, *The Corinthian Women Prophets: A Reconstruction through*

SHAMING THE HEAD (VERSES 2-6)

*I praise you because you remember all that I taught and, just as I delivered
them to you, you observe the traditions* (1 Cor. 11.2). Where, in spite of
this, traditions have not been faithfully observed, Paul does not
praise. He is sharply critical, as in the case of the Corinthian
practice of the Lord's Supper (11.17–34): 'As for the following
instructions, I do *not* praise you, because your assembling
together is not for the better but for the worse' (v. 17). It seems
likely that the uncovered heads of the Corinthian women
represent not an aberration but the established tradition at
Corinth, which Paul now seeks to change – in the light,
perhaps, of the universal practice of 'the churches of God'
elsewhere (v. 16). 'But I want you to know . . .' (v. 3) signals the
intention not of correcting an abuse but of announcing a
supplement to the traditions that will interrupt and modify
existing practice. To continue to observe the traditions 'just as I
delivered them to you' would now be to disobey the living voice
of the apostle.[2]

Paul's Rhetoric, Minneapolis: Fortress Press, 1990). Fiorenza is rightly critical of
interpreters who 'characterize the Corinthians as foolish, immature, arrogant, divisive, individualistic, unrealistic illusionists, libertine enthusiasts, or boasting spiritual-
ists who misunderstand the preaching of Paul in terms of "realized eschatology"'
(389). 'A cursory look at scholarship on 1 Corinthians indicates that Paul is a skilled
rhetorician, who, throughout the centuries, has reached his goal of persuading his
audience that he is right and that the "others" are wrong' (390). Fiorenza wishes to
distinguish between 'the historical argumentative situation, the implied or inscribed
rhetorical situation as well as the rhetorical situation of contemporary interpretations'
(388): a 'historical argumentative situation' marked by the genesis of an incipient
feminist theology at Corinth can both be reconstructed from the Pauline text and
used to counter the 'implied or inscribed rhetorical situation' as rendered in that text.
Two main problems arise at this point. First, the project of recovering the suppressed
voices of early Christian women reflects historical-critical scholarship's over-opti-
mistic assessment of its own ability to reconstruct entire historical complexes from the
few ambiguous fragments that survive. Second, the polarity of androcentric text and
suppressed voices simply reverses the privileging of the Pauline perspective over that
of his addressees, and assigns to the interpreter the privileged role of opponent of the
text. But a generalized 'hermeneutic of suspicion' along these lines may not be the
most appropriate or effective strategy for theological reflection on issues of gender.

[2] The text does not support the view that an 'overrealized eschatology' has 'involved
some kind of breakdown in the distinction between the sexes', as women at Corinth
argued for the right to pray and prophesy 'without the customary "head covering" or
"hairstyle"' (G. Fee, *The First Epistle to the Corinthians*, NICNT, Grand Rapids: Eerdmans, 1987, 498). This view derives from the assumption that a coherent, distinctive

But I want you to know that the head of every man is Christ, the head of woman is man, and the head of Christ is God (v. 3). The traditions as originally delivered and faithfully maintained are interrupted by a threefold dogmatic statement that lends itself to rearrangement in the form of a hierarchy. If the third statement is placed at the beginning, the result is a *descending* hierarchy that runs from God to Christ to man to woman. If the first statement is placed second, the result is an *ascending* hierarchy, from woman to man to Christ to God. Rearranged like this, the threefold statement serves as a pattern for later Christian or pseudo-Christian accounts of being as hierarchy and discloses the simple assumptions about gender that will so often underlie their apparent complexities. It also indicates that a hierarchical account of gender, in which male and female are related to one another as higher to lower, may be sustained by what will later be identified as an 'Arian' christology in which human pre-eminence and subordination find their ontological grounding in the relation of God to Christ. Hierarchical accounts of being require not only relationships of pre-eminence and subordination but also a chain of connections that links the highest member in the series with the lowest and blurs the absolute distinction between creator and creature. Yet these world-views will often be unconscious of their Arian or neo-Platonic affinities. They will feel no need to defend themselves against the charge of heterodoxy, and will for centuries be accepted as authentically Christian. Although the Pauline statement *lends itself* to hierarchical rearrangement along these lines, it is not its *intention* to assert any such account of being as hierarchy. As the threefold statement stands, there is no descending or ascending hierarchy: only a series of assertions in which a 'head' is assigned to man, to woman and to Christ. The reference is probably to pre-eminence and authority rather than to relations of origin.[3] The sequel will show that it is only the first two

Corinthian theology can be deduced from 1 Corinthians and used as the primary background for the interpretation of the letter.

[3] The claim that *kephalē* in v. 3 means 'source' is rejected by David Horrell, *The Social Ethos of the Corinthian Correspondence: Interest and Ideology from 1 Corinthians to 1 Clement,*

assertions that play any role in the argument, that they are applied to the single issue of the covering or uncovering of the head, and that the covering of the head gives woman the 'authority' to proclaim the word of God to the congregation irrespective of her relation to any other 'head'. The fact that 'the head of woman is man' is a potential deterrent to woman's proclamation which the covering of her head will effectively nullify. As a theological basis for the proposed new custom, the threefold statement of verse 3 is entirely unconvincing in the light of the radical divine deconstruction of worldly dualities of wisdom and folly, power and weakness, that has earlier been announced (1 Cor. 1.18–31). Yet the grounding of the new custom in woman's relationship to man remains significant, however poorly this relationship is here articulated.

Every man praying or prophesying with his head covered shames his head (v. 4). 'With his head covered' translates *kata kephalēs echōn* ('having down the head'). The meaning of this phrase is established by Esther 6.12, where, after his defeat by Mordecai the Jew, Haman returns to his home grieving *kata kephalēs*: the underlying Hebrew can only refer to the covering of the head as a sign of mourning, and a later Septuagintal editor rightly paraphrases the cryptic Greek phrase as *katakekalummenos kephalēn*, '[his] head covered'. That men cover their heads in situations of distress is confirmed by the example of David who, according to Josephus, covered himself (*katakalupsamenou*) as he mourned the death of Absalom (*Antiquities*, vii.254). Paul, however, is uninterested in the mourning custom: his concern is with the covering of the head while speaking to or from God in the midst of the assembly.

It now becomes clear that the 'head' metaphors of the previous verse arise out of this concern with the literal, physical head. The metaphors (Christ as head, man as head) provide the

Edinburgh: T. & T. Clark, 1996, 170–1. Horrell notes that Paul uses this word 'not to talk about authority and subordination but *precisely because* he wants to talk about the way in which men and women must attire their *kephalē* in worship. Nevertheless, the theological legitimation which the *kephalē* analogy provides clearly gives man priority over woman' (171).

key to the word-play of the following verses, in which literal and metaphorical referents are juxtaposed. In the light of this key, it is clear that the head that is shamed is not the head that is covered. The covered male head shames Christ, who is the head of every man. Paul wishes to impose the covering of the head on women but not on men, and the hypothetical notion of the covered male head serves to justify the distinction the new custom draws between men and women.[4] The objection is anticipated that, if women are to cover their heads, then men should do likewise; and this objection is ruled out on the grounds that the physical heads of men and women represent different metaphorical realities that require the uncovering of the one and the covering of the other. But if man (the head of woman) is shamed by her uncovered head, why is Christ (the head of man) shamed when his head is covered? What is it about the relation of woman to her 'head' that requires the covering of her physical head, when the relation of man to his 'head' prohibits any such covering? To be subject to a 'head' does not in itself entail the covering of the physical head. At this point, pure arbitrariness appears to reign; in other words, the underlying issue is still completely unclear.

But every woman praying or prophesying with head uncovered shames her head . . . (v. 5a). In recent scholarship, 'uncovered' is often taken to mean 'with unbound hair' rather than 'unveiled', on the basis of Septuagintal usage. The term *akatakaluptos* ('uncovered')

---

[4] According to J. Murphy O'Connor, the problem addressed in 1 Cor. 11.2–16 'involved both sexes', and the references to male head-covering are therefore not merely hypothetical ('Sex and Logic in 1 Corinthians 11:2–16', *CBQ* 42 (1980), 482–500; 483). On this view, v. 14 suggests that *kata kephalēs* in v. 4 refers to long hair, which in a male was 'associated with homosexuality' (485). 'The issue was not so much long hair in itself, but long hair as the indispensable prerequisite for an elaborate arrangement' (488): thus, for women, what is criticized is not short hair but untended, unbound hair that was 'not neatly arranged in the fashion becoming a woman' (488). In defiance of accepted conventions, Corinthian men paraded the trappings of homosexuality while Corinthian women took pride in looking wild and dishevelled: 'Scandal was the symbol of their new spiritual freedom; the more people they shocked, the more right they felt themselves to be' (490). This vivid and imaginative portrayal of 'the situation at Corinth' derives, once again, from the hermeneutical assumption that interpretation must be controlled by a hypothetical 'background' reconstructed by the interpreter – even where the text itself is silent about any such background.

occurs only in Leviticus 13.45, where the leper is instructed to wear torn clothes and to leave his head uncovered (*hē kephalē autou akatakaluptos*, an accurate rendering of the Hebrew); that is, he is to let his hair hang loose. But the term does not refer to loose hair as such, but to loose hair as the uncovering of a head that has previously been covered – perhaps by an arrangement of the hair, but equally possibly by an article of clothing such as a turban. This Septuagintal usage is quite compatible with the traditional view that the woman who prays or prophesies with uncovered head is 'uncovered' in the sense that she does not wear a veil. This view is confirmed by the Septuagintal use of the verb *katakaluptein*, which occurs three times in 1 Corinthians 11.6–7, and the cognate noun *katakalumma*. In Genesis 38.15, the patriarch Judah mistakes his daughter-in-law Tamar for a prostitute because her face was covered (*katekalupsato gar to prosōpon autēs*): here the reference can only be to a veil. At the trial of Susanna, the elders who falsely accuse her of adultery demand that her face be unveiled (Sus. 32: *hoi de paranomoi ekeleusan apokaluphthēnai autēn, ēn gar katakekalummenē*). As for the noun, the 'virgin daughter of Babylon' is commanded in Isaiah 47.2 to put off her veil (*apokalupsai to katakalumma sou*). Septuagintal usage seems conclusively in favour of the traditional interpretation of this passage: the Corinthian women's head-covering is specifically a covering for the *face*. Like Moses but unlike other men, they are to conceal their face behind a veil (*kalumma*, 2 Cor. 3.13).[5]

---

[5] W. Schrage's arguments in favour of the 'unbound hair' view represent a broad consensus in recent scholarship (*Der Erste Brief an die Korinther (1 Kor. 6,12–11,16)*, EKK VII/2, Solothurn and Düsseldorf: Benziger Verlag AG; Neukirchen-Vluyn: Neukirchener Verlag des Erziehungsvereins GmbH, 1995, 491–4). (1) Paul does not mention the veil in this passage, but he does mention the topic of hair-length (vv. 4, 6, 14–15). (2) There is extensive evidence that women took part in Graeco-Roman religious rites with unbound hair. (3) The term *akatakaluptos* is found in the LXX only in Lev. 13.45, where it refers to unbound hair. It is remarkable how Lev. 13.45 is so often cited without any reference to Septuagintal usage of *katakaluptein*, which Paul uses three times in 1 Cor. 11.6–7. As for the first point, the celebration of woman's long hair as her 'glory' (v. 15) is hardly an effective argument *against* unbound hair. The references to hair-length must be understood as supporting arguments for the imposition of the veil. If the 'unbound hair' interpretation is preferred, however, the interpretation of the passage in terms of the erotic attraction of man to woman is still viable. In one of the parabolic visions of the *Shepherd of Hermas*, there appear 'twelve women, very beautiful to look at, clothed in black, girded, and their shoulders bare and their hair

It is true that Moses' veil is said to cover his 'face' (*prosōpon*), whereas the Corinthian women are to cover their 'head' (*kephalē*). This might suggest a form of head-covering that leaves the face free. The new custom is explicitly associated with the 'head' in verses 5, 7, 10; the influence of the head imagery of verse 3 is apparent in the wordplay of verse 5, and perhaps still in verse 7. But Paul can also speak of woman's being 'covered' in absolute terms and without specific reference to the head (*ei gar ou katakaluptetai gunē*, v. 6; *katakaluptesthō*, v. 6; *gunaika akatakalupton*, v. 13); this absolute usage is exactly parallel to Susanna 32, which can only refer to the face. Cognate terminology in 2 Corinthians 3.12–18 explicitly refers to the face (*mē anakaluptomenon*, v. 14; *anakekalummenō prosōpō*, v. 18; *kalumma*, vv. 13, 14, 15, 16; cf. *kekalummenon*, 4.3).[6]

The passage from 1 Corinthians was associated with the veiling of women at least as early as the latter part of the second century (well before Tertullian's extensive treatment of it, which will be discussed later). In 1 Corinthians 11.10, Irenaeus attests a reading that substitutes *kalumma* for *exousia*: 'For this reason a woman should have *a veil* upon her head . . .' (*Adversus haereses*, i.8.2). Irenaeus cites a gnostic exegesis of the text in which it is linked with Moses' veil as an indication that Achamoth (the misshapen feminine being that resulted from the passion of Sophia (i.4)) 'drew a veil over herself through modesty' at the

---

loose [*tas trichas lelumenai*]. And these women looked to me to be cruel' (*sim.* ix.9.5). Later, certain of the 'servants of God' are 'deceived by the beauty of these women' with their 'loose hair' (ix.13.7–9). Hermas and his readers obviously recognize unbound hair as a symbol of illicit sexual attraction.

6 The view that the head-covering does not include the face is represented by C. Wolff: 'Bei der Kopfdeckung, auf die korinthische Frauen verzichteten, handelt es sich nicht um einen das Antlitz verhüllenden Schleier; denn Paulus spricht nicht von einer Verhüllung des Gesichtes, sondern vom Bedecken des Kopfes' (*Der erste Brief des Paulus an die Korinther*, ThHKNT 7/II, Berlin: Evangelische Verlagsanstalt, 1982, 67). Wolff appeals to evidence from the synagogue at Dura Europos for a form of head-covering that leaves the face free. A. Jaubert shows that later Jewish texts require the covering of the hair on the grounds that 'les cheveux sont un ornement pour la femme mais un danger pour l'homme, parce qu'ils sont pour lui un attrait' ('Le Voile des Femmes [I Cor. XI.2–16]', *NTS* 18 (1971–2), 419–30; 425–6). Although my own interpretation of the passage assumes that the head-covering includes a covering of the *face*, the crucial point is the basis of the head-covering in the erotic attraction of the male for the female.

approach of the masculine Saviour from above (i.8.2). This reading of 1 Corinthians 11.10 therefore predates Irenaeus and may be traced back to Valentinus or his disciple Ptolemaeus (*Adv. haer.*, i.1.2). Irenaeus does not dissent from the association of the Pauline passage with the veil, and later indicates that he has his own reasons for interest in the passage. In opposition to 'Montanist' appeal to the Johannine theme of the coming of the Paraclete, some have argued that the Gospel of John itself should be rejected. Irenaeus is scathing: 'Wretched men indeed! who wish to be pseudo-prophets, indeed, but who set aside the gift of prophecy from the church . . . We must conclude that these men cannot admit the Apostle Paul either: for in his Epistle to the Corinthians he speaks expressly of prophetical gifts and recognizes men and women prophesying in the church' (iii.11.9). This defence of women prophets demonstrates Irenaeus' own Montanist sympathies; and in the light of his reading of 1 Corinthians 11.10, it is likely that he associates the women prophets of the Pauline text with the veil.[7]

Paul links the absence of this head-covering with 'shame'. The unveiled woman 'shames her head' (*kataischunei tēn kephalēn autēs*, 1 Cor. 11.5, a reference to her husband or perhaps to 'man' in general). This 'shame' appears to be the shame of physical nakedness. (If so, this is a further indication that the head-covering conceals the face, and not just the hair. For Paul, woman's hair is already equivalent to a 'garment' (*peribolaion*, v. 15), and the absence of a hair-covering cannot be associated with nakedness and shame.) Shame and nakedness can be virtual synonyms. The daughter of Babylon is to put off her veil, strip off her robe and uncover her legs, so that 'your shame shall be seen [*anakaluphthēsetai hē aischunē sou*]' (Is. 47.2–3). The shame of nakedness arises from the uncovering of the face no less than the legs, and – although the passive verb conceals this – it also presupposes the presence of a male onlooker who makes the virgin daughter of Babylon the object of his contemptuous and lustful gaze. The correlation of the naked female face with the

---

[7] Translation adapted from *The Ante-Nicene Fathers*, vol. 1, reprinted Grand Rapids: Eerdmans, 1975. The Victorian translator's assumption that Irenaeus is here writing *against* the Montanists makes nonsense of the passage.

desiring male onlooker is, however, more explicit in the story of Susanna, which at several points offers crucial insights into the meaning of the Pauline text.

Susanna is a devout woman of great beauty (*kalē sphodra kai phoboumenē ton kurion*, Sus. 2) who becomes the object of lustful infatuation. Seeing her walking each day in her husband's garden, two elders – appointed that year as judges of the people – are overcome with desire for her. One hot day she sends her maids to fetch oil and ointments so that she may bathe, and finds herself trapped by the elders who have secretly been watching her: if she will not lie with them, they will testify that they caught her in the act of adultery with a young man. She chooses 'not to sin in the sight of the Lord', and is duly accused. The trial is held the next day at her husband's house, and Susanna is called in – a woman, we are reminded, 'of great delicacy and beautiful in appearance [*truphera sphodra kai kalē tē eidei*]' (v. 31). 'And the wicked men commanded her to be unveiled [*apokaluphthēnai*] – for she was veiled [*ēn gar katakekalum-menē*] – so that they might be satisfied with her beauty [*hopōs emplēsthōsin tou kallous autēs*]. But her family [*hoi par' autēs*] and all who saw her wept' (vv. 32–3). Susanna is convicted, but is saved as she is led out to die by the intervention of Daniel, who demonstrates that the elders' testimony is false.[8]

The moment of unveiling is the satisfaction of the elders' desire for Susanna. Having failed to persuade her to lie with them, the 'desire' they announce to her (*en epithumia sou esmen*, v. 21) remains unfulfilled. But the sight of her naked, unveiled face at her trial provides a substitute for what Susanna refused them: in a climactic moment, they look and are satisfied. At this point, however, a persistent misreading of the text comes to light. The text does not say that Susanna was naked when the elders accosted her in the garden. She had announced her intention to bathe, she had sent her servants out to fetch oil and

---

[8] Like the patristic church, Jerome and other translations, RSV prefers Theodotion's version of the Susanna story to the shorter LXX one (details in R. H. Charles (ed.), *The Apocrypha and Pseudepigrapha of the Old Testament in English*, vol. I, Oxford: Clarendon Press, 1913, 638–43). In the LXX version, the phrase *ēn gar katakekalummenē* is absent from v. 32.

ointments, and, 'when the maids had gone out, the two elders rose and ran to her . . . ' (v. 19). The elders must act during the brief interval when the maids are absent; they have no time to watch Susanna undress and enter the water, and the text says nothing of this. In any case, it is perhaps the maids who will undress her. Yet it is generally assumed that Susanna, like Eve, was naked in the garden (described here as a *paradeisos*); and the real moment of nakedness – the unveiling of the face at the trial – is downplayed.[9]

The non-existent moment is captured by Rembrandt, who painted it twice. In the earlier version (c. 1637), the naked Susanna rises from a seated position in order to enter her bath, slipping her shoes off her feet as she does so. Behind her lie her clothes, although with her right hand she continues to clutch the lower part of a garment across her thigh. Her left hand (nearest the viewer) crosses her breast in order to disentangle her long hair. Bracelets, necklace and head-band signify her wealth. Her face is turned towards the viewer, and she shows no apprehension. But in the dense foliage behind her there is concealed a single male face that watches her – the dark *alter ego*, perhaps, of the male viewer, who also looks at her in her nakedness. In the later painting (1647), Susanna is stepping into the water and the elders have now emerged from their conceal-ment. Immediately behind her, the first of them grasps with his left hand the robe with which she conceals her modesty, as if to pull it away from her. His clenched right hand expresses his tense excitement, while, behind him, the face of the second elder betrays his pleasure at the spectacle – forgetful now of the physical weakness of age which compels him to walk with the aid of a stick. Susanna's anxious face is turned towards the viewer, as if appealing for help.

[9] C. A. Moore refers to 'the bathing scene' as actually taking place (*Daniel, Esther and Jeremiah: The Additions*, Anchor Bible, New York: Doubleday, 1977, 97). According to Amy-Jill Levine, 'The narrative renders us voyeurs, looking on with the elders at the naked Susanna at her bath and at her trial. Like Susanna, we cannot leave the garden without shame' ('"Hemmed in on Every Side": Jews and Women in the Book of Susanna', in A. Brenner (ed.), *A Feminist Companion to Esther, Judith and Susanna*, Sheffield: Sheffield Academic Press, 1995, 303–23; 308).

Why has the artist insinuated this moment of nakedness into the text, so plausibly that its later readers continue to believe that they have found it there?

In the background of both paintings there stands a large building with a tower. If the tower can be seen from Susanna's garden, then Susanna can be seen from the tower. In these paintings, however, the tower remains unoccupied – although a sketch for the later one replaces it with a distant stone column upon which a statue of a male figure surveys the scene. This figure has, as it were, crossed over from another painting (1643), in which King David watches from a tower in his palace as the naked Bathsheba prepares for her bath. It is the biblical narrative of David and Bathsheba that underlies the conversion of Susanna's intention to take a bath into these visions of her naked form exposed to male onlookers. But the result of this insertion from another narrative is that the lifting of Susanna's veil at her trial has hardly been noticed. The artist knows of it, but he has allowed this motif too to wander into another painting: for in his rendering of the encounter between Christ and the woman taken in adultery (1644), the elder who tells of the kneeling woman's sin raises the veil from her face as he does so – enabling onlookers and viewers to find their satisfaction in her humiliated and threatened beauty. The artist has rightly sensed actual affinities between the story of Susanna and the earlier and later narratives, but he has chosen to develop them in such a way that the projection of Bathsheba's naked form into Susanna's garden displaces the unveiling-motif into the Johannine narrative. There are profound reasons for his choice. For the artistic tradition in which he stands, the primary erotic object is not the unveiled female face but the unveiled female body. Susanna's unveiled face is not without erotic interest, as her surrogate in the rendering of the Johannine story indicates. But in the presence of Christ, eros must take subdued forms. In the case of Susanna, whose physical beauty the narrative itself twice emphasizes, the expressed intention to take a bath is sufficient textual basis for the insertion of the Bathsheba motif of full bodily unveiling. So Susanna comes to share Bathsheba's nakedness, just as she shares her exposure to a male gaze that is represented within the painting itself.[10]

In the biblical Susanna narrative the links with Bathsheba are real but marginal, and the erotic climax occurs not in the garden but in the unveiling of the face. The narrator distances himself and his readers from the elders' erotic satisfaction by emphasizing their depravity, and by presenting a more appropriate response to Susanna's humiliation in the form of her weeping family (v. 33). Yet the story does presuppose a tradition in which the female face is an object of such intense erotic concern that, in the public realm outside the immediate sphere of the family, it must be concealed behind a veil. Susanna's entire bodily beauty is concentrated in her face, and the narrative assumes that the uncovering of the face is itself sufficient to satisfy male desire. That is why her family weeps. And that is also why 'every woman who prays or prophesies with uncovered head shames her head'. Susanna is shamed by her own public unveiling, and her parents, husband, children and relatives share in her shaming. Susanna was unveiled under duress, but the woman who deliberately appears in public with unveiled face, displaying herself as the object of the erotic male gaze, must be held responsible for the shame that falls especially upon her husband. Or so one might conclude if, like Paul, one shared the cultural assumptions implied in the Susanna narrative.

It is now clear why men who pray and prophesy must do so with uncovered head whereas women must conceal their face behind a veil. Eros is construed asymmetrically as the desire of the male subject for the female object, aroused and perhaps even satisfied by an act of looking that transfixes its object, depriving it of subjectivity and movement and subjecting it to its own power. Such a construal is admittedly an abstraction, indeed a fantasy; for the male gaze is always embedded in

[10] According to M. Miles, depictions of Susanna in western art 'attempt to reproduce, in the eyes of an assumed male viewer, the Elders' intense erotic attraction, projected and displayed on Susanna's flesh . . . Viewers are directed – trained – by the management of lights and shadows to see Susanna as object, even as cause, of male desire' (*Carnal Knowing: Female Nakedness and Religious Meaning in the Christian West*, Boston: Beacon Press, 1989, 123).

networks of relationships in which its potential and actual objects continue to exercise their subjectivity and their relative freedom of movement. The art-work that holds the naked female form steady and immobilized before the eyes of the male viewer corresponds to a fantasy that is only imperfectly realized within actual erotic relationships. In claiming that the woman who prays or prophesies with unveiled face makes herself the object of the male gaze, Paul need not assume that eros will simply overwhelm and erase her speech, making it inaudible as the eye supplants the ear; but he must assume that the availability of the look may distort and impair the reception of her speech. She speaks the word of the Lord or the human response to that word, but her face as it appears to the gaze of eros is incommensurate with that speech. It is a barrier to hearing – not because of what it is in itself but because of the mode of its appearance as the passive object of erotic fantasy. The purpose of the veil is to remove the hindrance to reception by depriving the fantasy of its object – not as a first step towards refusing woman the right to speak at all, as the unfortunate later gloss would have us believe (1 Cor. 14.34–5), but precisely in order to secure that right to speak and to ensure that what is spoken is duly heard.

Paul knows that the new custom he proposes will be contentious (11.16). It will perhaps be seen as representing 'eastern' and 'Asian' cultural assumptions that are alien to the Greeks and the west.[11] But objections to it are not simply an expression of cultural differences; there are also good theological reasons why the proposed new custom should be rejected. Is it really the case that in eros the male is the active subject and the female the passive object? May a woman not look at a man and desire him, and, if so, ought not *men* to conceal their faces behind a veil when they pray or prophesy? In fact, the new custom grossly exaggerates the potential of the look to hinder the reception of the word. It insults women by compelling them to reckon with the male look as a fundamental problem of their

[11] The Jewish and oriental provenance of the veil is emphasized by A. Oepke, in G. Kittel (ed.), *Theological Dictionary of the New Testament*, ET Grand Rapids: Eerdmans, 1966, 3.561–3.

existence, even within the sphere of the Christian congregation. It insults men by stereotyping them as the helpless victims of eros, depriving them of true subjectivity by offering them protection from a false subjectivity that they may well disown. It undermines the familial dimension of the Christian community, within which the fellow-Christian is addressed as 'brother' or 'sister'. It is a barrier not so much to eros as to agape. Within the Christian congregation, it must surely be possible for men and women to behold the glory of the Lord together, with unveiled faces.

For these or other reasons, most subsequent Christian communities have not been persuaded by Paul's argument here.[12] Yet, clumsy and ill-conceived though it surely is, this passage is not simply to be rejected as the later passages that silence women altogether are to be rejected. The Pauline veil may be taken to represent not a viable practical proposal but an invitation to think through the difference between eros and agape, on the assumption that genuine concerns of individual and corporate Christian existence may indeed be bound up with this distinction. We may therefore persist in the attempt to hear what Paul is saying, from behind the veil of his questionable theological arguments.

Every woman praying or prophesying with uncovered head shames her head; it is one and the same thing as having herself shaved. If a woman refuses to veil herself, let her have her hair cut short. But if short hair or shaven head is shameful for a woman, let her veil herself (vv. 5–6). Paul cannot rely on his readers to agree that woman's unveiled face is an occasion for shame, and he therefore attempts an argument by analogy. They will not deny that it is shameful for a woman to have her hair cut short or her head shaved altogether, even though that is not the case with a man (v. 14). But what is the precise mechanism of shame here? The shame is the shame of nakedness. Hair is given to a woman 'for a covering' (v. 15), as a garment provided by nature itself so that the shame of her nakedness may not be seen. It is just a small step, although a

---

[12] The history of the interpretation of this passage is summarized in W. Schrage, *I Korinther*, 2.525–41.

necessary one, from the covering of woman's head by her hair to the covering of her face with a veil.

Shame-language proves a more useful support for the new custom than the christologically oriented 'head' metaphors of verse 3, which have now dropped out of sight. But an attempt is now made to find an alternative theological basis for the new custom in the created order as described in Genesis 1–2 (vv. 7–12). Despite the appearance of seemingly arbitrary and inconsistent statements here, the theological substance of this attempt to delimit eros from agape as the basis for the relation of man and woman 'in the Lord' deserves close attention.

THE GLORY OF MAN (VERSES 7–9)

For man ought not to cover his head, since he is the image and glory of God; but woman is the glory of man (v. 7). Is this a second hierarchy in the making (God–man–woman), similar to the first although grounded not in christology but in the created order? Is woman now deprived of her participation in the image of God, which in Genesis defines her humanity as a co-humanity shared with man? The passage lends itself to such a reading, it drifts towards it without sufficient forethought, but it is not this that it intends to say. It intends to support the claim of the preceding verses that the veil is proper to woman but improper to man, and we may expect to find here not so much a 'hierarchy' as a further development of the theme we have already identified: the asymmetrical account of eros in which the male subject fixes his gaze on a female object. This account may be one-sided and flawed, but it is not unrelated to the problematic realities of eros – whether these stem from nature, from culture or from both.

Man and woman were previously distinguished by their relation to different 'heads'; now they are distinguished as the 'glory' of their respective 'heads'. The head of man is Christ and the head of Christ is God; the head of woman is man. If, in the context of creation, we omit 'Christ' as the connecting link between man and God, a symmetrical pattern emerges. Man's head is (indirectly) God, woman's head is man; man is God's glory and woman is man's glory. Man would dishonour his head

by covering his head, woman would dishonour her head by
leaving her head uncovered; man's status as the glory of God
forbids his covering his head, woman's status as the glory of
man forbids her to appear with uncovered head. The crucial
term in this elegant but obscure patterning is perhaps 'glory'
(*doxa*). Man is 'image and glory of God': 'glory' is intended to
gloss the scriptural term, 'image', which is understood here as
manifestation or revelation. If man is the manifestation of God,
then man cannot veil what God has revealed. Woman should
be veiled, for she is the glory not of God but of man. But in
what sense is she the glory of man, and what has that to do with
her veiling herself? If man is the image and glory of God in the
sense that he is the revelation of God, is woman the glory of
man as the revelation of man? That seems unlikely: for, unlike
God, man is not hidden and does not need a manifestation
external to himself. Even if he did, why would it need to be
concealed behind a veil?

The moment of theological substance here is concealed
within a semantic slippage between the two occurrences of *doxa*.
Man is the glory of God as the manifestation of God which
should not be veiled; yet woman is veiled not as the manifestation of man but as 'the glory of man' in a rather different sense.
In 1 Thessalonians 2.20 Paul writes: 'You are our glory and our
joy [*hē doxa hēmōn kai hē chara*]'. In Philippians 3.19 it is said of
certain persons that 'their glory is in their shame [*hē doxa en tē
aischunē autōn*]'. In one case the object of glory is an appropriate
one, in the other it is inappropriate – but in both cases *doxa* is
the object of a person's joy, love and devotion. This sense of *doxa*
makes 1 Corinthians 11.7 comprehensible: man as the manifestation of God should not be veiled, but woman as the object of
man's erotic joy, love and devotion should be veiled. Why?
Because it is her face that is the focal point for the male erotic
drive, which – contrary to our earlier, more negative impression
– may intend to honour her and may be gladly reciprocated in
the mutuality to which eros aspires, but which has no place
within the agape at the heart of the congregation's being and
life. This human attraction to the glory of the other is real
enough, and the congregation will have to accommodate it and

will not wish simply to deny it. But, as a sign that the togetherness of man and woman 'in the Lord' is not the togetherness of
eros, it is appropriate that the glory should lie concealed behind
a veil. The Pauline veil invites theological reflection not on the
problem of a 'hierarchical' ordering of the sexes and the
possibility of an 'egalitarian' alternative, but on the difference
between agape and eros as the basis for the togetherness of man
and woman in Christ.[13]

*For man is not from woman but woman from man; and man was not
created for woman but woman for man* (vv. 8–9). Within a few
sentences, this asymmetrical and irreversible relationship – man
is not from woman but woman from man – will be reversed and
symmetry will be restored: as woman is from man, so too man is
through woman (v. 12). If the relationship of origin is reversible,
so too is the teleological relationship. As woman is for man, so
too man is for woman. The order, in which one is irreversibly
from and for the other, is precarious and can only be maintained as a fleeting moment within a larger picture of male and
female togetherness 'in the Lord' (v. 11). Yet, for a moment, this
abstraction does occur, and the order is asserted. The intention
is to substantiate the claim that 'woman is the glory of man' and
should therefore veil herself.

Why is woman the glory of man, the object of his erotic joy,
love and devotion? It is because 'it is not good for the man
[*hā-ādām*] to be alone' (Gen. 2.18). 'Adam' is 'man', and if
solitude is not good for the first man then it is not good for man
as such. Man is 'not without woman' (1 Cor. 11.11). Although the
creator looks on all of his works and pronounces them to be
'good', in the case of the solitary man formed from the dust of

---

[13] The interpretation of *doxa* in v. 7b as the object of joy and love is crucial to this
interpretation of the passage in terms of the eros problematic. Even if in association
with 'image' *doxa* can mean 'reflection', it is hard to see how this sense can be carried
over into the second half of the verse – as Conzelmann advocates (*1 Corinthians*,
Hermeneia, Philadelphia: Fortress Press, 1975, 186–7). The grave inscription cited by
Conzelmann (*hē doxa Sophroniou Loukilla eulogēmenē*) is hardly to be translated '[Here
lies the one who was] the reflection of Sophronius, blessed Lucilla' (187n); it is much
more likely that Lucilla is the 'glory' of her husband as the object of his love and
devotion. Annie Jaubert rightly paraphrases *doxa andros* as 'la gloire de l'homme – ce
qu'il a de plus précieux et de plus beau' ('Le Voile des Femmes', 423).

the ground he acknowledges that his work is 'not good' – not good, that is, in itself and in its abstraction and its solitude. Solitary man, this being that in its abstraction and self-containment is 'not good', needs a helper that even God cannot be: a helper *kenegdô*, who corresponds to him and is his counterpart, like him but also different and therefore not a mere repetition of the same, let alone an inferior imitation. Pure likeness would be a repetition that would merely replicate the original solitude. Pure difference would leave man and the other separated by an abyss of mutual incomprehension, and solitude would remain unbroken. Although the creation of the animals establishes a relative rather than an absolute difference, in which some elements of likeness remain and therefore some possibility of mutuality, it is mentioned only to highlight the distinctiveness of the 'helper corresponding to him', in whom difference and likeness must be equally original.[14]

The creation of the counterpart from out of man's own flesh and bone signifies not inferiority – an inferior helper would be another animal, not a counterpart – but the co-presence in this other of likeness and difference. It is in this sense that woman is created 'from' and 'for' man: not as a sign of secondariness and inferiority but so that her being can make good a being that is 'not good' without her. The Pauline language and the Genesis narrative are 'androcentric' in the sense that woman's being is determined by the being of the man; her existence rectifies the deficiencies of his, and nothing is said of the meaning of her existence in itself and apart from his. Yet his own existence in itself and apart from her has been described as 'not good'. If man-in-himself is an abstraction contrary to the will of the creator and the nature of the creature, then he hardly constitutes a 'centre' in relation to which woman's existence is peripheral and dependent. If she is dependent on him, then he is also dependent on her if his being is to display the goodness proper to the creature rather than languishing in the impossible limbo of the not-good. She is the helper he needs to draw him

---

[14] For the interpretation of *kenegdô* as 'corresponding to him, his counterpart', see H. Gunkel, *Genesis*, ET Macon, Georgia: Mercer University Press, 1997, 11; C. Westermann, *Genesis 1–11: A Commentary*, ET Minneapolis: Augsburg, 1984, 227.

out of this limbo. Her help is not a help that he could in the last resort do without; unlike the help of the animals, it is essential to his being. If he stands at the centre of God's creation, he does not do so without her.

The second creation story substantiates the Pauline claim that 'woman is not apart from man nor man from woman' (1 Cor. 11.11), but it also substantiates his claim that there is an order in this relationship. Man is not from woman but woman from man; man was not created for woman but woman for man. This is an androcentrism that draws woman into the centre to share that centre with man – but for man's sake (*di' anthrōpon*), so that *his* existence may be good rather than not-good. When woman is brought to man, she does not address him, naming him and identifying him in relation to her own being and its needs. It is he who speaks – speaking *of* her in the third person rather than addressing her directly, and finding in her being from his own bones and flesh a relationship of likeness and derivation that must be mirrored in the medium of language: woman is from man and is therefore called *ishshah*, which is from *ish*. But this act of naming is not like the naming of the animals that the man had earlier carried out, in accordance with the divine will. Here, the naming stems from an ecstatic moment of recognition: 'This at last is bone of my bones and flesh of my flesh . . .' (Gen. 2.23). In this other he recognizes the counterpart, like him in her difference from him and different in her likeness to him. The likeness arises from the intimacy of an original physical identity of bone and flesh, and it is this likeness within the medium of otherness that is expressed in the event in which man and woman become 'one flesh', naked yet unashamed despite the absence of the veil (vv. 24–5). The recognition of the helper and counterpart reaches its goal in physical union; and it constitutes woman as 'the glory of man'.[15]

[15] According to Gunkel, this passage is 'the prototypical example of an aetiological myth . . . The question here is, "How is it that man strives for union with woman?" The myth answers, "Man desires to become one flesh with woman because he was originally one flesh with her". In love that which was originally one is reunited . . . The nature of the love [the narrator] intends is very clear from the expressions he uses: it is sexual union' (*Genesis*, 13). While it is true that the narrative is concerned

In the Genesis narrative and its Pauline interpretation, eros is construed asymmetrically as the movement of man towards woman, arising out of the moment of recognition and culminating in the union of flesh – the movement in which 'a man leaves his father and his mother and cleaves to his wife . . .' (v. 24). That is not to say that in eros the male is merely 'active' and the female merely 'passive'. Male activity over against female passivity would be difference without likeness, difference hardened into opposition, and it is not this that the erotic moment of recognition intends – except when it takes the pathological form of the gaze to which Susanna is subjected. The recognition of the counterpart seeks an answering recognition. The asymmetry of eros, as rendered in these texts, is one of initiative and response. Yet there seems to be no compelling reason for this asymmetry, outside the constraints of cultural assumptions. Thus, in contrast, the erotic dialogue of the Song of Solomon is evenly distributed between the male and the female speakers, and the initiative passes from one to the other. On occasion she can acknowledge his initiative as calling for her response: 'My beloved speaks and says to me: Arise my love, my fair one, and come away . . .' (Cant. 2.10). But she too may claim the initiative, even if she fails to attain her object: 'Upon my bed by night I sought him whom my soul loves; I sought him but found him not, I called him but he gave no answer' (3.1). Indeed, within this enclosed world of eros the idea of 'initiative' is purely relative and may drop out of view. If 'my beloved is mine and I am his', then 'initiative' is subsumed and dissolved into mutual belonging. The partners see themselves as responding to an initiative not of the other but of eros itself, and as subject to an ethical imperative to allow this to be so. Thus, the 'daughters of Jerusalem' are twice adjured 'that you stir not up nor awaken love until it please' (3.5, 8.4). Sexual initiative may result in the form of love without the reality. Mechanically, the partners go through the motions of love; but the reality is absent not because the woman has taken the initiative rather

with 'the creation of humankind which reaches its goal in the complementary society of man and woman', it is implausible to rule out a concern with 'the origin of the mutual attraction of the sexes', as Westermann does (*Genesis 1–11*, 232).

than the man but because both partners have failed to subject themselves to the initiative of love itself. When they speak of love as strong as death and claim that many waters cannot quench it (8.6–7), they are speaking not primarily of themselves but of the suprapersonal quasi-divine power that holds them in its grasp and demands their obedience. In this world, the lovers' language shows that as woman is the glory of man so man is the glory of woman.

Paul, however, is dependent on the Genesis model of eros in terms of male initiative and female response. (If this model is inadequate, as it is, it is no more so than the erotic fantasy of absolute and unbroken mutuality within an enclosed garden cut off from the external world.)[16] Woman is the glory of man, but man is the glory not of woman but of God; it must therefore be woman's face that is concealed behind a veil if eros is to be restrained from penetrating the internal life of the community, insinuating itself into the agape that binds the congregation together and secretly subverting it. Woman's veil ensures that the male gaze will not find its object. Yet eros is not simply cast out. A barrier is placed in its way to prevent its extending itself beyond its limits, but its right to existence within its limits is not denied. To identify woman as the glory of man is to acknowledge not only the reality but also the validity of the erotic look of recognition. Nor is this merely the pragmatic concession of one whose real belief is that 'it is good for a man not to touch a woman' (1 Cor. 7.1). Pragmatism can speak of 'conjugal rights', 'self-control' and 'passion' (7.3, 5, 9, 36), but it will not speak of 'glory' or of an original eros that is older even than original sin and that still participates in the goodness of the first creation. Within the limit marked by the veil, the eros that unites man and woman as one flesh is good, and its exclusion from the agape that unites the congregation as one body is not a rejection or a denial. To mark a limit is not to deny. The importance of

---

16 Phyllis Trible's comments exemplify the modern tendency to idealize the lovers of the Song of Songs: 'Their love is truly bone of bone and flesh of flesh, and this image of God male and female is indeed very good . . . Testifying to the goodness of creation, then, eroticism becomes worship in the context of grace . . . In this setting, there is no male dominance, no female subordination, and no stereotyping of either sex' (*God and the Rhetoric of Sexuality*, Philadelphia: Fortress Press, 1978, 161).

this distinction comes to light if the Genesis narrative is set alongside an alternative account of the origins of man and woman.

According to Plato's *Timaeus*, the goodness of the world's divine maker guarantees that, so far as possible, the world too will be good.[17] Desiring to reduce the disorder of the primitive chaos to order, he implanted in it soul and intelligence, the principle of orderly temporal movement manifested supremely in the heavens that makes them 'a moving image of eternity' – the timeless world of the ideas that the maker used as his pattern (37D). The first of the gods is the earth herself, but other gods are created out of fire and entrusted with the task of making the remaining creatures; immortal seed is given to them in order that they may blend it with what is mortal. This seed is composed of soul, which the maker divided up into as many souls as there are stars, allocating each soul to its star. 'And setting them as if in a chariot, he showed them the nature of the universe [*tēn tou pantos phusin*] and told them the laws of their destiny – how the first birth [*genesis prōtē*] would be one and the same for all, so that no-one might be unfairly treated by him; and how each would be sown in its appropriate instrument of time and be born as the most god-fearing of living things; and how, since human nature is twofold [*diplēs ousēs tēs anthrōpinēs phuseōs*] the superior sex [*to kreitton genos*] was that which would be called "man". And when, by necessity [*ex anagkēs*], they should be implanted in bodies, subject to physical gain and loss, they would all inevitably be endowed, first, with a common faculty of sensation [*aesthēsis*], dependent on external stimulation; second, with desire [*erōta*] mingled with pain and pleasure; and, in addition, with fear and anger and their accompanying feelings, and also with their opposites. If they mastered these, they would live justly, but if they were mastered by them, wickedly. And the one who lived well for his appointed time of life would return home to his native star and live an appro-

---

[17] My translations from the *Timaeus* and the *Symposium* draw on the Loeb editions (Plato, vols. IX (1929), III (1925) respectively), from D. Lee, *Plato: Timaeus and Critias* (Harmondsworth: Penguin Books, 1971), and from W. Hamilton, *Plato: The Symposium* (Harmondsworth: Penguin Books, 1951).

priately happy life; but anyone who failed to do so would be changed into woman's nature at the second birth [*eis gunaikos phusin en tē deutera genesei metaboloi*]. And if in this form too he continued to do wrong, he would be changed into some animal suitable to his particular kind of wrongdoing . . . After the sowing, he gave to the newly made gods the task of forming mortal bodies, and of framing whatever of the human soul still needed to be added, with whatever pertained to it, and of governing the mortal creature in the best way possible – so long as it did not become a cause of evil to itself' (41E–42E). These instructions were duly carried out, and the human frame was constructed – the prototype that would in subsequent genera- tions be transformed in a descending scale into 'women and other animals' (76E). In due course, 'the men of the first generation [*tōn genomenōn andrōn*] who were cowardly or passed their lives in wrongdoing were . . . transformed into women at their second birth [*en tē deutera genesei*]. So that was when the gods created sexual love [*ton tēs xunousias erōta*] . . . ' (90E–91A). In the male, a modification to the urinary tract enabled it to serve also as a means of generation. 'Thus in men the nature of the genital organs is to be disobedient and self-willed [*autok- ratēs*], like a creature deaf to reason [*anupēkoon tou logou*], attempting to dominate all because of its frenzied desires' (91B). In the female, the gods provided 'a living creature within them which longs to bear children' (91C). The mutual distress of male and female is assuaged only when 'the mutual desire and love [*hē epithumia kai ho erōs*] unites them, and, as if picking fruit from a tree, they sow the ploughland of the womb with germs of life, unformed and too small to see, which take shape and grow big within; after which they bring them forth into the light and complete the generation of the living creature' (91C–D).

As in Genesis, man is formed first and then woman. But in Genesis, woman is formed in order to remedy the not-goodness of man's solitary state; in the *Timaeus*, she incarnates the not- goodness of his moral choices, so that – as in the Pandora myth – her being is his punishment.[18] The plunging of the soul into

---

[18] The Pandora myth occurs in Hesiod's *Works and Days*, ll. 52–104.

the chaos of matter subjects it to a disorder that it can and must overcome through the practice of virtue and philosophy. The original all-male generation face a difficult task as they struggle to come to terms with their incarceration in the body – although their task is not impossible and they can rely on the help of the gods and of the godlike principle within themselves. Yet a gradual decay from generation to generation is inevitable, and its first manifestation is the woman who is, as it were, designed around the modified male bodily parts that are now to serve as organs of generation, and who mirrors their irrational behaviour. The erotic union of man and woman engulfs them in the disorder of passion, and, like woman's very existence, is an unfortunate side-effect of the original male's lapse from virtue and philosophy.

At the beginning of the *Timaeus*, Socrates summarizes the previous day's discussion in which he had outlined his ideal state. He had spoken then of the role of women, arguing that so far as possible the differences between men and women should be erased: 'Their natures were to be harmonized with the men's, and all occupations, both in war and in the rest of life, were to be common [*koina*] to all' (18c). The assumption here that woman is capable of the life of virtue is in tension with the later claim that she is the first step in man's downward path that leads beyond her into the existences of birds, mammals, reptiles and fish. Might there have been a quite different Platonic myth of origins that assigned to woman a position of equality rather than inferiority? The problem is that, in contrast to Genesis, the cosmology within which man and woman come into being is for Plato already gendered. The world is a visible and changing copy of an intelligible and unchanging pattern, and as such it is the product of two principles, intelligence and necessity. The necessity that is both the medium for the expression of intelligence and its limit is described as the 'receptacle, as it were the nurse, of all becoming' [*pasēs geneseōs hupodochēn auto, hoion tithenēn*] (49A), about which it is hard to speak accurately because its unstable elements (earth, air, fire and water) undergo constant transformations. 'Having no stability, they elude the designation "this" or "that" or any other term that

expresses permanence' (49E).[19] The receptacle 'is established by
nature as raw material for everything, formed and shaped by
the figures that pass into it, so that it appears different at
different times. And the things which pass into and out of it are
copies of the eternal realities [*tōn ontōn aei mimēmata*], receiving
their stamp in a way hard to describe . . . It is appropriate to
describe that which receives [*to dechomenon*] as the Mother, the
originating model [*to hothen*] as the Father, and the nature they
produce between them as the Offspring' (50C–D). Because of
her shifting, unstable and impermanent character, 'the mother
and receptacle of all sensible things' – the matter out of which,
on their maternal side, they are constituted – is not to be
identified with any individual elements or compounds but can
only be described as 'invisible and formless, all-receptive [*pan-
dechēs*], partaking in the intelligible [*tou noētou*] in a way that is
perplexing and very hard to grasp' (51A–B). The receptacle is
also the 'ever-existing space' (52B) within which all things come
to be, and in its pure, primeval form as 'the nurse of becoming'
it lacks even the relative stability of the sensible world of our
experience, since its contents are in constant process of movement and separation. Thus the world is a kind of compromise
between a paternal principle of intelligence and order and a
maternal/material principle of necessity and disorder. In a
world so constituted, the being of woman *must* be a step
downward from the being of man into the irrational chaos; for
the chaos is itself woman, the womb of becoming. The first
generation of men is poised precariously between the starry
heights of paternal intelligence and the irrational maternal
abyss.[20]

[19] A. E. Taylor points out that 'necessity' (*anagkē*) in the *Timaeus* 'is something disorderly
and irregular', quite unlike the necessity 'of the myth of Er, or of the Stoics, which
are personifications of the principle of rational law and order' (*Plato: The Man and his
Work*, London: Methuen, 1926, 455). While it is true that necessity is 'plainly not
meant to be an independent, evil principle, for it is plastic to intelligence' (*ibid.*), it is
nevertheless the source of evil in a world shaped by a wholly good intelligence.

[20] Taylor believes that he detects in Plato's account of the origin of man and woman an
'unmistakably playful' note, which 'should not be taken as seriously as has been done
by some interpreters' (*Plato*, 460). 'As in the tale of Aristophanes in the *Symposium*, we
are really dealing with a playful imitation of the speculation of Empedocles about the
"whole-natured" and double-sexed forms with which evolution in the "period of

That is also essentially the situation of the present generation of men – the men of whom and to whom Plato speaks. In the *Symposium*, Pausanias (the second speaker) distinguishes between two goddesses of love, and this distinction is foundational for Socrates's final unveiling of the 'truth' of eros (which takes the form of a reported speech by a woman, Diotima, who is perhaps assigned her revelatory role in preference to a man partly as the embodiment of *philosophia*, partly in order to rule out the possible complication of an erotic relationship between Socrates and the revealer). According to Pausanias, Phaedrus (the first speaker) has made the mistake of assuming that love is single. Although he has spoken primarily of the love of men and boys, he has claimed that women too may demonstrate love's willingness to sacrifice itself for the sake of the beloved. Alcestis' love for her husband has been placed in the same category as Achilles' love for Patroclus. Phaedrus has failed to identify precisely what the eros is in whose praise he has agreed to speak. 'If there were a single Aphrodite there would be a single Eros, but since there are two of her there must also be two Eroses [*duo Erotē*]. How can anyone doubt that the goddess is double? One is the elder, the motherless daughter of Ouranos, whom we call Aphrodite the heavenly [*Ouranian*]. The other is younger, the child of Zeus and Dione, and is called Aphrodite the common [*Pandēmos*]. It follows that the Eros which is the partner of the latter should be called common Eros and the other heavenly Eros' (180D–E). The devotees of common Eros are 'the meaner sort of men', who 'first of all love women as well as boys; second, they love the body rather than the soul; third, they choose the most ignorant objects, looking only to the gratification of desire . . . This love is from the goddess, far the younger of the two, who partakes in her origin of both male and female. But the love which is from the heavenly Aphrodite partakes not of the female but only of the male – and this is the love of boys [*ho tōn paidōn erōs*]; also, being the elder, she is free from wantonness. And so those who are inspired by this love are attracted towards the male sex as being by nature the stronger

strife" began' (461). The coherent metaphysical context of the account in the *Timaeus* suggests that any 'playful' elements here should be taken seriously.

and more intelligent' (181B–C). The heavenly love of man and
boy is older than the common love of man and woman: and this
claim may be read back into the *Timaeus*. Heavenly male Eros is
original, and may be traced back to the first generation of men.
That is the meaning of the ancient myth of an Aphrodite who
originates purely from the male. In contrast, heterosexual Eros
is degenerate and secondary, deriving from that younger, fallen
world in which genitality and woman represent the victory of
the primal Mother over the primal Father in the struggle for the
first men's allegiance. The homoerotic relationship should
exclude genitality because genitality is essentially feminine; the
purity of Aphrodite Ourania is corrupted by the intrusion of
feminized bodily parts which in their chaotic resistance to
rational control represent in the male person the downward
pull of the Mother. Aphrodite Pandemos is passion, and passion
is a woman.[21]

The eros of man and woman has no place at the symposium's
celebration of eros. It belongs to the feminine sphere of the
passions and pleasures, which it is philosophy's vocation to

---

[21] According to Foucault, Pausanias's theory distinguishes 'not between a heterosexual
love and a homosexual love' but between a love that 'only looks to the act itself' and
a 'more reasonable love that is drawn to what has the most vigour and intelligence,
which obviously can only mean the male sex' (*The History of Sexuality*, vol. II: *The Use of
Pleasure*, ET London: Penguin Books 1987, 188–9). Foucault argues that 'the Greeks
did not see love for one's own sex and love for the other sex as opposites, as two
exclusive choices, two radically different types of behaviour' (187); they 'did not
recognize two kinds of "desire", two different or competing "drives", each claiming
a share of men's hearts or appetites . . . To their way of thinking, what made it
possible to desire a man or a woman was simply the appetite that nature had
implanted in man's heart for "beautiful" human beings, whatever their sex might be'
(188). If the *Symposium* is read against the metaphysical background of the *Timaeus*,
these claims have to be qualified. Foucault's account of the love of man for boy
effectively shows that this relationship was held to be problematic and that the
notions of 'tolerance' and 'intolerance' are 'completely inadequate to the complexity
of the phenomena' (190). But he overlooks the distinction – crucial in Alcibiades'
speech in the *Symposium* and in Socrates' speech in praise of love in the *Phaedrus* –
between a same-sex love that abstains from genital expression and one that succumbs
to it. As the *Timaeus* shows, genitality represents the downward pull of the female
within the male person. There is some truth in the criticism, anticipated by Foucault
himself, that he evades 'the biologically established existence of sexual functions for
the benefit of phenomena that are variable, perhaps, but fragile, secondary, and
ultimately superficial', that he 'speak[s] of sexuality as if sex did not exist' (*The History
of Sexuality*, vol. I: *An Introduction*, ET London: Penguin Books, 1990, 150–1).

combat.[22] In the Platonic dialogue, philosophy strives to re-create the all-male society of the first generation. (Thus, on the day of Socrates' death, Xanthippe must be sent home before the final dialogue can get under way (*Phaedo*, 60A).) In contrast, in the Pauline text 'woman is the glory of man'. She is created from and for man, but her secondariness is not that of the inferior whose being represents the decline from original perfection towards the maternal abyss, but that of the counterpart whose being contradicts and overcomes the imperfection of an original being that is not-good in its abstract solitude. In her, that original being finds its *telos*. But that means that the male does not here represent the pure original moment. Woman too belongs to the moment of origin, and in the erotic union of man and woman as one flesh that moment of origin is still present, however distorted its empirical expression. The eros of man and woman is given space within the world – a demythologized space in which the archaic myth of a world that arises from the conjunction of male and female principles has been supplanted by the ungendered relation of the creator *ex nihilo* to the creature.

Eros is given space within the world, but it is a limited space. Within the new creation, it no longer belongs at the centre of the relationship of man to woman. At this centre is now the community of those who are in Christ, in which the relationship of man and woman reflects the pattern of Christ's agape. The word of the Lord which founds this community is proclaimed

[22] If the issue of gender is set aside, the philosophical question put to the *Symposium* may be that of the value of love of the *particular* within a metaphysic in which eros strives to encompass the whole. Thus, Martha Nussbaum argues that the movement from the particular to the universal in Diotima's speech is initially countered by Alcibiades' speech in praise of a particular beloved object (Socrates) and yet ultimately confirmed by the detachment and remoteness of this object. 'Socrates, in his ascent towards the form, has become, himself, very like the form – hard, indivisible, unchanging . . . Socrates refuses in every way to be affected. He is stone; and he also turns others to stone. Alcibiades is to his sight just one more of the beautifuls, a piece of the form, a pure thing like a jewel' (*The Fragility of Goodness: Luck and Ethics in Greek Tragedy and Philosophy*, Cambridge: Cambridge University Press, 1986, 195). The *Phaedrus* can then be read as Plato's recantation, influenced perhaps by his erotic relationship with Dion (228–33). Nussbaum treats the text's exploration of the eros of man for boy as paradigmatic of all human erotic relations, and the text's gendered hierarchy of value is downplayed.

by women as well as by men, and they too articulate the community's answering word. As a sign of the new limit assigned to eros, a veil is interposed between the woman who prays and prophesies and the men to and for whom she speaks. Otherwise (Paul believes), her voice may not be heard. For the sake of the word of God, the glory of man must be concealed.

THE AUTHORITY OF THE VEIL (VERSES 10–16)

For this reason the woman should have authority on her head, because of the angels (v. 10). 'For this reason . . . ' – because woman is the glory of man, created from and for man; but also, 'because of the angels'. Yet the veil is not the *sign* that woman is the glory of man. On the contrary, it is the sign that, 'in the Lord', the limitations of this status are overcome. As the glory of man, woman responds to a prior male initiative. In the Lord, as she prophesies and prays on behalf of the congregation, she represents both God's initiative and the human response; and she can do so because in this case the pattern of initiative and response is no longer gendered. Conceivably, it might be otherwise. The divine initiative might be represented by the male prophet, the human response by the praying woman; or men might lay claim to both the 'masculine' and the 'feminine' roles, thereby asserting the deity's special affinity to the male. In reality, however, both the divine initiative and the human response are embodied in the figure of Jesus who, as the agent of the new creation, creates anew and does not simply underwrite the gender roles inscribed in the old creation or in the cultures built on that foundation. 'Old things [*ta archaia*] have passed away – behold, new things [*kaina*] have come!' (2 Cor. 5.17). In the sphere of the new creation, the vanishing *archaia* include the male erotic gaze as the centre and foundation of the relation of men and women. Negatively, the veil is the sign of this decentering of the old. Positively, it is the sign of the new reality in which 'your sons and your daughters shall prophesy' because the Spirit has been poured out on all flesh (Joel 2.28, Acts 2.17). The veil is 'authority' (*exousia*) on the head of the woman who prophesies because it declares and enacts the passing away of the old and the dawning of the new.[23]

The sign of the new *exousia* is needed not only because, in the created order, 'woman is the glory of man' but also 'because of the angels'. Are these the 'sons of God' who, according to Genesis 6.2, 'saw that the daughters of men were fair, and took to wife such of them as they chose'? Or are they the angelic guardians of the created order? There is perhaps no need to choose between these two interpretations. The angels are 'guardians and stewards', they are 'the elemental spirits of the universe' (*ta stoicheia tou kosmou*) to whom God has entrusted the administration of the world until the 'fulness of time' and the sending of his Son; but those who have received the Spirit of God's Son are no longer the slaves of these 'weak and impoverished' beings (Gal. 4.1–9). The angels are 'the rulers of this age, who are passing away' (1 Cor. 2.6). Appointed by God, it is not yet clear how far they were faithful to their stewardship; that will only be known on the day when 'we shall judge angels' (6.3). These angels or *stoicheia* are the foundations of the old order, the shadowy powers that stand behind and guarantee the visible powers operative in the human and the natural realms. If the male erotic drive towards the female is one of those visible powers, it is imaginable that we also encounter here the quasi-transcendence of a non-divine being that is nevertheless, from the standpoint of the old order, suprahuman. Eros is not a god, but its pseudo-divinity is easily mistaken for actual divinity: that is perhaps the significance of the old legend of the angels' unions with human women and of the similar tales told among the Greeks.

The woman prophet does not cower behind her veil, fearful of attracting the angels' erotic attentions. The Pauline attitude

---

23 That *exousia* in 1 Cor. 11.10 must refer to the woman's authority, and not to her subordination to male authority, was shown by Morna Hooker in an article dating from 1964 (reprinted in *From Adam to Christ: Essays on Paul*, Cambridge: Cambridge University Press, 1990, 113–20). 'The head-covering which symbolizes the effacement of man's glory in the presence of God also serves as the sign of the *exousia* which is given to the woman; with the glory of man hidden she, too, may reflect the glory of God. Far from being a symbol of the woman's subjection to man, therefore, her head-covering is what Paul calls it – authority: in prayer and prophecy she, like the man, is under the authority of God' (119–20).

to these beings is more contempt than fear. The veil is a prophetic sign to the angels that the new creation has dawned and that their jurisdiction has passed away. They may be named impressively as 'thrones and lordships, rules and authorities [*archai, exousiai*]' (Col. 1.16), but the *exousia* of the woman prophet, represented by the veil, is greater than theirs; for if anyone (man or woman) is in Christ, there is new creation (2 Cor. 5.17), and that is what the veil proclaims. The *archai* belong to the *archaia* that are passing away. Christ has freed us from their dominion; he has demythologized them.

But neither is woman apart from man nor man apart from woman, in the Lord (v. 11). Woman must have authority on her head because, from the standpoint of the first creation, she is the glory of man and because, from the standpoint of the new creation, her being is no longer limited by this original identity. Yet, in its negative and positive aspects, the veil is a complex symbol that will easily be misunderstood. A disclaimer is therefore necessary. In decentering eros in the name of the agape of the new creation, the veil introduces a physical barrier between man and woman. Her voice can still be heard, but her face is concealed behind a blank screen. The veil will all too easily solidify into a symbol of a division in which man and woman are apart from one another: and Paul perhaps writes his disclaimer precisely in order to pre-empt this obvious objection from a sceptical Corinthian readership.

The disclaimer is all too necessary, for the danger of misunderstanding is real. In this very passage, Paul himself has come perilously close to losing sight of his true theme – the oneness of man and woman in Christ. If in the old creation woman is the glory of man (v. 7), how is it that, even in the new creation, man is still the head of woman (v. 3)? Is the new merely a repetition of the old? Why is the language of 'new' and 'old' not used here, and why is there no explicit affirmation and celebration of woman's prophetic ministry and of the pouring out of the Spirit on all flesh? Why is the meaning of the veil as a sign of authority over the powers merely hinted at? Throughout the passage, we recognize genuine theological concerns that belong at the heart of Paul's gospel. But they lie beneath the surface of his text; he does not himself identify them clearly enough, and his language betrays uncertainty and anxiety. The disclaimer – in the Lord woman and man are together, not apart – is addressed in part to himself. Yet our concern is not with the text in relation to its author, but with the theological issue of the standing of woman and man 'in the Lord' that we must articulate with the help of his text.

What would happen if the veil became a symbol of division between man and woman? What would happen is what does happen a few chapters later, where a later editor has inserted the fateful words: 'As in all the churches of the saints, the women should keep silence in the churches. For they are not permitted to speak, but should be subordinate, as even the law says. If there is anything they desire to know, let them ask their husbands at home. For it is shameful for a woman to speak in church' (1 Cor. 14.33b–35). Even here, the separation of man and woman is not absolute. Women are silent in church, it is only men who speak, but women are still physically present. Through the Spirit, their silent listening and their asking questions at home will not be in vain. But although elements of the togetherness of man and woman in the Lord survive even here, the theological loss is disastrous. The barrier between those who speak and those who are silent makes it possible for men to define themselves apart from women and for women to define themselves apart from men. First the veil makes woman invisible, and then a further instruction makes her inaudible too.[24]

---

[24] The view that 1 Cor. 14.34–5 is the work of a later editor is widely although not universally accepted. The following points favour this view: (1) A number of textual authorities (D F G a b vg^ms Ambst) place vv. 34–5 after v. 40. This uncertainty about the placing of the passage suggests a later insertion. It also suggests that the insertion did not include v. 33b. (2) In the light of the explicit reference to both men and women prophets in 11.4–5, the exhortation in 14.1 to seek the gift of prophecy would naturally be read as applying to women as well as men (cf. 14.5, 24–5, where the potential universality of the gift of prophecy is emphasized). (3) 'Let the women be silent in the churches' (v. 34a) is an un-Pauline formulation, explicitly addressing an exhortation to all the churches and ignoring the constraints of the epistolary genre. (4) Equally un-Pauline is the unsubstantiated appeal to 'the law' as authority for women's subordination. (5) 'Did the word of God originate from you, or is it only you that it has reached?' (v. 36) is an appropriate conclusion to the plea of vv. 26–33 that prophetic utterance should be orderly. (6) The parallel passage in 1 Tim. 2.11–15

Traces of the distorted self-definitions that result from this
hardening of the veil into a dividing-wall may be found in the
pastoral epistles. Once again, silence and submissiveness is
required of women in the most emphatic terms (1 Tim.
2.11–12), on the grounds that 'Adam was formed first, then Eve;
and Adam was not deceived, but the woman was deceived and
became a transgressor. Yet she shall be saved through child-
bearing . . . ' (vv. 13–15). As Adam is Man, so Eve is Woman.
Revealing in her conduct the general untrustworthiness of
womankind, Eve disqualifies all her daughters from exercising
authority in the church. Man may exercise that authority
because he is Adam, who was not deceived. Man is first,
Woman is second; he is to lead, she must follow. So inferior is
her status that she can normally be ignored. So superior is his
status that he can identify himself and his perspective as the
norm and the truth, without reference to her. Disillusioned by
Eve's untrustworthiness, Adam leaves her to her child-bearing
and goes out to create a world or a church in his own image. He
does not entirely succeed. He cannot escape the togetherness of
man and woman, in the first creation or in the Lord. But his
self-definitions apart from woman are not without damaging
effect.

Silenced within the public space of the church, woman is
banished to the private space of the home. There she is still
permitted to ask questions, and there she may choose to
construct her own self-definitions, apart from man. The author
of 2 Timothy knows of certain men who 'make their way into
homes and capture little women [*gunaikaria*], overwhelmed by
their sins and swayed by various desires, always eager to learn
but incapable of reaching a knowledge of the truth' (2 Tim.
3.6–7). Under firm paternal authority in church, women have
greater freedom at home. There are men who are prepared to
treat women as thinking people and not just as child-rearers,
and women can choose to admit them into their homes, asses-
sing what they have to say in complete independence from the

suggests a deutero-Pauline origin. These are strong points, although not absolutely
decisive. But even if Paul did write 1 Cor. 14.34–5, a passage so at odds with its
immediate and broader contexts can be regarded as an unfortunate aberration.

truth handed down in the church. Excluded from the church's all-male teaching ministry, women react by thinking independently at home. In reaction against their exclusion, they define themselves as Outsiders. The author may perhaps have been right to complain that such people 'turn away from listening to the truth and wander into myths' (4.4). But he has failed to notice his own responsibility for their decision to define themselves in terms of these myths and to reject ecclesial truth; for it is he who has decreed that men are the only reliable mouthpieces of ecclesial truth and that women's calling is to submit in silence. Where man defines himself apart from woman, then woman will define herself over against man. Even in the pastoral epistles, that is not the whole truth of the relation of man and woman in the Lord. The church leader is to treat older women like mothers, younger women like sisters, without using his authority as a pretext for harshness or sexual exploitation (1 Tim. 5.2). Widows are to be honoured for their life of prayer, and where appropriate the church is to give them financial support (5.3–8). Timothy's own acquaintance with holy scripture seems to derive from the teaching he received in childhood from his mother Lois and his grandmother Eunice (2 Tim. 3.15, 1.5). The author's frequently expressed concern for decency and respectability in family life is not necessarily misplaced. Yet, although vestiges of the truth that man and woman are together in the Lord survive even here, the impact of distorted self-definitions in which man and woman hold themselves apart from one another is palpable.[25]

Paul's disclaimer – that in the Lord woman is not woman apart from man and man is not man apart from woman – is all too necessary. But its function is not only to answer the objection that the effect of the veil will be to separate men and women; it is also a positive affirmation. In itself, it lacks definition. All kinds of more or less satisfactory social and ecclesial arrange-

---

[25] As a general judgment about the pastoral epistles, it seems an over-simplification to say that 'their tone (especially as regards women and their roles) is negative to the point of ferocity' (Linda Maloney, 'The Pastoral Epistles', in E. Schüssler Fiorenza (ed.), *Searching the Scriptures*, vol. II: *A Feminist Commentary*, London: SCM Press, 1995, 361–80; 361).

ments might claim to represent the togetherness of man and woman in the Lord. It is the context that gives this affirmation the clarity and the critical edge it might seem to lack as a general principle. Clarity and critical edge are still lacking where this text is understood as a general affirmation of the 'equality' of man and woman, over against the 'hierarchical' language of the preceding verses. Like 'togetherness', 'equality' begs a number of questions. What sort of equality? What forms will it take, and why? In itself, the notion of a 'discipleship of equals' is purely negative and polemical, and has nothing to say about the nature, form and basis of this equality except that it excludes every kind of inequality. The Pauline text is best understood on the basis of its own polarity of togetherness and apartness, within a broader context marked by the symbol of the veil.

The togetherness which this text articulates is a togetherness of *speech* – the distinctively Christian speech of proclamation and prayer. This speech is the speech of men, and it is the speech of women. The veil that differentiates them is intended to preserve the distinctively Christian character of this speech as the dialogue of God and the community, by screening out the erotic look – the irrelevant and impertinent intrusion of the old creation, in which woman is the glory of man, into the new creation in which the Spirit is poured out upon all flesh. The togetherness of man and woman will not be the primary *content* of this speech. The divine word and the thankful human response refer to the event in which 'God was in Christ reconciling the world to himself' (2 Cor. 5.19). That alone is their foundation and content, and it can never be replaced by any other. 'No other foundation can anyone lay than that which is laid, which is Jesus Christ' (1 Cor. 3.11). 'I decided to know nothing among you except Jesus Christ and him crucified' (1 Cor. 2.2): Paul's proclamation is the paradigm for the prophet's. It is true that the reconciliation of the world through the crucified Christ entails a social embodiment in which there is reconciliation between humans – Jew and Greek, slave and free, male and female. But the divine reconciliation of the world cannot be *reduced* to this social embodiment. In the speech that enacts the dialogue between God and the community, the community is not simply speaking about itself. Responsibility for this speech is shared between men and women, and this shared responsibility relates more immediately to the *form* of the speech than to its content.

What takes place when, in the midst of the congregation, man or woman *speaks* in proclamation or prayer? In the first instance, woman (or man) makes the divine-human speech at the heart of Christian and ecclesial existence her own speech. She assumes responsibility towards it. This is always a *shared* responsibility. Even as one who speaks, she must continue to listen to others' speech; for her speech is not hers alone but the speech of God to the community and of the community to God, and the word of God and of the community is not exhausted by her word. Her word is subordinated to that general word – the old word that has already been spoken and heard, sedimented in the form of a tradition, and the new word that now comes to expression on the basis of the old. If the tradition is living and not dead, it is always in need of new articulation, and the new word is therefore not an impersonal repetition of a static tradition but an ever-new event. It is not a word-in-general that comes to expression through her voice and mouth; it is genuinely *her* word, no less her own for being a contemporary articulation of the living word of tradition. Yet a word that was *exclusively* her own would be incomprehensible to its hearers, an instance of the pure *glossolalia* whose tendency to exclude its hearers from participation will later be criticized (1 Cor. 14.1–19). In taking responsibility for the word in which God speaks to the community and the community speaks to God, the woman who prophesies and prays makes the word her own.

In speaking rather than remaining silent, the one who prays or prophesies refuses the temptation to withdraw from responsibility and to leave that responsibility to others. If he or she leaves the speaking to others, speaking and hearing will both be impaired as speakers and hearers are divided from each other. Where speech is met by silence, it fails to attain its object – even if the silence is the silence of attentive listening rather than that of indifference. Speech seeks to evoke speech; communication intends dialogue, as the circular movement of the divine speech and the human response indicates in paradigmatic form. Where speech is met by unbroken silence, the speaker is not heard but *over*heard talking to himself. There is no response, and no further impartation to others. The responsibility of speech may indeed be assumed in various ways, outside as well as inside the formal meetings of the community for worship. Even though she is not permitted to teach or have authority over men, Timothy's mother proclaims the word of the Lord to her young son and articulates on his behalf the prayer that answers it. Nevertheless, the circular movement of authentic Christian speech will be impaired if, in communal worship, an absolute distinction is drawn between those who speak and those who either remain silent or who speak only in the impersonal language of the first person plural.

The one who assumes the responsibility of speech does so in the presence of others. Her appropriation of speech is a public act, and the movement out of silence into speech is a venture that exposes her to risk. She undertakes this movement because she is called to do so through the Spirit, who bestows on each the *charisma* that is to be used for the common good. It is the Spirit who opens her mouth and gives her utterance and who ensures that, however it is received, that utterance is not in vain. Since utterance is undertaken for others' sake, it is grounded in the agape that desires the true well-being of the other – her own love for the other insofar as it arises out of the divine agape that is the content of her proclamation and her thanksgiving. But she participates in the divine agape through the mediation of the congregation, whose true life, apart from all accidents and distortions, is the life of agape. The love for the other that impels her to speak is a love that has first comprehended her in its scope – a human love that is also a divine love, not partly human and partly divine but wholly human and wholly divine, the one because it is also the other: for, without compromising the distinction between divine and human, 'divine' here refers to a reality that is turned towards humanity rather than enclosed in itself, and 'human' refers to a reality that is not left in its own self-enclosure but drawn into the koinonia of the divine agape.

In the Lord, man and woman are together and not apart because they participate alike in the divine-human agape. But their togetherness should also be manifested in a shared responsibility for speech. Within the meeting of the congregation, women as well as men must articulate the distinctive Christian word in its circular, dialogical form. This 'must' does not simply reflect the fact that the Spirit happens to bestow his gifts indifferently on both men and women. Nor is it the case that a woman must speak so as to enable other women to 'identify' with her, as male listeners 'identify' with a man who speaks. That would be division, not togetherness. The man who speaks is not man-in-abstraction, and the woman who speaks is not woman-in-abstraction – man or woman turned away from the other and addressing his or her own kind. The one who speaks is the man who is not apart from woman or the woman who is not apart from man. If man alone speaks, he will represent only the abstraction of a man who is apart from woman, an absolutized and distorted maleness. Woman must speak as well as man so that the divine-human discourse at the heart of the church's life may be represented and enacted not by an abstraction but by a full and genuine humanity – full and genuine in both man and woman when each is not apart from the other. Here too, it is 'not good for the man to be alone'.

However ambiguously and questionably, the Pauline veil intends to preserve this koinonia in Christian utterance rather than undermining it. Inappropriate in practice, it retains its symbolic theological significance. Woman is to speak from behind a veil in order that the agape that is the motivation and the content of her speech should reach its intended goal and not be turned aside by an intrusion from the old order. It is a sign that the mythologized, quasi-transcendent authority of eros is excluded from the koinonia of agape, since it intends the possession of the other in the form of bodily union rather than the other's divinely determined well-being. The erotic koinonia of man and woman is – we might almost say – a parody of the true koinonia of man and woman in the Lord.

For as woman is from man, so too man is through woman . . . (v. 12). Following his affirmation of the togetherness of man and woman in the Lord, Paul unexpectedly reverts to the sphere of creation in order to support this affirmation. 'Woman is from man': the wording (*hē gunē ek tou andros*) is almost identical to v. 8 (*gunē ex andros*), where the point was to assert an imbalance between man (the glory of God) and woman (the glory of man) – an imbalance in the first creation that the veil is to screen out in the new creation. Having moved forward from the old creation to the situation 'in the Lord' (vv. 7–10), Paul is now in a position to look back at the old creation from the new perspective and to see the togetherness of man and woman in the Lord already foreshadowed there. The new creation re-dresses an imbalance in the old; but, seen retrospectively, the old creation is also prophetic of the new. Anticipations of the togetherness of man and woman in the Lord may be found in the simplest and most obvious phenomena of the first creation. Woman is from man: as we have already seen, this intimate original unity is represented by the Genesis narrator as the basis of the erotic movement of man towards woman which is the original foundation of their relationship. But, even in the first creation, the relation of man and woman is not wholly deter-mined by eros. Woman is from man, but man is also through woman. Man is the origin of woman, but it is no less true that woman is the origin of man. Christ himself is 'born of woman' (Gal. 4.4). Eve claims: 'Through God, I have created a man [*ektēsamēn anthrōpon dia tou theou*]' (Gen. 4.1). The relation of mother to son is no less fundamental and original than the relation of man to his wife. As man becomes one flesh with woman in sexual union, so woman is one flesh with man in conception, pregnancy, birth and nurture. The symmetry is inscribed in woman's very body, as the Pauline 'through' indicates. In the light of this original togetherness with woman, the notion of male autonomy and primacy appears as a post-Oedipal myth, a denial of the maternal origin that attempts to redress the perceived imbalance of man's dependence on woman for his very being. In the Genesis text, however, the imbalance is redressed not by the myth of an autonomous masculinity but by an erotic drive that is not a helpless reversion to infantile dependence on the mother but a genuine initiative towards a woman who is not the mother: a man *leaves* his father and mother and is joined to his wife, so that the movement from woman to woman is not circular but linear. From woman's perspective, the movement of the man towards union with her flesh is balanced by a corresponding movement of man out of and away from her flesh. In neither case does the togetherness of man and woman take the form of a stifling embrace in which their distinctiveness is dissolved. In their togetherness, they are allowed their own space.[26]

From the standpoint of the togetherness of man and woman in the Lord, these complex and emotionally charged realities may be seen as imperfect but actual anticipations of the divine-human koinonia of agape. Incorporated into this broader context, the eros of man and woman is no longer a parody of agape but a parable.

. . . *and all things are from God* (v. 12b). The dialectic of male and female, origin and initiative, identity and union is a purely creaturely reality that is relativized by the acknowledgment that all this and the world in which it occurs is 'from God' as its absolute origin. That divine origin is the basis for the fact that the togetherness of man and woman in the created order can serve as a parable of the koinonia of agape: for the two realities, distinct though they are, have a common source. In the relation of the human creature to the divine creator, gender is relativized and transcended; and this too is a parable of the divine-

---

[26] The different approaches to creation in vv. 7–9 and v. 12 are rightly emphasized by Judy Gundry-Wolf ('Gender and Creation in 1 Corinthians 11:2–16: A Study in Paul's Theological Method', in O. Hofius *et al.* (eds.), *Evangelium – Schriftauslegung – Kirche: Festschrift für Peter Stuhlmacher zum 65. Geburtstag*, Göttingen: Vandenhoeck & Ruprecht, 1997, 151–71). According to Gundry-Wolf, this passage indicates that creation 'can be construed in a patriarchal sense . . . but also in an egalitarian sense . . . The latter reading comes through viewing creation from the perspective of the new eschatological life in Christ; it is a specifically Christian reading of creation. The former comes through viewing creation through the lens of patriarchal culture' (170). But the polarities between the patriarchal and the egalitarian, the cultural and the specifically Christian are too broad to capture the specificities of this text.

human agape of the new creation in Christ. In Christ there is neither Jew nor Greek, male nor female, slave or free, and this relativizing of difference is anticipated in the relation of creature to creator that precedes and grounds it. Gender is a creaturely reality; the divine–human relation is not itself gendered. There is no more a feminine other that would constitute God as masculine than there is a masculine other that would constitute God as feminine. The creature does not play a feminine role in relation to a masculine initiative of the creator, for what passes for masculine initiative in the creaturely sphere does not even attain the level of a caricature of the divine *creatio ex nihilo*. There is an absolute qualitative difference between the two realities.

The gendering of the one who creates *ex nihilo* is the fabrication of an image, in defiance of the second commandment. A particularly clear example, expressive of a platonizing homoeroticism and misogyny, may be seen on the ceiling of the Sistine Chapel. In the most celebrated painting of this series, the hidden source of the creator's masculinity is revealed in the erotic look that evokes the answering look of the awakening Adam – a look whose sacrament is the gesture in which the divine lover's index finger reaches out to meet the rising finger of the human beloved. The heavenly archetype of this homo-erotic relationship is represented by the creator's simultaneous embrace of the naked and youthful Son, who looks upon the human beloved not as a rival but as a counterpart. In the next panel, in stark contrast to the grace and lightness of the first, Eve stumbles awkwardly into being. The masculinity of the creator has already been established by the homoerotic encounter with Adam, and the creation of woman is the first step downwards towards the Fall. Here the creator has lost his ease and grace of movement. He stands motionless, his back bent. He is the Ancient of Days, and he looks his age. His right hand appears to ward off the approach of the emerging Eve, refusing her the gesture of love spontaneously imparted to Adam. The gracelessness of the figures in this panel contrasts with the beauty of the naked youths at its corners, who variously gaze at one another and display themselves in an attempt to restore the

all-male harmony that Eve's irruption has broken. This painting is in fact a concession to orthodoxy, for in the next panel
Eve's true origins are revealed. This time it is her turn to recline
languidly on the ground, to gaze into the eyes of a divine other,
and to reach up to touch an outstretched hand – the hand of a
female figure with a serpent's body coiled around a tree. In her
rapt devotion to her counterpart, Eve is oblivious of Adam's
urgent warnings. ('Adam was not deceived, but the woman was
deceived and became a transgressor' (1 Tim. 2.14).) As in the
Timaeus, Man represents the Father from above, Woman the
Mother from the chaos below. Man and Woman enjoy same-sex
relationships with the divinities they acknowledge, and their
apartness from one another is projected into the divine realm.

If 'all things are from God' and if gender is a purely
creaturely reality, then the projection of gender onto divinity is
exposed as misogynistic and idolatrous.[27]

*Judge for yourselves: is it proper for a woman to pray to God with uncovered
head?* (v. 13). Earlier, it was the woman who 'prays or prophesies'
who is to be veiled (v. 5); now, it is the woman who 'prays to
God'. When prayer is associated with prophecy, it is clear that
the woman in question is articulating the word of God to the
congregation and the responsive word of the congregation to
God. But when prayer is mentioned without prophecy, her role
as leader is less clear and her veiling may now become the
condition of her presence at Christian worship. Her veiling will
then correspond to her silence: within Christian worship, she
will be both invisible and inaudible. It is only in the single
reference to prophecy (v. 5) and in the identification of the veil
as women's *exousia* (v. 10) that this passage explicitly resists
assimilation to the later silencing of women in church (14.34–5).

---

[27] In the opinion of E. H. Gombrich, 'It is hardly an exaggeration to say that the
picture of God the Father – as it has lived in the minds of generation after generation,
not only of artists but of humble people, who perhaps have never heard the name of
Michelangelo – was shaped and moulded through the direct and indirect influence
of these great visions in which Michelangelo illustrated the act of creation' (*The Story
of Art*, London: Phaidon Press, 16th edn 1995, 312). If there is any truth in this, then
the theological need for a critique of these paintings is obvious. William Blake shows
more perception than most in his 'Elohim creating Adam' (c. 1795), a savage
caricature of Michelangelo's painting.

By the time of 1 Clement, the silence of women has become – at least for the author – the traditional norm to which the church at Corinth is recalled out of 'the abominable and unholy uprising [*stasis*], alien and foreign to the elect of God, which a few rash and self-willed persons have kindled . . . ' (1 Clem. 1.1). Before the trouble started, the young were taught subservience to their rulers and women were instructed to remain 'in the rule of submission' (*en tō kanōni tēs hupotagēs*) to their husbands (1.3). But then, 'the dishonourable rose up against the honourable, the unknown against the renowned, the foolish against the wise, the young against the elders [*tous presbuterous*]' (3.3). The cause of the uprising was 'jealousy' (*zēlos*), which 'has estranged wives from husbands and made of no effect the saying of our father Adam, "This is now bone of my bone and flesh of my flesh"' (6.3). The young and the women are again set over against the elders as the author appeals for a return to the church's traditional order. 'Let us respect those who rule us, let us honour the elders [*tous presbuterous*], let us instruct the young in the fear of God, let us lead our women to what is good . . . Let them make the gentleness of their tongue manifest by their silence [*to epieikes tēs glossēs autōn dia tēs sigēs phaneron poiesatōsan*], let them not give their affection in a partisan spirit [*kata proskliseis*], but in holiness to all alike who fear God' (21.6–7).

The silencing of women means that the link between the veil and the authority to speak is broken, so that the veil becomes the uniform condition of woman in church. According to Tertullian, the Corinthian church understands the apostle's imposition of the veil to apply to all women alike (*De virginibus velandis*, 8); indeed, this is the custom of the majority of churches throughout Greece, although some impose the veil only on married women (2). Tertullian commends the Corinthian practice to the churches of the west, where the less stringent practice is the norm. The veil that the apostle imposes on 'every woman' (including 'virgins') seems consistent with the fact that 'it is not permitted to a woman to speak in the church, or to teach, to baptize, to offer, or to lay claim to a male function such as the priestly office' (9). Despite this, the veil is for Tertullian the symbol of woman's power, and not of her weakness or subordination.[28]

In his treatise *On the Veiling of Virgins*, Tertullian both extends the discipline of the veil to unmarried women and insists that married women should conceal their heads fully, and not just partially. At both points, he is conscious of flying in the face of local custom, but – under the influence of Montanism – he claims that the new practices have been revealed by the Paraclete through prophetic utterances. A Christian woman has reported a visionary experience in which she was chastised by an angel for appearing in church with an uncovered neck. 'To us, the Lord has measured the extent of the veil by way of revelations. For a certain sister of ours was thus addressed in visions by an angel, beating her neck as if in applause: "Elegant neck, and deservedly bare! You should uncover yourselves from the head down to the loins, so as to take full advantage of the freedom of your neck!"' (*De virg. vel.*, 17). This supernatural sarcasm is taken as a sign that total concealment of the head and neck is required of all women in church. If women are 'scandalized' by the stringent addition of invisibility to their existing inaudibility, they should 'learn to acknowledge their own evil' (3) – for it is only their own lust that makes them want to be seen. 'The same kind of eyes reciprocally crave after each other. Seeing and being seen belong to the self-same lust [*eiusdem libidinis est videri et videre*]' (2). A woman 'must necessarily be imperilled by exposing herself in public, as she is penetrated by the gaze of untrustworthy and multitudinous eyes, as she is is caressed [*titillatur*] by pointing fingers, as she is too well loved, as she feels a warmth creep over her amid ardent embraces and kisses. So the forehead hardens; so the sense of shame [*pudor*] wears away' (14). On the other hand, 'Who will have the audacity to intrude with his eyes upon a covered face [*faciem clausam*], an unfeeling face, a face with the appearance of a frown? Every evil thought will be destroyed by that expression of severity' (15). Women should realize that their face endangers

---

[28] Translations from Tertullian's *De virginibus velandis*, *De exhortatione castitatis* and *De resurrectione carnis* are adapted from *The Ante-Nicene Fathers*, vols. III, IV, reprinted Grand Rapids: Eerdmans, 1976.

their Christian brothers, young or old: 'All ages are imperilled in your person' (17). The story of the seduction of the sons of God by the daughters of men is a terrible warning. 'A face so fair as to cast stumbling-stones as far as heaven itself must surely be shaded' (7).

This is a theology of women's *power* – a power which can be used in the service of the flesh or of the spirit. It is a power to which women themselves lay claim, for the demand for full concealment of the head by all women was revealed by the Paraclete through a woman prophet. In demanding women's total withdrawal from the male gaze, Tertullian seeks to enforce not his own opinion or even the requirements of holy scripture but a divine commandment revealed through a woman prophet who is his own contemporary. After the ages of the Law and the Gospel, representing infancy and youth, the present age of the Paraclete represents maturity: those who 'demand that virgins be wholly covered' do so because they have heard the Paraclete 'prophesying to the present time' (1). Women and men who absent themselves from the sexual games prevalent even in the church are promised that they too will prophesy. 'Through the holy prophetess Prisca [= Priscilla] it is proclaimed that the holy minister must know how to administer holiness of life [*sanctimoniam*]. For purification (she says) produces harmony, and they see visions; and turning their face downward, they also hear salutary voices, as clear as they are secret' (*De exh. cast.*, 10.5). The downturned face speaks of woman's silence and invisibility in church, here representing not her weakness but her power – the power to see visions and to receive heavenly revelations. The sphere of woman's silence is penetrated and shaped by her prior speech, which in the name of the Paraclete can override the authority of tradition itself. The precondition of this speech is the sexual self-purification whose symbol is the veil which marks woman's definitive rejection of the conventional games of seeing and being seen. Yet it would be wrong to understand the veil as a rejection of the flesh itself. In another of the revelations of the Paraclete through Prisca, it is said of those who deny the resurrection of the flesh that 'they are fleshly, and yet they hate the flesh' (*De res. carn.*, 11). Through the licentiousness of their lives, the enemies of the flesh are its greatest friends. But from another point of view, it is those who impose sexual continence on the flesh who honour it most highly as God's workmanship. In both temporal and eternal matters, 'the flesh, which is accounted the minister and servant of the soul, turns out to be also its associate and co-heir' (7). Virginity and sexual restraint within marriage are themselves 'fragrant offerings to God paid out of the good services of the flesh' (8).

In this remarkable appropriation of the Pauline symbol of the veil, it is women's power that makes it improper for them to worship with uncovered head. The rule of faith – that there is one God, the creator, whose son Jesus Christ was 'born of the Virgin Mary, crucified under Pontius Pilate, raised again the third day from the dead, received in the heavens, seated now at the right hand of the Father, destined to come to judge quick and dead through the resurrection also of the flesh' (*De virg. vel.*, 1) – requires that the flesh that is eternally honoured by God should also be honoured within the church by disciplines revealed through the Paraclete to prophetically gifted women.[29]

Does not nature itself teach you that it is dishonourable for a man to have long hair, while for a woman long hair is her glory? For her hair is given to her as a garment (vv. 14–15). In itself, this might suggest that the issue at Corinth is not the covering of the face with a veil but the covering of the head with the hair. If long hair is already a 'garment' (*peribolaion*) provided by nature to conceal the nakedness of the female head, what need is there to supplement nature's provision with the artifice of the veil? The issue would then be that women at Corinth have had their hair cut short, like men; it would be in that sense that their head is 'uncovered' (vv. 5, 6, 13). This interpretation makes good sense of the movement of thought from verse 13 – 'Is it fitting for a woman to

---

[29] A notorious passage at the beginning of his *De cultu feminarum* has created the mistaken impression of Tertullian as an arch-misogynist. This widespread view is effectively criticized in F. Forrester Church, 'Sex and Salvation in Tertullian', *HTR* 68 (1975), 83–101. The recognition of Montanism's significance for feminist theology (see Susanna Elm, 'Montanist Oracles', in E. Schüssler Fiorenza (ed.), *Searching the Scriptures*, II.131–8) should encourage reassessment of Tertullian.

pray to God uncovered?' – to verses 14–15, where the covering of the head is the long hair that is nature's gift.[30] Yet the earlier use of concealment language would be surprising if the issue is simply hair-length; and in verse 6 Paul asserts that the woman who refuses to be covered *should* have her hair cut short or shaved off altogether – in which case her hair is not *at present* cut short, so that this cannot be the point at issue. Verses 14–15 also offer no support for the view that Paul is trying here to persuade the Corinthian women to bind up their unbound hair, thereby 'covering' their heads. On that view, the idea that long hair is woman's glory and that as such it is a garment provided by nature would be indistinguishable from the Corinthians' own position. As in verses 5–6, the point is that women's long hair (as opposed to men's short hair) is *analogous* to the additional covering represented by the veil. In seeking to impose this extra covering on women but not on men, Paul is following the example of nature itself, which has similarly seen fit to provide women with an extra covering.

The limitations of this argument are already noted by Calvin, who writes: 'Paul here sets nature before them as the teacher of what is proper. Now, he means by "natural" what was accepted by common consent and usage at that time, certainly as far as the Greeks were concerned. For long hair was not always regarded as a disgraceful thing in men. Thus the poets are in the habit of speaking about the ancients and applying to them the epithet "unshorn". In Rome they did not begin to use barbers until a late period, about the time of Africanus the Elder. When Paul was writing these words, the practice of cutting hair had not yet been adopted in Gaul or Germany. Yes, and more than that, indeed, it would have been a disgraceful thing for men, just as much as women, to have their hair shaved or cut. But since the Greeks did not consider it very manly to have long hair, branding those who had it as effeminate, Paul

---

[30] The view that Paul is criticizing the Corinthian women for their short hair is advocated by W. J. Martin, 'I Corinthians 11:2–16: An Interpretation', in W. Ward Gasque and R. P. Martin (eds.), *Apostolic History and the Gospel: Biblical and Historical Essays presented to F. F. Bruce on his 60th Birthday*, Exeter: Paternoster, 1970, 231–41.

considers that their custom, accepted in his own day, was in conformity with nature' (*1 Corinthians*, 235).[31]

But if anyone wishes to be argumentative, we have no other custom, nor do the churches of God (v. 16). Many readers of Paul's text have indeed wanted to argue with it and with him, and have found in this final verse the collapse of a weak and incoherent argument into a bare appeal to authority. Paul, writes John P. Meier, 'seems to have a sinking feeling that none of these arguments from Scripture, reason and nature is going to carry the day against his opponents, people who are contentious, obstinate, dogmatic, more interested in having a fight and winning it than in the truth (*philoneikos*). Well, if anyone wants to be contentious –, at this point, Paul does not even complete his sentence. He breaks off all reasoned argument and delivers his *fiat* on the basis of universal tradition . . . As some commentators have noted, it is ironical that in the charismatic Paul, the great Apostle of freedom, we have the beginnings not only of natural law and natural theology in the Christian Church, but also of apodictic canon law. One does wonder, in the light of verse 16, why verses 3–15 even exist. The appeal to universal church practice as the definitive arbiter of a question does make theological reasoning look like so much window dressing' ('On the Veiling of Hermeneutics', 223).[32] Meier's purpose is to compare the doubtful argumentation of the Pauline text with the equally doubtful argumentation of the *Declaration on the Question of the Admission of Women to the Ministerial Priesthood* (or *Inter Insigniores*), published by the Congregation for the Doctrine of the Faith in 1977. In both cases, an unthinking appeal to what is supposed to be unchanging tradition partially conceals itself behind the 'window dressing' of pseudo-theological argument. At the root of the problem is the fact that 'the Declaration does not take historical-critical exegesis seriously' (226). That is, it

---

[31] Translation from *The First Epistle of Paul the Apostle to the Corinthians*, in D. W. Torrance and T. F. Torrance (eds.), *Calvin's New Testament Commentaries: A New Translation*, Grand Rapids: Eerdmans, 1960.

[32] John P. Meier, 'On the Veiling of Hermeneutics (1 Cor 11:2–16)', *CBQ* 40 (1978), 212–26.

does not make sufficient allowance for the historical conditioning of the deliverances of tradition on the question of women's ministry, from the Pauline texts onwards. If we read the assertions of Paul, Augustine or Aquinas within the context of their own philosophical presuppositions and pragmatic strategies, we must recognize that they can no longer be regarded as normative.

To 'take historical-critical exegesis seriously' is evidently to read the biblical texts as a whole – and not just this Pauline passage – in the light of the antithesis between that which is 'historically conditioned' and that which is 'normative'. At point after point, what purports to be 'normative' will turn out to be 'historically conditioned'. Thus, one legalistic hermeneutic gives rise to another, as the old law of the text is overthrown by a new law derived from the insights and prejudices of the present – a law which judges the text, finds it wanting, and discards it.

In opposition to the hermeneutics of historicism, it is more productive of theological insight to refuse the role of the adversary and to allow the text to unfold itself in its own way, attending carefully and patiently to an underlying logic that is not always manifest, and criticizing misleading statements only in order to attain a better understanding of the real subject matter of this passage: the togetherness of man and woman in the Lord, within the koinonia of agape.

PART II

Concupiscentia: Romans 7

The veil signifies the exclusion of eros from the inner life of the Christian community, in which man and woman belong together in agape. Does this mean that it also signifies the 'negative attitude towards sexuality and the body' for which Christian faith is so often held to be responsible? This thesis presupposes a contrast between an earlier era of sexual repression (variously associated with 'Victorian hypocrisy' or with Paul and Augustine) and the present era of sexual enlightenment. Freud is conventionally seen as the turning-point from one era to the other, since it was he who first gave voice to sex, enabling sex to speak for itself and without shame. Paul and Augustine on the one hand, Freud on the other, mark the opposite poles of contemporary telling and retelling of the story of our sexual enlightenment.

Augustine's view of sexuality is based on the Pauline analysis of desire (*epithumia, concupiscentia*) and of the ego caught within the opposition between 'the law of God' and 'the law of sin that is in my members' (Rom. 7). In his later theory of the ego as exposed to the contradictory demands of super-ego and id, Freud shows himself to belong to the Pauline-Augustinian tradition. Far from underwriting the modern assumption that we (unlike our predecessors) have now discovered sexuality to be unproblematic, Freud recovers the Pauline-Augustinian sense of the intractability of this sphere of human experience. Paul's *epithumia*, Augustine's *concupiscentia* and Freud's *libido* all refer to the same impersonal, quasi-divine power to which human existence is subjected. The purpose of a reading of Freud along these lines is to make it possible to re-read the

Pauline text (and its Augustinian interpretation) as a *critique* of the contemporary discourse of sex, which overlooks or represses the phenomena that contradict its claim that, for us, sexuality is essentially unproblematic (chapter 3).

The Pauline-Augustinian critique is no more than a negative corollary of a trinitarian theology of divine *grace* which represents the fundamental ethos of the Christian community (chapter 4). Here, there is a service of God in the newness of the Spirit and not in the oldness of the letter – the letter of a law which, as the narratives of Israel's experiences in the wilderness testify, both embodies God's claim on human life and is implicated in the genesis of human resistance to this claim. The law of the Spirit of life gives *freedom* from the law of sin, and fulfils the promise of life which is the true goal of the law of God. Christian sexual ethics is therefore not to be seen as a set of perhaps rather archaic restrictions on sexual life, which need to be accommodated to the insights and conventions of our own time if they are to have any continuing 'relevance'. The 'restrictions' are simply a consequence of the gift of freedom to participate, together with others, in the eternal intradivine life opened up to us in the death and resurrection of Jesus and through his Spirit. As such, they belong to the gospel. They are good news, not bad; compassionate and merciful, not harsh or judgmental. They limit eros or concupiscence only in the name of agape.

'Do not be conformed to this world but be transformed by the renewal of your mind, that you may prove what is the will of God, what is good and acceptable and perfect': the Pauline injunction applies also to the sphere of sexual life. This nonconformity to the world and renewal of the mind gives a certain critical detachment from the destructive myths underlying the contemporary discourse of sex.

CHAPTER THREE

Sex: a critique

It is a familiar story, and it goes like this:

Sex is natural. Sex is good. Sex is enjoyable. There is no need to be ashamed of it. Indeed, we inflict serious psychological damage on ourselves if we attempt to repress our sexuality. Repression stems from a negative view of the body, for which Christianity is largely responsible. But to be embodied is to be innocent not guilty, and the sexual conjunction of bodies celebrates this innocence in the play of paradise. It is these truths about the human condition that our own age has rediscovered; Eros, demonized for so long, is again found to be a god who bestows on his devotees the bliss of participation in his own divinity. We are now at last at home with our bodies, we are no longer ashamed of them. And we are no longer ashamed to *speak* of that which so intimately concerns our bodies. Sexual liberation is also (or even primarily) the liberation of *speech*. What was formerly unsayable can now be spoken freely, without fear or shame.

Or so it is said. The story of our sexual liberation is told and retold in many different versions; it is constantly updated, so as to incorporate new emphases overlooked by earlier renderings; and various qualifications and nuances may be added or subtracted. But in all these variations it is recognizably the same story that is told and retold, so compelling that it imposes itself as self-evidently true.

The story is inscribed in language itself. 'Sex' – as a synonym for 'sexual intercourse', as in the phrase 'to have sex with' – appears to be a coinage only of the past fifty or sixty years.

Originally used simply in the sense of 'gender', this word acquired increasingly 'sexual' connotations from around the 1890s onwards – as exemplified in formulations such as 'sex-act', 'sex-life', 'sex-drive', 'sex-organs', 'sex-appeal', popular in the early decades of the twentieth century. These formulations prepared for the moment when it became possible to use 'sex' in a (relatively) independent secondary sense, as referring not to gender but to the act of sexual intercourse itself. Unlike 'sexual intercourse' or 'sex-act', 'sex' is no longer a circumlocution. In itself, 'intercourse' refers to the dialogical movement of contact and communication between persons; and 'sexual' identifies the 'intercourse' in question as that which is characteristic of persons as male and female, as differentiated from one another and related to one another by the polarity of sex. The vagueness of 'intercourse' is given the necessary precision by the adjective – so effectively that 'intercourse' itself is often now equivalent to 'sexual intercourse', and can be used in a non-sexual sense only with difficulty. Originally as vague as the equivalent terms in phrases such as 'sexual relations', 'sexual connection', 'sexual conjunction', 'sexual union' and 'sexual act', 'intercourse' has succumbed, as it were, to the gravitational pull of 'sex' and its semantic range has been restricted. ('Copulation', 'coition' and 'make love' have suffered the same fate.) Yet 'sexual intercourse' retains its circumlocutory feel; the original vagueness of 'intercourse' continues to lend it a certain neutrality and non-assertiveness. 'Sex', on the other hand, is more assertive. And what it asserts is the right of the act in question to have its own proper name, to announce itself in all its nakedness, without veiling itself in circumlocution and without shame. To assert that 'sex' is natural, good, enjoyable and not shameful is simply to articulate the ideology inherent in the word itself. And yet the word strives to conceal its ideological content and its assertiveness by laying claim to something of the neutrality of 'sexual intercourse'. 'Sex' just *is* what the act in question is called; it *is* what the participants in the act 'have' with each other. 'Sex' has no intention of transgressing the limits of linguistic decorum. Aspiring to neutrality, it denies its own assertiveness; wishing to be a natural feature of language, it conceals its own very recent

origin. Thus an English speaker may express surprise to discover that a particular foreign language has no word for 'sex' –
although English itself has only recently acquired its word for
'sex'.[1]

Sex is natural, sex is good, sex is enjoyable; it speaks freely,
without shame. Yet 'sex' has so far been unable to establish itself
securely as the proper, unproblematic, non-circumlocutory
name for the act in question. Had it succeeded in this, 'sexual
intercourse' would now be redundant. The persistent use of this
expression – although in a limited range of mainly literary
contexts – registers a continuing preference for the circumlocutory veil rather than direct naming. Circumlocution arises out of
an enduring sense of the shame of semantic nakedness – in spite
of the claim of 'sex' that the nakedness of direct utterance is
proper to the natural, good and enjoyable act that speaks in it.
'Sex' and 'sexual intercourse' divide over the question of shame.

'Sex' is supported by a profusion of 'popular', less formal
expressions which variously assert or assume the innocence, the
enjoyableness, the excitement, the physicality or the comic
incongruity of the sexual act. For example, there is no trace of
shame in expressions such as 'sleep with/together' or 'go to bed
with/together'. These expressions evoke the excitement of an
initial moment of 'breakthrough' into a sexual relationship –
the excitement not only of the sexual partners but also of third
parties for whom the fact that *A* has 'gone to bed with' *B* or that
they 'sleep together' may be an important and absorbing topic
of conversation. To 'sleep together' or 'go to bed together' is the
act of free agents considered in abstraction from any prior
commitments. This language does not normally refer to the

---

[1] Philip Larkin's poem, 'Annus Mirabilis' opens with the lines: 'Sexual intercourse
began / In nineteen sixty-three / (Which was rather late for me) – / Between the end
of the *Chatterley* ban / And the Beatles' first LP' (*Collected Poems*, London: The Marvell
Press; Faber and Faber, 1988, 167). Strictly speaking, it was perhaps 'sex' that began in
1963, not 'sexual intercourse'. The poem as a whole is an ironic rendering of the
standard modern narrative of sexual enlightenment, in a retelling popular in the
1960s and 1970s. According to the second stanza: 'Up till then there'd only been / A
sort of bargaining, / A wrangle for a ring, / A shame that started at sixteen / And
spread to everything.' But now at last the new age has dawned: 'Then all at once the
quarrel sank: / Everyone felt the same, / And every life became / A brilliant breaking
of the bank, / A quite unlosable game.'

repeated, more or less regular sexual acts that occur within marriage. Although husbands and wives go to bed together and sleep together, husbands are not said to 'go to bed with' their wives and wives are not said to 'sleep with' their husbands. 'Sleeping together' and 'going to bed together' derive their *frisson* of excitement from their primary association with extra-marital rather than marital 'sex'. One sleeps with or goes to bed with a *new* sexual partner, and it is the newness of the ensuing situation that is newsworthy and that creates the need for a specialized vocabulary. In this vocabulary, the free, transgressive excitement of the 'extra-marital' is tacitly contrasted with what are taken to be the unexciting, repetitive routines of the 'marital'.

'Sex', aspiring to neutrality and comprehensiveness, relativizes the distinction between the marital and the extra-marital by asserting that it is the same act that is performed on both sides of the boundary. Married couples and unmarried 'lovers' all 'have sex'; what they 'have' is the same, irrespective of the legal status of their relationship. 'Sex' rejects – that is, it makes archaic – the earlier distinction between 'conjugal union' (or 'marital relations') and 'fornication' – a term now regarded as tactless to the point of offensiveness. 'Sex' has nothing in common with those acts in which wanton men satisfy 'their carnal lusts and appetites, like brute beasts without understanding' – to cite the gloss on the term 'fornication' offered by the Book of Common Prayer.[2] Those who 'have sex' do not want to be compared to brute beasts without understanding. 'Sex' may be natural, but it has nothing to do with the copulation of animals; animals do not have sex any more than they go to bed together. Those who have sex are free agents, freely exercising their right to do what they wish with their own bodies.[3] It is true

---

[2] The reference to 'men's carnal lusts and appetites' occurs in an exhortation not to undertake marriage itself 'unadvisedly, lightly, or wantonly'. Marriage was 'ordained for a remedy against sin, and to avoid fornication', and to undertake it wantonly would be to convert marriage itself into fornication. In the 1928 revision, the carnal lusts and brute beasts have been eliminated; and 'ordained for a remedy against sin, and to avoid fornication' is replaced by 'ordained in order that the natural instincts and affections, implanted by God, should be hallowed and directed aright' – a sign of modern fastidiousness and reticence about sexual matters.

[3] As Linda Woodhead writes: 'When and where sex takes place between consenting

that sex may on occasion be unfree: it may be said of a rape victim, for instance, that she was 'forced to have sex', whereas it would not be said that she was 'forced to make love'. As the proper, primary and comprehensive term for the sexual act, 'sex' must cover unfree as well as free sexual acts. But its bias is towards a construal of the act as the free choice of unconstrained partners. It is suspicious of what it sees as the unwarranted intrusion of negative moral judgments into its amoral paradise or playground. To have sex is to make love; love is good, and it is good to make what is good; it is therefore good to have sex. The logic is unanswerable because it has already been written into the terminology itself.

The hegemony of 'sex' over this semantic field is challenged on the one side by the circumlocution 'sexual intercourse', which ought to have become redundant but has not, and on the other side by the overpoweringly negative connotations of the term 'fuck', which may function as verb, noun or expletive, or in the quasi-adjectival 'fucking'. Like the analogous 'shit', 'fuck' as an expletive draws attention to the speaker's intense annoyance and frustration by a wilful violation of linguistic decorum. The force of 'shit' as an expletive seems to derive from disgust at what it names, human excrement – although the expletive is not in itself an expression of disgust. The still more negatively charged 'fuck' may be explained along similar lines – in which case it preserves a reaction of intense disgust at the sexual act, from which it derives its transgressive force. The fact that 'fuck' is more negatively charged than 'shit' would then imply that the sexual act evokes a still more intense disgust than does excrement. 'Fuck' appears to imply that 'sex' is or can be disgusting and shameful. Yet, as we have seen, 'sex' is not disgusting or shameful, it is natural, good and enjoyable. A book entitled *The Joy of Sex* occasions no surprise, but a book entitled *The Shame of Sex* is inconceivable. In principle, then, 'sex' should either have

adults liberalism views it as sacrosanct *per se*. The freedom from which sexual activity arises is understood as the undisputed ground of its justification and sanctification. This holds good whatever forms such sexual activity may take, and whatever its social consequences' ('Sex in a Wider Context', in J. Davies and G. Loughlin (eds.), *Sex These Days: Essays on Theology, Sexuality and Society*, Sheffield: Sheffield Academic Press, 1997, 98–120; 100).

made 'fuck' redundant (as it should have made 'sexual intercourse' redundant), or it should have worked for its rehabilitation as a word that actually denotes something that is natural, good and enjoyable. Despite the advocacy of D. H. Lawrence, however, this word remains as transgressive as ever. Although familiar to all adult native English speakers, it is rarely if ever used by a significant proportion of them. Even hearing it uttered can be experienced as a gross violation, an insult to one's integrity. It is a word that is shunned and feared. Why? Because it evokes the knowledge – which 'sex' represses – that disgust and shame remain all too comprehensible as reactions to sexual acts in which we too may be implicated. This word exposes the limits and limitations of the sanitized world in which one 'makes love' or 'has sex'.

Although it takes pride in its own frankness and forthrightness, 'sex' is in fact deeply disingenuous. Wishing to know and to promote only the joy of sex, it represses the knowledge of the shame of sex. It denies the profound ambivalences registered, in their different ways, by circumlocution and expletive. It simplifies complexities. Its determination to maintain its own innocence makes it blind to the reality of guilt. Although it asserts its own neutrality, it aligns itself all too readily with the sentimentality of 'making love' and the casual frivolity of 'sleeping together'. Conversely, it is uneasy about the older framework within which 'conjugal union' or 'marital relations' used to take place – a framework in which a 'husband' and 'wife' are joined together in 'marriage', one of the purposes of which is to establish a 'family'. Under the impact of sex, these words – husband, wife, marriage, family – have acquired a 'conservative', slightly archaic ring, although the social arrangement they represent is still very common. The words are still in use, but they now generate a certain unease. Sex is not interested in marriage. All sex is 'extra-marital', in the sense that 'marital status' is irrelevant to it. If sex occurs within marriage, it does so irrespective of marriage; one does not speak of 'marital sex'. Sex favours a different language: that of 'relationships', which may be 'long term' or 'stable' but which are at every moment sustained purely by the free choice of the two 'partners'.

Integral to this sex is the concept of 'contraception', which ensures the integrity of sex as a self-contained field by protecting the partners from the unwanted epiphenomena of conception, pregnancy, birth and parenthood. Sex is natural, but sex needs technology to protect it from nature. Without the technology of contraception, sex is not sex.

These linguistic phenomena indicate that the hegemony that 'sex' has established since its entry into language is neither complete nor unproblematic. Although the characteristic modern usage of this term has achieved spectacular success, anomalies remain. The survival of circumlocution and expletive indicate that the shame and disgust they express remain comprehensible even within the new regime. The attempt to archaize and problematize 'husband', 'wife', 'marriage', 'family' flies in the face of a social reality in which traditional, premodern assumptions about 'adultery' or 'unfaithfulness' often survive intact, along with the terms themselves. Even in the more neutral 'having an affair', the relevance of marriage is acknowledged in the fact that this phrase is used only where at least one sexual partner is married to someone else. (The north American 'cheating on' makes this point still more clearly.) Although 'sex' does accurately represent certain kinds of social reality, there is also a curious and significant disjunction between the discourse of sex (the way 'sex' is theorized) and a complex social reality in which sexuality is associated not only with love, joy and pleasure but also with shame and reticence, betrayal and deceit, jealousy and anger, egotism and malice. 'Sex' turns a blind eye to all this. It represses it.

Sex is natural, good and enjoyable; it should speak itself freely and without shame. Although these assertions are inherent in the word itself, the tautologies have a purpose. They are directed against the repressive regime that is believed to have held sway until the dawning of modern sexual enlightenment. 'Sex' is a monument to this enlightenment and to its victory over the pre-modern darkness of 'Victorian hypocrisy' and of 'Christianity's negative attitude towards the body'.[4]

---

[4] The fact that the story of modern sexual enlightenment is precisely a story (and in some respects a very odd and implausible story) was demonstrated by Michel

Ideologies need heroes and villains, and the ideology of 'sex' has no difficulty in identifying suitable figures. If we ask who was responsible for 'Christianity's negative attitude towards the body', the answer is obvious: it was St Paul and St Augustine, those masters of repression. If we ask who was responsible for bringing the reign of 'Victorian hypocrisy' to an end, the answer is equally obvious: it was Sigmund Freud. Freud restored to light what Paul, Augustine and the Victorians concealed in darkness.

According to Paul, periods of sexual abstinence in marriage should be short-lived, 'lest Satan tempt you through lack of self-control'. The young do not sin if they marry, 'for it is better to marry than to be aflame with passion'. In such statements as this, as Peter Brown notes, 'The dangers of *porneia*, of potential immorality brought about by sexual frustration, were allowed to hold the center of the stage. By this essentially negative, even alarmist strategy, Paul left a fatal legacy to future ages . . . In the future, a sense of the presence of "Satan", in the form of a constant and ill-defined risk of lust, lay like a heavy shadow in the corner of every Christian church' (*The Body and Society: Men, Women and Sexual Renunciation in Early Christianity*, 55).[5] The depiction of the conflict of mind and flesh in Romans 7 establishes, in a mere hundred words or so, 'the future course of Christian thought on the human person . . . A weak thing in itself, the body was presented as lying in the shadow of a mighty force, the power of *the flesh* . . . "The flesh" was not simply the body, an inferior other to the self, whose undisciplined stirrings might even at times receive a certain indulgent tolerance, as representing the natural claims of a physical being. In all later Christian writing, the notion of "the flesh" suffused the body with disturbing associations' (48). In Augustine, the Pauline 'law of sin which dwells in my members' is traced back to the moment of the Fall when the bodies of Adam and Eve 'were

---

Foucault, in his *History of Sexuality*, vol. 1: *An Introduction* [1976], ET London: Allen Lane, 1979.

[5] New York: Columbia University Press, 1988. Although Foucault's significance is acknowledged (xvii–xviii), the 'repressive hypothesis' that he identified and criticized remains basically intact in Brown's work.

touched with a disturbing new sense of the alien, in the form of sexual sensations that escaped their control . . . A tiny but ominous symptom – in Adam's case, the stirring of an erection over which he had no control – warned them both of the final slipping of the body as a whole from the soul's familiar embrace at death' (416–17). 'In Augustine's piercing vision, the Roman city and the walls of the married household within it – those solid, magnificently self-reliant creations of an ancient Mediterranean way of life – were now washed by a dark current of sexual shame. Adam's shame knew no frontiers' (426–7). Augustine's 'distrust of sexual pleasure' was 'a heavy legacy to bequeath to later ages' (426).

It is this 'legacy' – so 'heavy' as to be 'fatal' – that our own century has at last definitively rejected in its rediscovery of 'the natural claims of a physical being'. For us, 'sexuality has come to wear a more comfortable face' (xvii). Comfortable with our bodies and our sexualities, we find it hard to understand how anything as innocent, natural and pleasurable as the symptoms of sexual arousal could ever have been found to be 'disturbing'. At home again with the 'indulgent tolerance' we think we see in pagan antiquity, we find Christian antiquity deeply enigmatic. And yet this enigma plays an indispensable role in the story of our sexual liberation: for narratives of enlightenment require a prior state of darkness if our own breakthrough into light is to be commemorated with due solemnity. The discovery of a 'sex' that is natural, good and enjoyable must be narrated precisely as a *discovery*, an uncovering of what had previously been concealed. Christianity's 'negative view of the body' may be enigmatic, but without it there would be no story of how we have learned to take a 'positive view of the body'. 'The body' must be initially defined in terms of 'sexual renunciation' (as in Brown's subtitle) so that we in turn may redefine it in terms of sexual fulfilment.

Narratives of enlightenment deny ambivalence and complexity by assigning negativity to a now-superseded past and positivity to a victorious present. They separate the light from the darkness; they are comedies, not tragedies. In comedy, a history of confusion and conflict resolves itself into the transparency of a happy ending. In tragedy, confusion and conflict prove intractable, and resolution can occur only within the severest constraints. Yet the Pauline and Augustinian narratives of the body cannot properly be classified as tragedies – for both Paul and Augustine believe that 'where sin increased, grace abounded all the more' (Rom. 5.20). The war of 'the law of my mind' with 'the law of sin which dwells in my members' (7.23) would only be a tragic conflict if the cry, 'Wretched man that I am! Who will deliver me from this body of death?' (v. 24) were the last word. But it is thanksgiving that has the last word: 'Thanks be to God through Jesus Christ our Lord!' (v. 25). If grace and thanksgiving are set aside, the tension between the mind and the flesh would indeed be the tragic truth of human nature. The mind, desiring to subject itself to the demands of the law of God in which it delights, finds itself unable to master the contrary desires of the rebellious flesh. Without grace and thanksgiving, this almost unendurable tension is perhaps integral to being human.

To put the point another way: the ego, desiring to subject itself to the demands of the super-ego, finds itself unable to master the desires that arise out of the id. To be human is to be subject to this intractable conflict. The language is, of course, Freud's. The father of twentieth-century sexual enlightenment turns out to be deeply rooted in the Pauline and Augustinian tradition – not at all what the narrative of sexual enlightenment had led us to expect.[6]

THE LUST OF THE FLESH

The Pauline text begins with a contrast between a past, 'when we were in the flesh' and when 'the passions of sins, aroused by the law, were working in our members to bear fruit for death', and a present in which we belong not to the law but to Christ,

---

[6] Gerd Theissen finds an 'astonishing proximity' between the Pauline triad of law, self, flesh and the Freudian super-ego, ego, id – despite the 'great historical distance' (*Psychological Aspects of Pauline Theology*, ET Philadelphia: Fortress Press; Edinburgh: T. & T. Clark, 1987, 244). The 'proximity' is only 'astonishing' if one overlooks the phenomenon of *Wirkungsgeschichte*.

who 'has been raised from the dead in order that we may bear fruit for God' (Rom. 7.5, 4). Freed from the law, our service of God is now 'in newness of the Spirit and not in oldness of the letter' (v. 6). The letter is the law's inscribed demand, 'Thou shalt . . .' or 'Thou shalt not . . .' In this model of the divine– human relationship, God is characterized as the one who subjects humans to his command and humans are characterized as those who are thereby subjected. The divine–human relationship is a master–slave relationship. That does not make it unjust. 'The commandment is holy and just and good' (v. 12) – its goodness is twice reiterated in subsequent verses (vv. 13, 16). The command of this divine master to this human slave is 'just' because it addresses the human being as a creature whose very being is derived *ex nihilo*, without remainder, from the creative act of the divine being; and it is 'good' because it is addressed to the human creature not to compel it to sacrifice its own well-being for the well-being of its master, but to ensure that in the service of its divine master it finds its own true well-being. *This* master–slave relationship, as promulgated by Moses and actualized within Judaism, derives from God's own holiness, justice and goodness, and in it the human subject rightly finds satisfaction and joy (vv. 16, 22):

The law of the Lord is perfect, reviving the soul. The testimony of the Lord is sure, making wise the simple. The precepts of the Lord are right, rejoicing the heart. The commandment of the Lord is pure, enlightening the eyes. The fear of the Lord is clean, enduring for ever. The ordinances of the Lord are true, and righteous altogether. More to be desired are they than gold, even much fine gold; sweeter also than honey and drippings of the honeycomb. (Ps. 19.7–10)

Every human master–slave relationship is a caricature and distortion of the divine–human relationship as characterized by the Law of Moses. To find in Judaism a heteronomy which unjustly denies the proper autonomy of the human subject is a slander deriving from Gentile malice and ignorance of God.

Yet all this is declared to be 'old', surpassed, superseded and transcended in the redefinition of the divine–human relationship accomplished by Jesus (a Jew) and his Spirit, and proclaimed by the apostle (also a Jew). If the Law is understood in abstraction from Christ, as the definitive account of the divine–human relationship and not as preliminary and provisional, a radical flaw appears which prevents the divine goodness from attaining its goal, which is true human well-being. The flaw is not in the Law itself, or in God ('By no means!' (Rom. 7.7)). The flaw arises from a catastrophic event that has overtaken the human partner in the divine–human relationship: the coming of the Law has manifested and brought to the surface a previously latent resistance to God. The Law forbids even the desire for the objects it prohibits, and the unforeseen result is that the forbidden desire springs to life, overwhelming the self and depriving it of the life and well-being in communion with God that the Law intends (vv. 7–13). The human body, originally identical to the human ego and at the same time its vehicle, becomes 'flesh' (vv. 5, 18, 25), the site of uncontrolled 'passions' (v. 5) and 'desire' (vv. 7–8). The body as 'flesh' is withdrawn from the control of the ego, and the ego, aligned with the Law of God, looks on helplessly as it sees how 'my members' are obedient to 'another law' (v. 23), whose authority I reject but which has nevertheless taken up residence at the heart of my being and established its authority. The ego, longing to enjoy the life and well-being intended by the Law, finds itself trapped in a body that obeys a quite different logic. This analysis of the human self as caught in the tension between the Law and the Flesh has evoked echoes that continue to reverberate.

In Augustine's reading of this passage, the 'desire' (*epithumia*) that overwhelms the ego and prevents the doing of the good is pre-eminently sexual desire (*concupiscentia*).[7] 'The law of sin which is in my members' (v. 23) is therefore not distributed among my members in anarchic fashion, each member being impelled along its own path independently of the others. The Law of Sin is far from anarchic. Having removed the body as a whole from the control of the ego (or 'mind' (vv. 23, 25)), Sin

---

[7] My paraphrase of Augustine's reading of Rom. 7 and Gen. 3 is based on passages such as the following: *De spiritu et littera*, 21; *De natura et gratia*, 28, 58, 61, 62; *De nuptiis et concupiscentia*, i.6–8, 24, 27, ii.14, 53; *Contra duas epistolas Pelagianorum*, i.31–5 (ET in *The Nicene and Post-Nicene Fathers: St Augustine*, vol. v: *Writings against the Pelagians*, repr. Grand Rapids: Eerdmans, 1971).

subjects the bodily members to the primacy of a single member, which it appoints as its surrogate and through whom it exercises its power. This is clear from the Genesis narrative of the Fall. When Adam and Eve transgressed the divine commandment, their first act was to conceal their genitals in shame at their nakedness. They did so because their assumption of control over their own bodies, in the act of eating the forbidden fruit, had met its due retribution in the loss of control over their own bodies that accompanied the new perception of the nakedness of the other. In the presence of the other as naked, involuntary physiological changes took place – most obviously in the case of Adam, in the erection of his penis, but no less actually in the case of Eve, whose desire is already for her husband (Gen. 3.16), and is manifested in corresponding symptoms such as the engorgement of the genital region and the lubrication of the vagina. These physiological changes were not in themselves new, for they were already entailed in the creation of humans as male and female and in the divine command to be fruitful and multiply. Sexual intercourse was corrupted by the devil, but it was not invented by the devil; the devil lacks the divine creativity that is still evident even in the corrupted form of the sexual act (the only form known to us). What was new was the fact that the physiological changes were no longer subject to the control of the mind but now seemed to obey an alien power. Until now, the bodily movements associated with sexual inter-course had been as voluntary as the bodily movements associated with eating. Like eating, sexual intercourse was pleasurable, but in both cases the pleasure was commensurate with the natural, divinely ordained goal underlying the gratification of desire: the maintenance of life in the one case, the reproduction of life in the other. The pleasures of food and sex were therefore orderly pleasures, in the sense that they fitted harmoniously within the orderly rhythm of a life ordained by God and oriented towards God.

Through the eating of the forbidden fruit, sexual pleasure falls out of that orderly pattern and becomes disordered and disordering. In place of a previously orderly desire, Adam and Eve are overwhelmed by a tidal wave of *concupiscentia* that they can no longer control. In the presence of the other's nakedness, the whole body is reordered around the genitals and the longing for bodily union which is visibly and palpably expressed in them. The body, which had been both identical to the person and the vehicle of the person, is now charged with an intense and impersonal energy which holds the body of the other within its field of attraction, and threatens to deprive it of all power of movement other than the movement of physical union. *Concupiscentia* is both the promise of pleasure and the threat of unfreedom, and it is the body itself – the naked body, which is also the natural body, created by God – that is the site of its promise and threat. The body is no longer simply the person as such or the vehicle of the person; it has become an intensely ambivalent object, fascinating and enticing but also overpowering and disturbing. In the symptoms of sexual arousal that (according to Augustine) follow the eating of the forbidden fruit, Adam and Eve involuntarily acknowledge both their own body and the body of the other as charged with an impersonal power that threatens their freedom of movement – a power that demands discharge through sexual union and orgasm. This power, previously one among a number of mutually limiting, beneficent powers to which human life was subject, has now taken control of the body as a whole: the natural body, received from the hand of God as the physical manifestation of the person, has become the 'naked' body, the genitally oriented body that incites sexual arousal. The threat that this distorted body poses to oneself and to others can be warded off only by concealing it. With rudimentary garments of fig-leaves, Adam and Eve conceal their nakedness; that is, although leaving most of their flesh exposed and naked, they conceal their genitals and thus the new reality of the genitally oriented, libidinally charged body that has supervened upon the natural body created by God. Humans clothe themselves as a defence against the power of concupiscence. Forced underground by this act of repression, concupiscence may at any time break through the surface, as if without warning, aroused perhaps by the mere sight of flesh or even by the hints of the shape and texture of flesh that clothing continues to permit. If this seems a trivial and innocent phenomenon, it is worth recalling that the purest expression of the reality of concupiscence is found in the event of rape. Rape is what happens when concupiscence is uninhibited by social constraints and finds itself capable of direct expression.

For Augustine as for Paul and for Freud, there is much more to be said about the human condition than that it is subject to the disruptive power of *concupiscentia, epithumia* or *libido*. Yet, for Augustine and Paul although differently for Freud, it is at this point that symptoms of the intransigence of human resistance to God are most clearly visible. Thus the present-tense section of Romans 7 (vv. 14–25) can be read as a vivid rendering of the ego's experience of itself as caught in the tension between the law of God and the exorbitance of sexual desire. For Augustine, this is the experience of the ego that has become conscious of its true situation, the ego as enlightened by divine grace and re-empowered by divine grace at least to will the good, even if not to fulfil it. The speaker wills what is good but does what is evil, not in the sense that there is no true human love of God or of neighbour (which would be to deny the reality of grace) but in the sense that love of God and of neighbour is never pure (except in the case of Jesus) but is always mingled with the residue of concupiscence.

Freud too sees the ego as caught in the tension between 'law' and 'flesh', or, in his own terminology, between super-ego and id. As we shall see, the concept of the 'super-ego', first clearly outlined in a relatively late text dating from 1923, marks a shift from a Platonic model of the self to a Pauline and Augustinian one.

MODELLING THE PSYCHE

Eager to establish that psychoanalysis is a true 'science', and thus a genuine contribution to the project of 'science' as a whole, Freud at one point inscribes the resistance to the new science within the history of resistance to science that looms so large within science's self-image. This resistance arises from science's destruction of the illusions projected by 'men's naïve

self-love'. Human self-love suffered a first blow when Coper-
nicus established 'that our earth was not the centre of the
universe but only a tiny fragment of a cosmic system of scarcely
imaginable vastness'. The second blow came when, 'not
without the most violent contemporary opposition', Darwin,
Wallace and others 'destroyed man's supposedly privileged
place in creation and proved his descent from the animal
kingdom and his ineradicable animal nature'. All that is past
history. But now, 'human megalomania suffers its third and
most wounding blow', as psychoanalysis shows that the human
ego 'is not even master in its own house, but must content itself
with scanty information of what is going on unconsciously in its
mind . . . Hence arises the general revolt against our science'
(1.326).[8]

This attempt to write psychoanalysis into the story of the rise
of science actually subverts that story at a crucial point. The
story of the rise of science is at the same time the story of the fall
of religion; science rises precisely as, point by point, it brings
about religion's downfall. In its quest for an illusory consolation
through the projection of a divine father-surrogate, religion
belongs to the childhood of the human race; and 'men cannot
remain children for ever' but must allow science to initiate them
into adulthood by providing them with an 'education to reality'
(12.233). Psychoanalysis proves its scientific credentials by
furthering the scientific critique of religion. Yet its claim that
the ego 'is not even master in its own house' is actually
analogous to the religious critique of the comforting illusion of
the autonomous, self-sufficient ego (an illusion that helps to
generate the scientific ego and to make its fictions plausible). In
pointing to the universality of repressed, prohibited impulses,
'psychoanalysis is simply confirming the habitual pronounce-
ment of the pious: we are all miserable sinners' (13.129). The
pious have never believed that the ego is master in its own
house. They have always known that the ego is subject to
impulses prohibited by the law of God which continue to
torment and seduce it, and that order can be restored only

---

[8] Here and elsewhere in this chapter, page references are to *The Penguin Freud Library*, ed.
Angela Richards and Albert Dickson, Harmondsworth: Penguin Books, 1973–85.

when the ego abandons the foolish project of becoming master in its own house and allows the house of the body to become the temple of the Holy Spirit. In the psychoanalytical account of redemption, it is psychoanalysis itself which ministers to the ego in its distress and enables it to survive its own overthrow.[9]

The ego is not even master in its own house because it lacks the freedom to determine who shall gain admittance to it. In the *Introductory Lectures on Psychoanalysis* (1915–17), the house image is developed into a full-scale picture of the topography and dynamics of the human mind. We are invited to

compare the system of the unconscious to a large entrance hall, in which the mental impulses jostle one another like separate individuals. Adjoining this entrance hall there is a second, narrower, room – a kind of drawing-room – in which consciousness, too, resides. But on the threshold between these two rooms a watchman performs his function: he examines the different mental impulses, acts as a censor, and will not admit them into the drawing-room if they displease him . . . The impulses in the entrance hall of the unconscious are out of sight of the conscious, which is in the other room; to begin with they must remain unconscious. If they have already pushed their way forward to the threshold and have been turned back by the watchman, then they are inadmissible to consciousness; we speak of them as *repressed*. But even the impulses which the watchman has allowed to cross the threshold are not on that account necessarily conscious as well; they can only become so if they succeed in catching the eye of consciousness. We are therefore justified in calling this second room the system of the *preconscious*. (1.336–7)

The ego (or consciousness) at least appears to be master in its own drawing-room. Guests enter and circulate, and the ego attends to them or disregards them, as it chooses. The mind is full of latent, pre-conscious ideas and images that can be summoned up when required, at a moment's notice. The ego cannot attend to all its guests at once, but they remain *its* guests. Their faces are familiar; they are the fixed points around which mental life circulates, giving it its own particular identity and texture. It is memory that ensures the stability and security of

[9] Quotations in this and the preceding paragraph are taken from the *Introductory Lectures on Psychoanalysis* (1917), *The Future of an Illusion* (1927), and *Totem and Taboo* (1913).

the ego within the sphere of its dominion. Yet the ego has overlooked something. Master of its own drawing-room, it has failed to notice that its entrance hall is occupied by an unruly proletarian mob, and that it is only the vigilance of the servant at the doorway that prevents the masses from bursting into the drawing-room itself, inflicting insult and injury on the ego and its guests. The guardian of the threshold distinguishes genuine guests from the mob by various means. Those who are to gain admittance must be appropriately attired for the drawing-room; those who are turned back are improperly dressed, and some indeed are entirely naked – worse still, they flaunt their nakedness and their sexuality with flagrant disregard for all the rules of propriety. Those who gain admittance indicate that they are worthy to enter by their speech and their deportment; those who are turned back reveal their unworthiness in the vulgarity of their speech and gestures. Occasionally a member of the mob will elude the vigilance of the 'watchman' or 'censor' and take a few steps over the threshold before being ejected. On the whole, the servant is remarkably successful at concealing from his master the gross disorder that is occurring within his own walls. Yet the concealment is not entirely successful. Even the most diligent servant cannot prevent one from becoming aware, perhaps through the tiniest of symptoms, that all is not well. The guests themselves will be marked by the trauma of their entrance.[10]

The ego, the watchman and the unruly passions: this anthropological model is reminiscent more of Plato than of Paul. In Plato's *Republic* (414B), the governing of the proletariat is assigned to two classes, the 'rulers' (*archontes*) or 'guardians' (*phulakes*) and the 'auxiliaries' (*epikouroi*) or 'assistants' (*boēthoi*); it is the role of the auxiliaries to put into effect the decisions of the rulers. The just ordering of the life of the individual follows this model of the just ordering of society. In the soul, there is a

---

[10] The 'censor' image occurs already in *The Interpretation of Dreams* (1900), where the dream-censor plays a crucial role in distorting and concealing the true meaning of a dream. 'This censorship acts exactly like the censorship of newspapers at the Russian frontier, which allows foreign journals to fall into the hands of the readers whom it is its business to protect only after a quantity of passages have been blacked out' (4.676–7).

rational element (*to logistikon*) and an element that is irrational, concerned only with the appetites and pleasures (439D); a third, intermediate element, corresponding to the 'auxiliaries', may be seen in the 'spirit' or 'indignation' (*thumos*) which allies itself with the ruling *logos* in its struggle to control the desires (*epithumiai*) or passions (440B). This third element may be compared to a sheep-dog who controls the unruly sheep in obedience to the will of the shepherd (440D). Without the auxiliaries, the rulers would be powerless to control the much more numerous class of those who devote themselves solely to pleasure and the passions. In Freud's version of this model, the role of *thumos* is played by the watchman at the door, whose forcible ejection of would-be intruders protects the ego or reason from being overwhelmed. Yet Freud's watchman keeps the ego ignorant of the fact that the entrance hall has been occupied by the mob. His task is not simply to *suppress*, as in Plato, but to *repress* – to suppress so effectively and thoroughly that the act of suppression is not even perceived as such. The Platonic *logos* knows exactly who is its enemy and who is its ally; the Freudian ego remains pathetically ignorant of its enemy, and is at a loss to explain the symptoms of disorder that make themselves felt even in the orderly world of its own drawing-room – despite the efforts of the watchman. In addition, the pleasures and passions that oppose the control of the Platonic *logos* live elsewhere in the city, not in the ruler's own home. Policing them is not a problem. In Freud, they have left the slums and tenements on the other side of the city and have taken up residence within the elegant mansions of the ruling classes. The autocracy of the police state is threatened by proletarian revolution: at this point Freud's lectures, published in 1917, correspond to the unfolding political situation in Petrograd or Moscow. Psychoanalysis aligns itself with the insurgents in their hostility to the guardian of the threshold. It seeks to compel the uncomprehending ego to recognize what is going on under its own roof, to acknowledge that it is not master even in its own house, and to negotiate some new *modus vivendi* with the libidinous occupants of the entrance hall. In psychoanalytic interpretation, the work of the over-zealous watchman is undone: what is unconscious is transformed into what is conscious, and the ego becomes 'conciliatory towards the libido and inclined to grant it some satisfaction', its repugnance being diminished 'by the possibility of disposing of a portion of it by sublimation' (1.508).

In *The Ego and the Id* (1923), a new, more precise terminology is introduced. The realm represented in the image by the entrance hall is now described as the 'id' (*das Es*); and the anonymous watchman or censor who guards the boundary between the realms of id and ego (*das Ich*) is now named the 'super-ego' (*das Über-Ich*) Once a servant, corresponding to the Platonic 'auxiliaries', he is now master of the ego; no longer content with the role of repression or censorship, he has taken upon himself the task of judging and criticizing the ego itself. The super-ego is the internalized representative of authority figures such as parents and parent-substitutes, and its harsh commands and prohibitions ('Thou shalt . . . ' and 'Thou shalt not') are an important element in the genesis of religion. Thus the Platonic model of the self is replaced by a Pauline model in which the ego is torn between the conflicting imperatives of the super-ego ('the Law of God') and the id (the realm that is under the sway not of the ego but of 'the Law of Sin'). The promotion of the watchman or censor to 'super-ego' results in a transformation of the earlier model, and we must trace the rationale for this transformation.

Fundamental to psychoanalysis is the distinction between 'conscious' and 'unconscious', which originates in the discovery that an important class of mental events, perceptible only through their symptoms, is unconscious. Yet an identification between the conscious realm and the ego and between the unconscious realm and the repressed turns out to be misleading. As we have seen, the ego which receives its guests in its drawing-room is not conscious of all of them at once, but directs its consciousness from one to another in turn.

A state of consciousness is characteristically very transitory; an idea that is conscious now is no longer so a moment later, although it can become so under certain conditions that are easily brought about. In the interval the idea was – we do not know what. We can say that it was *latent*, and by this we mean that it was *capable of becoming conscious* at any time. Or, if we say that it was *unconscious*, we shall also be giving a correct description of it. (11.352)

Unconsciousness or pre-consciousness is therefore fundamental to the life of the ego itself. Thus 'we have two kinds of unconscious – the one that is latent but capable of becoming conscious, and the one which is repressed and which is not, in itself and without more ado, capable of becoming conscious' (11.353). This situation may be represented by the symbols *Cs.* (conscious), *Pcs.* (pre-conscious) and *Ucs.* (unconscious); since the *Cs.* derives its ideas not only from the *Pcs.* but also from sense-perception, the symbol *Pcpt.* is also required. But there is also a third kind of unconscious (in the broader sense), which, like the *Pcs.*, belongs to the ego, but which, like the *Ucs.*, is subject to repression. When, during psychoanalysis, a patient's free associations fail, this is a sign both that he is approaching the realm of the repressed and that he is experiencing a resistance to his proceeding any further. We tell him that he is encountering a resistance,

but he is quite unaware of the fact, and, even if he guesses from his unpleasurable feelings that a resistance is now at work in him, he does not know what it is or how to describe it. Since, however, there can be no question but that this resistance emanates from his ego and belongs to it, we find ourselves in an unforeseen situation. We have come across something in the ego itself which is also unconscious, which behaves exactly like the repressed – that is, which produces powerful effects without itself being conscious and which requires special work before it can be made conscious. (11.355–6)

The ego is, it seems, unaware of the activity of the guardian of the threshold, although he is the servant of the ego who faithfully carries out the ego's unconscious will.

Since the unconscious penetrates so deeply into the ego itself (in the form of the *Pcs.* and the as-yet unnamed analogue to the *Ucs.*), a division of the psyche into 'ego' and 'unconscious' is misleading. Another term is needed to set in opposition to 'ego', and this has been provided by the physician Georg Groddeck,

who is never tired of insisting that what we call our ego behaves essentially passively in life, and that, as he expresses it, we are 'lived' by unknown and uncontrollable forces . . . I propose to take [this] into account by calling the entity which starts out from the system *Pcpt.* and begins by being *Pcs.* the 'ego', and by following Groddeck in calling the other part of the mind, into which this entity extends and which behaves as though it were *Ucs.*, the 'id' . . . We shall now look upon an individual as a psychical id, unknown and unconscious, upon whose surface rests the ego, developed from its nucleus, the *Pcpt.* system . . . It is easy to see that the ego is that part of the id which has been modified through the medium of the *Pcpt.-Cs.*; in a sense it is an extension of the surface-differentiation. Moreover, the ego seeks to bring the influence of the external world to bear upon the id and its tendencies, and endeavours to substitute the reality for the pleasure principle which reigns unrestrictedly in the id. For the ego, perception plays the part which in the id falls to instinct. The ego represents what may be called reason and common sense, in contrast to the id, which contains the passions . . . Thus in its relation to the id [the ego] is like a man on horseback, who has to hold in check the superior strength of the horse; with this difference, that the rider tries to do so with his own strength while the ego uses borrowed forces. (11.362)[11]

The language and conceptuality here are still Platonic. The ego and the id correspond to the reason and the passions, identified respectively with 'reality' (Plato's 'truth') and 'pleasure'; and the image of the rider and his horse is descended from the myth of the charioteer in the *Phaedrus*. For Plato, the ego or reason originates 'from above'; it is a portion of the immortal soul-substance made by the demiurge himself. Its entanglement with irrational desire is alien to its true nature, and derives from the demiurge's decision that in the human person immortal soul or reason should be combined with the shifting elements of the maternal 'receptacle of becoming' (*Timaeus* 41A–47E). For Freud, the ego originates 'from below', out of the id. From the encounter between the desires of the id and external reality as conveyed by sense-perception, there arises, on and just beneath the surface of the id, that modification of the id that we know as the ego and that mediates between id and reality. This origin

---

[11] Freud acknowledges that Groddeck is indebted to Nietzsche for the distinction between *Ich* and *Es*. In *Beyond Good and Evil*, for example, Nietzsche criticizes the Cartesian *cogito* on the grounds that 'a thought comes when "it" wants, not when "I" want; so that it is a falsification of the fact to say: the subject "I" is the condition of the predicate "think". *It* thinks . . .' (§17; ET Harmondsworth: Penguin Books, 1973).

within the id means that, unlike the Platonic reason, the ego has no energy of its own and is forced to draw its energy from the id, 'the great reservoir of libido' (11.369n). Thus, for Freud in contrast to Plato, embodiment is proper to the human psyche. The absence of the older dualistic metaphysic can be traced back not just to the 'materialism' of modern science but to the Judaeo-Christian doctrine of creation. Yet, paradoxically, the difficulties of the embodied psyche are still greater for Freud than for Plato.

It is the concept of the super-ego that transforms this broadly Platonic model of the psyche into a Pauline one. The super-ego originates in the Oedipus complex, and since in 1923 – the date of *The Ego and the Id* – Freud's account of the distinctive female form of the Oedipal situation was still undeveloped, we follow the more familiar account, oriented towards the male.[12] For the small child, the original sexual object is the maternal breast, and the original relation to the mother therefore differs from the original relation to the father, which is characterized not by sexual attraction ('object-cathexis') but by 'identification'. The Oedipal situation arises when the father is perceived as an obstacle to the gratification of the child's sexual wishes in relation to the mother: 'His identification with his father then takes on a hostile colouring and changes into a wish to get rid of his father in order to take his place with his mother. Henceforth his relation to his father is ambivalent . . . ' (11.371). In 'normal' development, the small boy will be compelled to abandon his

---

[12] In *The Ego and the Id*, Freud still believed that the Oedipal conflict was 'precisely analogous' in boys and in girls (11.371). The distinctiveness of the female Oedipal situation is explored (controversially, of course) in 'Some Psychical Consequences of the Anatomical Distinction between the Sexes' (1925; 7.323–43), 'Female Sexuality' (1931; 7.366–92), and Lecture 33 of the *New Introductory Lectures* (1933; 2.145–69). In brief: 'The castration complex prepares for the Oedipus complex instead of destroying it; the girl is driven out of her attachment to her mother through the influence of her envy for the penis and she enters the Oedipus situation as though into a haven of refuge. In the absence of fear of castration the chief motive is lacking which leads boys to surmount the Oedipus complex. Girls remain in it for an indeterminate length of time; they demolish it late and, even so, incompletely. In these circumstances the formation of the super-ego must suffer; it cannot attain the strength and independence which give it its cultural significance, and feminists are not pleased when we point out to them the effects of this factor upon the average feminine character' (2.163).

desire for his mother and will identify himself all the more intensely with the father, the source of the original prohibition. This identification will express itself positively in a desire to be like the father, and negatively in submission to the paternal prohibition: certain things are indeed the father's prerogative, and the child must renounce all claim to them. In the emergence of the super-ego or ego ideal, the Oedipus complex is overcome. The paternal decree, forbidding possession of the mother, has now been accepted and internalized. (A later variant of this decree is the paternal prohibition of infantile masturbation, a genital substitute for the original oral sexual satisfaction which is countered with the threat of castration.) The ego, originally motivated solely by the id and its quest for libidinous pleasure, has been forced by reality to turn against the desires of the id and to repress them. The super-ego is constituted by that moment of turning, in which the Oedipus complex is overcome:

The child's parents, and especially his father, were perceived as the obstacle to a realization of his Oedipus wishes; so his infantile ego fortified itself for the carrying out of the repression by erecting this same obstacle within itself. It borrowed strength to do this, so to speak, from the father, and this loan was an extraordinarily momentous act. The super-ego retains the character of the father, while the more powerful the Oedipus complex was and the more rapidly it succumbed to repression (under the influence of authority, religious teaching, schooling and reading), the stricter will be the domination of the super-ego over the ego later on – in the form of conscience or perhaps of an unconscious sense of guilt. (11.374)

It is because the super-ego 'retains the character of the father' that it is no longer the servant of the ego – the guardian of the threshold, the censor – but its master:

Although it is accessible to all later influences, it nevertheless preserves throughout life the character given to it by its derivation from the father-complex – namely, the capacity to stand apart from the ego and to master it. It is a memorial of the former weakness and dependence of the ego, and the mature ego remains subject to its domination. As the child was once under a compulsion to obey its parents, so the ego submits to the categorical imperative of the super-ego. (11.389)

This 'categorical imperative' is like the Kantian one in that it demands compliance irrespective of inclination; it is unlike it in that it is not the self-imposed principle of the autonomous rational will but a heteronomous demand that the ego is compelled to internalize but that continues to stand over against it as the demand of the other. The Freudian 'genealogy of morals' reveals that human moral autonomy – whether in its Platonic, its Kantian or its Nietzschean form – is an illusion.

A further question arises at this point. 'How is it that the super-ego manifests itself essentially as a sense of guilt (or rather, as criticism – for the sense of guilt is the perception in the ego answering to this criticism) and moreover develops such extraordinary harshness and severity towards the ego?' (11.394). It seems that the super-ego redirects an aggressiveness originally directed towards others against the ego itself; hence the harshness and cruelty even of 'ordinary normal morality' (11.396). This aggressiveness may be traced back to the 'death instinct', which aims to lead organic life back into the inanimate state, in contrast to the sexual instinct, or Eros, which aims at the preservation of life. It is to be traced back not simply to the paternal prohibition in itself but also to the aggressiveness that this prohibition evokes in the child himself, which is then displaced onto the ego through identification with the father. Torn between the hyper-moral severity of the super-ego and the amorality of the id, the ego finds itself in an unenviable situation. 'Helpless in both directions, the ego defends itself vainly, alike against the instigations of the murderous id and against the reproaches of the punishing conscience' (11.395). The ego may well cry out: 'Wretched man that I am! Who will deliver me from this body of death?' (Rom. 7.24). On Freud's reading of the situation, 'The ego gives itself up because it feels itself hated and persecuted by the super-ego, instead of being loved' (11.400).

The introduction of the concept of the super-ego results in a model of the psyche analogous to the Pauline one in Romans 7. This analogy justifies an approach to Freud as a 'reader' of a Pauline text, whether or not he was himself familiar with it.[13] But his 'reading' might proceed in one of two directions. He might argue that psychoanalysis helps the ego to resist the super-ego's harsh demands by exposing its genealogy, that the particular form of the super-ego is merely a cultural construct, and that the reconstruction or re-education of the super-ego is therefore both desirable and possible. Since Freud's modelling of the psyche is inseparable from his account of sexuality, the outcome would be a call for the liberalization of traditional sexual morality. In terms of the Pauline text, this would be a

---

[13] In *Moses and Monotheism* (1939), Paul plays a crucial role in the transition from Judaism, the religion of the father, to Christianity, the religion of the son. Freud's Oedipus theory leads him to postulate as the origin of culture and religion an event in which the all-powerful father of the patriarchal horde is murdered by his sons – an event re-enacted in the murder of Moses. Moses was an Egyptian, a follower of the monotheistic Pharaoh Akhenaten, who led his supporters out of Egypt when the priests of Aten succeeded in overturning the monotheistic reforms. The theory that he was murdered is drawn from the Old Testament scholar Ernst Sellin, who in 1922 'found in the prophet Hosea . . . unmistakable signs of a tradition to the effect that Moses, the founder of their religion, met with a violent end in a rising of his refractory and stiff-necked people, and that at the same time the religion he had introduced was thrown off' (13.275–6). His supporters allied themselves with certain Midianite tribes, and the religion that arose at Kadesh (enshrined in the Pentateuch) was a compromise between Moses' monotheism and the Midianites' more primitive Yahwism. The result was a father-religion, a return of the repressed, primal father after a period of matriarchy, in which the ambivalence that is of the essence of the relation to the father was denied. 'There was no place in the framework of the religion of Moses for a direct expression of the murderous hatred of the father. All that could come to light was a mighty reaction against it – a sense of guilt on account of that hostility, a bad conscience for having sinned against God and for not ceasing to sin' (13.383). The ethical ideals of which Jews are so proud cannot 'disavow their origin from the sense of guilt felt on account of a suppressed hostility to God. They possess the characteristic . . . of obsessional neurotic reaction-formations; we can guess, too, that they serve the secret purposes of punishment' (13.383–4). It was Paul who first instinctively grasped that 'the reason why we are so unhappy is that we have killed God the father' (13.384). Paul 'seized upon this sense of guilt and traced it back correctly to its original source. He called this the "original sin"; it was a crime against God and could only be atoned for by death . . . A son of God had allowed himself to be killed without guilt and had thus taken on himself the guilt of all men. It had to be a son, since it had been the murder of a father' (13.330–1). Yet the new religion was simply a restatement of the old problem. 'Its main content was . . . reconciliation with God the Father, atonement for the crime committed against him; but the other side of the emotional relation showed itself in the fact that the son, who had taken the atonement on himself, became a god himself beside the father and, actually, in place of the father. Christianity, having arisen out of a father-religion, became a son-religion. It has not escaped the fate of having to get rid of the father' (13.385). Freud is dependent here on the well-known claim (already exploited by Nietzsche) that Paul was the real founder of Christianity. There is no sign of any knowledge of the Pauline texts.

critical, 'antinomian' reading that taught the ego to distance itself from the super-ego ('the Law of God') and to reappropriate the repressed forces of the id. Alternatively, Freud might argue that his model of the psyche is the presupposition of all particular cultural constructs, and that he has identified a conflict endemic to human existence as such. Pauline identification with the demands of the super-ego, with the ensuing anxiety and guilt, would then represent a moment of genuine insight. If 'sexual liberation' represents the enticing promise of a restored, natural, prelapsarian sexuality, without anxiety or guilt, this second Freudian reading of Paul would regard this promise with a degree of scepticism.

THE LIMITS OF FREEDOM

Conventional (or Christian) sexual morality, confining sexual activity to marriage, is perhaps to be seen as a 'cultural construct', whose advantages and disadvantages may be dispassionately weighed. If the disadvantages outweigh the advantages – and the grounds for this judgment may seem to be strong – then it can be modified or abandoned, giving way to new constructions in which older prohibitions and limits become fluid and new sexualities proliferate without shame or guilt. If there is an 'enlightenment project' in the field of sexuality, it consists in the critique of Christian sexual morality in the name of an open, unrepressed discourse on 'sex' and in the corresponding practices of 'sexual liberation'. If there is a 'postmodern' account of sexuality, it will emphasize the plurality of sexualities, seen now as the products of culture rather than as biological or natural imperatives. Yet the differences here between enlightenment and postmodernism are less striking than the continuities: they agree in their rejection of the single, monopolistic sexual morality supposedly inherited from the Christian past, they agree that new sexualities are possible and desirable, and they agree that the burden of guilt must be replaced by the innocence of play. The question is whether and how far Freud endorses the project of 'sexual liberation'; whether and how far he is the prophet or father of 'sex', as it is now construed, or whether he belongs within a 'critique of sex'.

Freud can indeed see sexual morality as a 'cultural construct' open to development and modification. In the first of the *Three Essays on Sexuality* (1905), he asserts that the boundary between 'normal' and 'abnormal' sexual behaviour may be a matter of convention:

> The use of the mouth as a sexual organ is regarded as a perversion if the lips (or tongue) of one person are brought into contact with the genitals of another, but not if the mucous membranes of the lips of both of them come together. This exception is the point of contact with what is normal. Those who condemn the other practices (which have no doubt been common among mankind from primaeval times) as being perversions, are giving way to an unmistakable feeling of *disgust*, which protects them from accepting sexual aims of the kind. The limits of such disgust are, however, often purely conventional: a man who will kiss a pretty girl's lips passionately may perhaps be disgusted at the idea of using her toothbrush, though there are no grounds for supposing that his own oral cavity, for which he feels no disgust, is any cleaner than the girl's. (7.63–4)

Certain sexual practices are rejected purely because they are found to be 'disgusting', not because there are any rational grounds for condemning them. This disgust is a matter of local convention, and cannot be traced back to any universal 'human nature'. The young man feels disgust at the thought of using the girl's toothbrush because he was taught as a child that his toothbrush is for his use only and that he in turn must not use the toothbrushes of other family members (even if he rinses them carefully before and after use). Implements such as forks and spoons come into contact with his 'oral cavity' without any such convention of exclusive ownership, and the arbitrariness of these oral conventions illustrates the difficulty of differentiating 'natural' or 'normal' sexual practices from 'unnatural' or 'deviant' ones.

The conventional character of sexual morality is, for Freud, also indicated by the factor of social class. Take the case of a middle-class child who engages in sexual games with the caretaker's daughter, who 'would have had an opportunity of observing a good deal of adult sexuality':

These experiences, even if they were not continued over a long period, would be enough to set certain sexual impulses to work in the two children; and, after their games together had ceased, these impulses would for several years afterwards find expression in masturbation. So much for their experiences in common; the final outcome in the two children will be very different ... [The caretaker's daughter] will go through her life undamaged by the early exercise of her sexuality and free from neurosis. With the landlord's little girl things will be different. At an early stage and while she is still a child she will get an idea that she has done something wrong; after a short time, but perhaps only after a severe struggle, she will give up her masturbatory satisfaction, but she will nevertheless still have some sense of oppression about her. When in her later girlhood she is in a position to learn something of human sexual intercourse, she will turn away from it with unexplained disgust and prefer to remain in ignorance ... [Thus] it will turn out that the well-brought-up, intelligent and high-minded girl has completely repressed her sexual impulses, but that these, unconscious to her, are still attached to her petty experiences with her childhood friend. (1.398–9)

Here, an analysis of sexuality as a social construct shades over into critique: conventional middle-class sexual morality all too easily deprives its victims (especially its female victims) of the possibility of sexual fulfilment. It tends to produce a disabling disgust not simply at sexual deviancy but at 'normal' sexual intercourse. As the result of its strictures, the trivial sexual explorations of childhood can assume a disproportionate significance. The straightforwardness of the caretaker's daughter is proof that all this need not be the case, and that it is possible to go through life regarding sexual activity as 'natural and harmless'. Yet Freud does not wish to deprive the middle-class girl of her 'higher moral and intellectual development' (1.399); he does not suggest that she should be given the same opportunities to observe adult sexual activity as the caretaker's daughter. If there are lessons to be learned from this cautionary tale, they represent only minor modifications to the status quo: adults, we might conclude, should be more tolerant towards the sexuality of childhood and should inculcate in their children an awareness of (marital) sexuality as natural and good, not a cause for shame. Freud himself does not draw even these modest conclusions, since he is more interested in subjecting sexual neuroses to psychoanalytic treatment than in advocating any particular reforms to the sexual code.

On occasion, Freud does campaign actively for change. In a paper entitled '"Civilized" Sexual Morality and Modern Nervous Illness' (*Die "kulturelle" Sexualmoral und die moderne Nervö-sität* [1908]), he poses the question 'whether sexual intercourse in legal marriage can offer full compensation for the restriction imposed before marriage', and finds 'an abundance of material supporting a reply in the negative' (12.46). If satisfying sexual intercourse within marriage is achieved at all, it will last only for a few years; and it may never be achieved, since the girl who has been kept in a state of sexual ignorance prior to marriage 'has nothing but disappointments to offer the man who has saved up all his desire for her' (12.50). 'To the uninitiated it is hardly credible how seldom normal potency is to be found in a husband and how often a wife is frigid among married couples who live under the dominance of our civilized sexual morality, what a degree of renunciation, often on both sides, is entailed by marriage, and to what narrow limits married life – the happiness that is so ardently desired – is narrowed down' (12.53).

It is medical science (and not psychoanalysis as such) that here lends its prestige to the campaign for reforming sexual morality. It is true that medical opinion is divided on this issue: the opposing view, 'that sexual abstinence is not harmful and not difficult to maintain, has also been widely supported by the medical profession' (12.45). But the view that sexual abstinence and repression endanger mental health is not a specifically psychoanalytical doctrine. As the opening pages of Freud's paper explicitly indicate, his twin themes of conventional sexual morality and nervous illness (or 'neurasthenia') are well-known current *topoi*; his assertion of a causal connection between the two will hardly have seemed untoward in the pages of a journal entitled *Sexual-Probleme*, and he asserts this connection simply as a 'physician' (12.34) and not in the name of psychoanalysis. In this paper, psychoanalysis aligns itself with a pre-existing discourse on sexuality and sexual reform, in much the same way as Freud will later align himself with a pre-existing ideology of science in his critique of religion as 'illusion'. This explains how an English translation of 1915 could in 1931 be reprinted as a pamphlet by 'Eugenics Publications, New York', and thus assimilated to a eugenicist discourse essentially alien to psychoanalysis. Psychoanalysis lends its weight to an existing discourse, and in turn avails itself of the power and prestige of that discourse; but in the process its own most characteristic features are temporarily set aside.

When Freud addresses the question of conventional sexual morality as a psychoanalyst, the outcome is rather different. Towards the end of the *Introductory Lectures* of 1915–17, he rhetorically imputes to his audience the view that psychoanalysis helps its patients by encouraging them to disregard conventional moral boundaries in their quest for sexual fulfilment. In fact, nothing could be further from the truth:

A recommendation to the patient to 'live a full life' sexually could not possibly play a part in analytic therapy – if only because we ourselves have declared that an obstinate conflict is taking place in him between a libidinal impulse and sexual repression, between a sensual and an ascetic trend. This conflict would not be solved by our helping one of these trends to victory over its opponent. We see, indeed, that in neurotics asceticism has the upper hand; and the consequence of this is precisely that the suppressed sexual tendency finds a way out in symptoms. If, on the contrary, we were to secure victory for sensuality, then the sexual repression that had been put on one side would necessarily be replaced by symptoms. Neither of these two alternative decisions could end the internal conflict; in either case one party to it would remain unsatisfied. (1.483–4)

Psychoanalysis is not in favour of conventional virtue, but it eschews the role of mentor and leaves the patient to make his own decisions. Above all, it emphasizes the severe constraints within which any modification of existing sexual practice must take place. The ego is suspended between the conflicting demands of super-ego and id, and although it may take certain measures to ease its situation it cannot rid itself of the tension. The optimistic assumptions that sex is natural, good and enjoyable, that repression is bad, and that these facts can straightforwardly be translated into harmonious and innocent sexual practice, are alien to Freud.

Paradoxically, it is the non-psychoanalytic Freud – the Freud who participates in the campaign against sexual ignorance and repression – who corresponds most closely to the 'Freud' of the general imagination. This image of Freud locates him at the turning-point between a nineteenth century in which sex was hypocritically repressed and a twentieth century in which sex has been rehabilitated as natural, good and enjoyable. This 'Freud' plays a key role in what Foucault has identified and criticized as 'the repressive hypothesis' that has shaped the modern discourse on sex. 'Until Freud', it is said, 'the discourse on sex . . . never ceased to hide the things it was speaking about' (*History of Sexuality*, 1.53); but after Freud, sex was able to speak freely, naming itself as 'sex'. Thus sex comes to be spoken of with evangelical earnestness. According to Foucault:

A great sexual sermon – which has had its subtle theologians and its popular voices – has swept through our societies over the last decades; it has chastised the old order, denounced hypocrisy, and praised the rights of the immediate and the real; it has made people dream of a New City. (1.7–8)

It is certainly legitimate to ask why sex was associated with sin for such a long time – although it would remain to be discovered how this association was formed, and one would have to be careful not to state in a summary and hasty fashion that sex was 'condemned' – but we must also ask why we burden ourselves today with so much guilt for having once made sex a sin. What paths have brought us to the point where we are 'at fault' with respect to our own sex? And how have we come to be a civilization so peculiar as to tell itself that, through an abuse of power which has not ended, it has long 'sinned' against sex? How does one account for the displacement which, while claiming to free us from the sinful nature of sex, taxes us with a great historical wrong which consists precisely in imagining that nature to be blameworthy and in drawing disastrous consequences from that belief? (1.9)

For Foucault, in opposition to the 'repressive hypothesis', the issue is no longer 'to determine whether one says yes or no to sex, whether one formulates prohibitions or permissions, whether one asserts its importance or denies its effects . . . ' (1.11). The aim is to investigate 'the way in which sex is "put into discourse"', irrespective of 'whether these discursive productions and these effects of power lead one to formulate the truth about sex, or on the contrary falsehoods designed to conceal that truth' (1.11–12). But one might also investigate the way in which 'Freud' is put into discourse, and so discover the extent to which this discourse conceals precisely that 'truth about sex' that Freud himself sought to uncover.

The insertion of Freud into the 'repressive hypothesis' serves to marginalize the distinctive content of the psychoanalytic discourse on sex. On this view, what occurs in Freud is simply that, having previously been silent, sex now speaks – it speaks itself, it calls itself by its proper name, 'sex', in token of the fact that reticence, shame and guilt are banished and innocence restored. 'Freud' *is* this speech-event; his discourse is the speech-act in which sex names itself and closes the era of silence. The specific content of this speech-act is not entirely unknown. That repression causes neurotic symptoms is a Freudian doctrine that the repressive hypothesis can readily make its own, enabling it to assert the superiority of modern, unrepressed sex over 'Victorian hypocrisy' with all the self-righteousness of the pharisee towards the tax-collector. But the Freudian doctrine that repression is an inescapable fact of human existence is passed over in silence. This doctrine challenges the repressive hypothesis at its core. By complicating the simple story of a passage from one sexual regime to another, it disturbs its complacency; and it must therefore be repressed.[14]

If, as Freud argues, the ego is constituted by the opposition between super-ego and id, and if this opposition is ultimately indissoluble, whatever adjustments may perhaps be possible

---

[14] This simplified image of Freud as enemy of the repressive super-ego and friend of the libidinous id is already firmly in place in W. H. Auden's 1939 poem, 'In Memory of Sigmund Freud' (*Collected Shorter Poems 1927–57*, London: Faber, 1966, 166–70). Here, Freud is 'no more a person / now but a climate of opinion / under whom we live our different lives'. Our lives are different because he showed us that true evil consists not in our reprehensible deeds but in 'our dishonest mood of denial, / the concupiscence of the oppressor' – that is, the oppressive super-ego. And he taught us 'to be enthusiastic over the night, / . . . because it needs our love'. (The night is of course the id.) Thus: 'Over his grave / the household of Impulse mourns one dearly loved: / sad is Eros, builder of cities, / and weeping anarchic Aphrodite.' If one becomes 'a climate of opinion', one is at the same time assimilated to an existing climate of opinion – with the result that significant qualifications and nuances are lost.

and desirable, then human sexuality is irreducibly *complex*. Freudian theory asserts this complexity in opposition not to 'Victorian hypocrisy' or 'Christianity's negative attitude towards the body' but to the modern, enlightened discourse of sexual liberation. Itself implicated in that discourse, it deconstructs it. The difference between the Freudian project and the project of sexual enlightenment is the difference between a Pauline model of the person as the site of the conflict between super-ego and id, law and flesh, and a 'liberal' model of the person as a property owner whose freedom in relation to the body is limited only by the property rights of others. Fundamental to the Freudian view of the person is the reality of 'guilt', which, as the subjective byproduct of objective structures of human existence, can more readily be seen as symptomatic of 'sin' than dismissed as an illusion created by a merely contingent repression. 'Sin', of course, requires a theological framework that Freud regards as no longer tenable in the age of science. But his own 'scientific' framework is still recognizably modelled on that older theological framework, especially in its Pauline-Augustinian form – just as the liberal view is modelled on the Pelagian view of the person as endowed with a purely neutral freedom limited only by the rights of others (notably God, although the liberal version of the Pelagian picture will discover that it has no need of that hypothesis).

Freud makes comprehensible again Augustine's understanding of concupiscence as 'the lust which lords it over the unchaste, has to be mastered by the chaste, and yet is to be blushed at by the chaste and the unchaste' (*De nuptiis et concupiscentia*, ii.59). For Augustine's Pelagian opponents, sexuality evokes no such ambivalence; there is no need to connect it with blushing. The 'vigour of the members' is cause for celebration not shame, even though it is beyond the control of the will. This involuntary erectile potency would surely have flourished in Paradise, for Paradise is its birthplace and home. There, 'it would always have been exercised and never repressed, lest so great a pleasure should ever be denied to so happy an estate . . . And so, should the motion of lust precede men's will, then the will would immediately follow it' (ii.59). But that is to project present sexual experience back into Paradise, thereby idealizing and mythologizing it by investing it with the innocent wonder of the first man and woman, who knew only of a pristine existence that unambiguously expressed the goodness of the Creator. In this Pelagian sex, Paradise is restored as a man and a woman are drawn by their desire for one another into the shared joy of sexual union. But for Augustine, there is discontinuity as well as continuity between the sexual experience of the present and of Paradise. That which the Creator intended has been overlaid by the human decision to establish an autonomous good and evil and by the ensuing judgment, which subjected human life to the anonymous power of a concupiscence in which excess, shame and violence have marred the original joy. Within marriage, and through the divine grace, something of the original joy at sharing in the work of creation may still be present. Yet even here, the clearest symptoms of shame persist. Augustine mentions just one of these symptoms: *blushing*, the visible, physiological manifestation of shame. Blushing occurs when the intention of concealment is overtaken by an accident: a careless turn of phrase, a lapse of discretion, the intrusion of a third party, an exposure of flesh. If the truth about 'sex' is simple – that it is natural, good and enjoyable, nothing to be ashamed of – then it is not clear why these utterly trivial events should evoke such profound discomfort.

Like Augustine, Freud regards such familiar but opaque phenomena as symptoms of a forgotten world of complexities and ambivalences. It is the knowledge of this world that the discourse of 'sex' strives to repress. The Freudian 'hermeneutic of suspicion' might diagnose in this repression a ruse of the ego. The ego 'is not only helper to the id; it is also a submissive slave who courts his master's love. Whenever possible, it tries to remain on good terms with the id; it clothes the id's *Ucs.* commands with its *Pcs.* rationalizations; it pretends that the id is showing obedience to the admonitions of reality, even when in fact it is remaining obstinate and unyielding; it disguises the id's conflicts with reality and, if possible, with the super-ego too' (11.398). 'Sex', we might say, is the product of just such a false consciousness. It is the ego's attempt to conceal the conflicts between id and reality by interposing an ideological screen, onto which is projected the fantasy-reality of the erotic Paradise. At the risk of seeming too 'negative about sex', it is the Pauline model of an ego torn by the conflict between law and flesh that can restore the reality that 'sex' represses.

CHAPTER FOUR

The Tombs of Desire

In the Freudian model of the self, Paul's portrayal of the ego as torn between the demands of law and flesh reappears in twentieth-century guise. The old language has been modernized, fitting it for a new career within a twentieth-century discourse on sex whose repeated announcements of a turning-point between the old era and the new it effectively subverts. Yet, if within Freud's texts there occurs a 'reading' of a Pauline text, this is clearly also a *misreading*. Little or nothing survives of the context in which the Pauline language has its natural habitat. That is of course deliberate: Freud's texts are resolute in their rejection of the 'illusion' on whose stories and traditions they continue to draw. But if we do not reject those stories and traditions, if we continue to regard them as embodying truth rather than illusion, the relationship of the ancient and the modern texts will be reversed. Paul will no longer be the precursor of Freud – a source for certain of his conceptual moves, apparently unrecognized by Freud himself or by his interpreters. Instead, Freud will be the precursor of Paul. A reading of Freud as subverting the discourse of sexual liberation is already a Pauline (and Augustinian) reading of Freud; and perhaps also – at least on some criteria – a misreading. The intention of this reading was to problematize the assumption that a negative, Christian attitude towards sex and the body has now at last been replaced by a positive one, and that this is all to the good. Freud is precursor to Paul in the sense that he may help to overcome some of the almost insuperable prejudices that prevent Pauline statements on sexuality from being heard. But in the end it is Paul (and not Freud) who must be heard –

insofar as he is acknowledged within the Christian community as an 'apostle of Jesus Christ' whose texts lie close to the centre of Christian canonical scripture. He is not to be heard simply as 'Paul' but, in accordance with his own self-designation, as 'Paul, a slave of Christ Jesus, called to be an apostle, set apart for the gospel of God' (Rom. 1.1). In this setting apart for the gospel of God there is also a setting apart from a merely individual 'Paul', some of whose personal idiosyncrasies may still be traced in his texts. What must be heard – if it can be heard – is the apostolic testimony to the gospel of God as it touches and transforms the sphere of sexuality and the body.

SPIRIT AND LETTER (VERSES 1–6)

Or are you unaware, brothers [and sisters] – for I speak to those who know the law – that the law exercises authority over a person only as long as he lives? (Rom. 7.1) We enter the discourse when it is already in full flow, and must begin by orienting ourselves. Who is addressed here? How are we who overhear related to these primary addressees? What has the theme of the discourse to do with us?

The discourse is addressed 'to all who are in Rome, God's beloved, called to be saints' (1.7), and it is addressed to them by one whose commission is to bring about 'the obedience of faith among all the Gentiles, for the sake of his name, among whom you too are called by Jesus Christ' (1.5–6). The particular addressees – Gentile Christians in Rome – are enclosed within the much wider category of 'all the Gentiles'; they are addressed as belonging to that category and as representative of it. But it is therefore 'all the Gentiles' who are themselves indirectly addressed, in the person of their representatives in first-century Rome. The address to a particular group of persons is not a limiting of the writer's universal commission; it is not a tacit admission that the abstract notion of a universal commission is unworkable in practice, and that the real commission is simply to the local groups that spring up in various places. The apostle's right to address those who are in Rome is in fact dependent on his universal commission to bring about the obedience of faith among all the Gentiles. It is on the basis of this commission that he addresses them, and this gives his address its comprehensive significance. He speaks to the Roman Christians not as private individuals or as members of purely local communities, but as particular representatives of the universal scope of the divine address to humankind embodied in Jesus and his Spirit. As Paul himself is not a private individual but represents that universal scope in his own person, so it is with his addresses. They are 'in Rome', but what is more important is that they belong to a wider group of people who are 'called by Jesus Christ' (1.6), who themselves represent the universal sphere of 'all the Gentiles' – 'Greeks and barbarians, wise and foolish' (1.14). The scope of Paul's testimony also extends into the future; by means of the written text, he continues to fulfil his commission to bring about the obedience of faith long after his death. It is not a mere accident of history that we are in a position to overhear Paul's discourse to the Romans, for the text itself intends a readership as broad as the apostolic commission – or rather, as broad as the grace of God in Jesus Christ, the basis for the apostolic commission.[1]

It is 'brothers' who are addressed in Romans 7.1. That *adelphoi* 'includes' *adelphai* is clear from the many greetings to women as well as men in Romans 16: those who are commended for their work in the Lord can hardly have been excluded from the circle of the letter's addressees. A commission to 'all the Gentiles' includes women as well as men within its scope. The addressees are 'brothers and sisters' on the basis of Jesus' saying: 'Whoever

---

[1] The significance of the prescript (Rom. 1.1–7) for determining the scope of the letter is rightly emphasized by Brevard Childs, *The New Testament as Canon: An Introduction*, London: SCM Press, 1984, 252–5). A 'canonical approach' to Romans seeks to avoid treating the letter as 'a timeless theological tractate', overlooking the historical particularities that are here given a canonical role, but it also distances itself from 'an interpretation which seeks to reconstruct an original context', guided by 'a herme- neutic of historical referentiality' (252). In a canonical approach, the 'purpose' of Romans would be a function of the text itself, not of the situation of Paul and the Roman Christians at the time of writing. That there is a *hermeneutical* issue here, and not just a historical one, is not sufficiently clear in most of the studies collected in K. P. Donfried (ed.), *The Romans Debate*, Peabody, Mass.: Hendrickson, 2nd edn 1991. My own *Paul, Judaism and the Gentiles: A Sociological Approach* (Cambridge: Cambridge University Press, 1986) assumes a 'hermeneutic of historical referentiality', and tends to exaggerate the significance of the historical context for interpreting the letter (88–176).

does the will of God is my brother, my sister and mother' (Mk. 3.35). Jesus, the Son of God, is 'the first-born of many brothers [and sisters]' (Rom. 8.29), who through him and with him address God as 'Abba, Father' (8.15).

They have not always been children of God, brothers and sisters of Jesus and of one another, but have previously been characterized as those who have experienced a moment of sharp discontinuity in their lives (Rom. 6). Behind them lies a transition from one way of life to another, and they are exhorted to preserve this difference from every encroachment of the old patterns of conduct. 'Just as you once subjected your bodily members to uncleanness and to every kind of lawless conduct, so now subject your bodily members to righteousness, for holiness' (6.19). The Christian brothers and sisters addressed in chapter 7 are said to 'know the law', but they also know what it is to devote their bodies to the service of 'uncleanness' (*akatharsia*). *Akatharsia* is the conduct of those who 'dishonour their bodies among themselves' (1.24), and is closely associated with *porneia*, sexual immorality (Gal. 5.19, 2 Cor. 12.21). The body that is dishonoured in *akatharsia* is therefore the body as subject and object of sexual union – the body under the primacy of the genitals, the 'bodily members' that acquire a privileged role in the service of *akatharsia* and *porneia*, in the pursuit of sex. If their maleness and femaleness now takes the form of a relationship between brothers and sisters, that has not always been the case. In their different ways, they once shared in a sexual culture that led them to do things of which, in the light of the new teaching they have received, they are now ashamed (Rom. 6.21). And they still live in the midst of the allurements of the sexual culture they have rejected. It has not rejected them. It continues to offer itself to them as a real possibility – perhaps even a Christian possibility. If we are under grace and not under law, what is 'sin' (cf. 6.1, 15)? Paul himself states that 'where there is no law there is no transgression' (4.15), and that 'sin is not reckoned where there is no law'. 'Transgression' and 'sin' are no more: under grace, it seems, a whole moral vocabulary has been erased. Under grace, in the absence of the harsh, condemning, moralizing law, might the joy of bodily union not be a sacramental expression of the Christian's union with Christ? Might grace not permit what the law forbids?[2] Whatever their past relationship to the surrounding sexual culture, Paul's readers still find themselves addressed by it in the present.

They are indeed under grace, not law. 'The grace of God and the gift in grace of the one man Jesus Christ have abounded for many' (5.15). Grace marks the limit of the law: 'Law came in, so that the trespass might increase, but where sin increased grace was all the more abundant' (5.20). At the beginning of chapter 7, too, the theme is the limit of the law: the law exercises authority over a person only during his or her lifetime. But as yet this notion of a life lived 'not under law but under grace' is opaque. What is it that motivates this disjunction? Is it merely a pragmatic response to contingent problems in the early church,

---

[2] Such arguments may take various forms, as three modern examples illustrate. (1) Although the Christian view of 'sex' has always tended towards 'legalism', Jesus himself 'boldly rejected all such legalisms', and endorses the view that 'whether any form of sex . . . is good or evil depends on whether love is fully served' (Joseph Fletcher, *Situation Ethics*, London: SCM Press, 1966, 139). This opposition between situational love and legalistic morality is an attempt to radicalize the Pauline-Augustinian antithesis of grace and law. Its motto is Augustine's *dilige et quod vis, fac* (79). (2) According to William Countryman, 'the demands of the gospel of grace are being constantly renewed and fitted to new situations by the Spirit who animates the church' (*Dirt, Greed and Sex: Sexual Ethics in the New Testament and their Implications for Today*, Philadelphia: Fortress Press, 1988, 239). Just as 'the New Testament rejected the imposition of the purity codes of the Torah on Gentile Christians', so today 'a Christian sexual ethic that remains true to its New Testament roots will have to discard its insistence on physical purity' (243). 'Purity' stands for the belief that 'a given sexual act is wrong in and of itself' (241), and is opposed by an ethic of 'sexual property' in which 'the individual is the primary arbiter of his or her sexual acts' (242). (3) In sexual love, one's sexual partner is 'the sacrament of God's joy, beauty and self-giving, the other as the sacrament of celebration . . . [I]n the deepest forms of sexual encounter there is a holiness, that is a purity and depth of recognition of the other, which speaks of the presence of the holy God' (T. J. Gorringe, *Discerning Spirit: A Theology of Revelation*, London: SCM Press, 1990, 101–2). This is a distinctively Christian view, for 'only Christian doctrine teaches that the divine can be not merely immanent or symbolized by material bodies but actually enfleshed, and only this doctrine could make such an articulation of experience permissible and therefore possible' (99–100). Although the ideal of lifelong commitment is to be respected, we must respond theologically to the fact that 'we may "fall in love" not once but several times' – an experience 'which always comes to us as a "given" and with the power of revelation' (106). To reject this experience in its full sexual expression 'will seem to those involved like the sin against the Holy Spirit, calling that which is good evil' (106).

or does it articulate something that is basic to Christian living as such? According to Augustine, 'the law was given that grace might be sought; grace was given that the law might be fulfilled' (*De spiritu et littera*, 34). 'The law says: Thou shalt not desire. Faith says: Heal my soul, for I have sinned against thee. Grace says: Behold, thou art made whole; sin no more, lest a worse thing befall thee' (52).[3] On that view, living under grace rather than law cannot be reduced to Gentile Christians' freedom from the obligation to practise Judaism. The 'law' that the antithesis excludes is the demand, 'Thou shalt . . .' or 'Thou shalt not . . .', insofar as it presupposes a free moral agent as its addressee. Grace closes off that apparent possibility. It is 'the Spirit of life in Christ Jesus' (Rom. 8.2) who establishes the human freedom to live in conformity to the will of God. Under this regime, the body is 'a living sacrifice, holy and acceptable to God' (12.1), and is no longer oriented towards *akatharsia*.[4]

---

[3] In this chapter, translations from Augustine are adapted from *The Nicene and Post-Nicene Fathers: St Augustine*, vols. I, III, v (repr. Grand Rapids: Eerdmans, 1971–9). In the case of the *Confessions*, I have also drawn on the translations of R. S. Pine-Coffin (Harmondsworth: Penguin Books, 1961), and H. Chadwick (Oxford: Oxford University Press, 1991).

[4] Here and elsewhere in this chapter, my use of Augustine as a Pauline interpreter is in reaction against recent attempts to replace the Augustinian-Lutheran reading of Paul with a 'new perspective', which emphasizes the irreducibility of the Jew–Gentile issues Paul faced to any more 'abstract' or 'universal' theological problematic. (My earlier book, *Paul, Judaism and the Gentiles*, is itself an exercise in that genre.) In Augustine, it is said, 'the Pauline thought about the Law and Justification was applied in a consistent and grand style to a more general and timeless human problem' (K. Stendahl, 'Paul and the Introspective Conscience of the West' [1963], repr. in his *Paul among Jews and Gentiles*, Philadelphia: Fortress Press, 1976, 78–96; 85). Paul's own concern was simply with 'the place of the Gentiles in the Church and in the plan of God' (84). In Rom. 7 – a crucially important text for the so-called 'introspective conscience of the west' – a commonplace observation about the goodness of the law and the wickedness of sin 'appeared to later interpreters to be a most penetrating insight into the nature of man and into the nature of sin' (93). Along similar lines, S. Stowers argues that Augustine 'internalized, individualized, and generalized such Pauline concepts as justification, sin, law, works, salvation, and election' (*A Rereading of Romans: Justice, Jews and Gentiles*, New Haven and London: Yale University Press, 1994, 13–14). He 'developed a way of understanding the gospel and of reading Romans that made the Jew the archetypical sinner and rebel against God's grace' (13). With due respect to Augustine and others, 'the historian of early Christian literature must imagine what it would be like to come upon Romans for the first time', and read it 'as a writing of antiquity', unencumbered by 'the purposes of the theologians and churchmen' (4). As for Rom. 7, Paul here uses the rhetorical device of *prosopopoeia* or speech-in-character to construct a fictional Gentile convert to Judaism, who confesses

For the married woman is bound by law to her husband as long as he lives; but if the husband dies, she is freed from the law of the husband. (v. 2) A slippage occurs between the first two sentences of the chapter. Initially it was said that the law is binding only during a person's lifetime, but now a law is specified that binds one party only during the lifetime of another. The general principle, that death marks the limit of the law's jurisdiction, is illustrated by a case in which the death of one marks the termination of the law's jurisdiction over another. The slippage is necessary to the theological position for which these general analogies prepare the ground: for to be 'under grace' is to be subject not only to a negation (a death) but also to an affirmation (a life beyond that death). To be under grace is to re-enact in daily conduct the pattern of Jesus' death and resurrection, in the negation of one mode of being and the affirmation of another that this pattern entails. The figure of the crucified and risen Jesus is already dimly discernible in the husband who dies and in the wife who survives him. 'Christ who has been raised from the dead dies no more, death no longer has dominion over him. As for his death, he died to sin, once for all; as for his life, he lives to God' (6.9–10). This is the pattern re-enacted in the Christian life: 'So you too must regard yourselves as dead to sin and alive to God in Christ Jesus' (6.11).

It is, then, the Christian who – following the pattern of Christ – is both the husband who dies and the wife who lives. That which is negated is the self apart from the grace of God, an abstraction that may have had a biographical counterpart in a life prior to conversion but that may also be understood in non-chronological terms as an *alter ego* or *shadow* that accompanies one on one's way, that bears one's own form, and that represents the enduring possibility of a selfhood on which the light that Paul encountered on the Damascus Road does *not* shine. The imperative, 'Regard yourselves as dead to sin . . . ', already

his difficulties with the practice of the law; the intention is to dissuade Gentiles from conversion to Judaism (264–84). Stendahl and Stowers show both that 'the historian' can indeed offer certain clarifications of the Pauline texts, and that hostility to their theological appropriation leads rapidly to banal and superficial exegesis.

implies a possible 'mode of being oneself' in which one fails to live in the light of the divine negation and affirmation but seeks out a quite different orientation by which to live – turning away from the light and finding one's self in the shadow. The divine negation and affirmation that occurs in Jesus' death and resurrection has put this shadow definitively behind us. The divine act differentiates the 'husband' who belongs to the past from the 'wife' who now lives apart from the husband; it forbids any attempt at a reunion in which the two again become 'one flesh'. It was once said: 'What God has joined let no one separate' (Matt. 19.6). The woman was bound by law to her husband. But now it is said: What God has separated let no one join. The woman is freed from the law of the husband. As God once separated light from darkness, so he has separated the self that is under grace from the self that seeks to exist apart from grace.

If, during her husband's lifetime, she joins herself to another man, she will be regarded as an adulteress; but if her husband dies, she is free from the law, so that she is not an adulteress if she joins herself to another man. (v. 3) There are two situations in which the woman can join herself to another man: illicitly, during her husband's lifetime, and lawfully, after his death. Christ's death is the divine judgment of a world which the law proved unable to restore to its proper subjection to God, and his life is the divine creation of a new world in which humankind attains its appointed *telos* in union with Christ. After her husband's death, the woman must join herself to another man rather than remain single: for Christ 'died for all so that those who live might no longer live for themselves but for him who for their sake died and was raised' (2 Cor. 5.15). Yet there are those for whom the law is the final, definitive divine address to humankind, and who believe humankind to be definitively constituted by this divine address. From their standpoint, the woman remains bound by the law of the husband, and the Pauline proclamation of grace sounds very much like an incitement to 'adultery'. There is a general belief in Jerusalem that Paul teaches 'all the Jews who are among the Gentiles to forsake Moses, telling them not to circumcise their children or observe the customs' (Acts 21.21).

He teaches unfaithfulness to the God of the fathers; and instead of instructing Gentiles in the Torah, he teaches them to do evil that good may come (Rom. 3.8). The Christian who joins herself to Christ because a death has occurred that frees her from the law will appear to be an 'adulteress' to those who do not recognize in the event of that death the divine judgment of the world.[5]

The issue here is not simply that of a 'Jewish identity', symbolized by the 'boundary-markers' that most visibly differentiate Jews from Gentiles. Earlier in Romans, Paul has addressed a fictional Jewish teacher (perhaps based in part on his own pre-Christian past) who understands himself to be 'a guide to the blind, a light to those in darkness, an instructor of the ignorant, a teacher of children' – on the basis not of his own wisdom and insight but of the divine law, in which he finds 'the embodiment of knowledge and truth' (2.17–20). On this basis, Gentiles as well as Jews are taught to discern the divine will: they are not to steal, commit adultery or worship idols (2.21–2). They are to live henceforth in a de-divinized, demythologized world, subject only to the divine categorical imperative. This mode of living is proper to them, as rational and moral agents created by God, and since it is proper to them it is also possible for them. This proclamation evokes immediate echoes in a world which is already not wholly ignorant of 'the decree of God' (1.32), even prior to the proclamation. If in this proclamation 'Jewish identity' is at stake, that identity consists not

[5] Throughout the discussion, I assume that the illustrations in vv. 1–3 can be fully integrated into the argument of vv. 4–6. This is in line with Karl Barth's interpretation, in which the addressees of Rom. 7 are identified with both the husband and the wife. In 7.1, 'the living man to whom Paul is referring, who is therefore subject to the law, is man "in the flesh" (7.5), who therefore lives as "the old man" (6.6) . . . In 7.2 a parable commences. As long as this man – the husband, it now says – is alive, his wife is tied to him by the law which binds him – and which, as long he is alive, binds her as well. In other words, as long as we (the husband) live in the flesh as that old man, and we (the wife) are governed by the law that binds him and therefore ourselves, we are in fact bound to become sinners properly speaking because of the law and to be accused as such by the law . . . Inasmuch as by the death of the old man we have been placed in a new situation, we are then no longer bound by that necessity: then the law has lost for us its power as instigator and accuser of our sin' (*A Shorter Commentary on Romans* [1956], ET London: 1959, 77–8). I do not understand why C. E. B. Cranfield rejects this interpretation as 'extremely complicated and forced' (*Romans I-VIII*, International Critical Commentary, Edinburgh: T. & T. Clark, 1975, 1.334).

simply in the distinctive pattern of life that binds a particular ethnic group together but in the vocation to bear witness among the nations to the will of the one true God. It is on the basis of that unique vocation that the teacher of the law 'calls himself a Jew' (2.17). He contributes to the formation of a 'Judaeo-Christian tradition' whose 'ethical principles' are said – most forcefully by Nietzsche – still to permeate the political-ethical discourse of modernity.

The dignity and majesty of the divine law appears to ensure the dignity and majesty of its human addressee. The human existence that sees itself as subject to the law's categorical imperative is an unbroken existence. It has not been crucified, nor has it been raised from the dead. From this standpoint, the idea that human life should be shaped by the pattern of Jesus' death and resurrection is simply another aberration of religious enthusiasm. Those who are seduced by it are unfaithful to the God in whose command humans approach most nearly to the mysterious constitution of reality-itself.

So, my brothers [and sisters], you too died to the law through the body of Christ, so that you might belong to another, to him who has been raised from the dead so that we might bear fruit for God. (v. 4) Reality-itself is in fact to be found in the rupturing and remaking of human existence in Jesus' death and resurrection. 'You died': the readers are identified with the 'husband' of verses 2–3, who is also the 'man' of verse 1. To 'die to the law' is to leave the sphere of the law's jurisdiction, as verse 1 has explained. 'So that you might belong to another': the readers are also identified with the 'wife' of verses 2–3, set free to remarry by her husband's death. The crucified Christ identifies himself with a human existence subject to the judgment of God; the risen Christ brings into being a new, fruitful human existence under the grace of God. Identifying himself with the first 'husband' in his death, he becomes the second 'husband' in his resurrection. The point of this language is not to 'legitimate patriarchal marriage'. It is rather to use whatever language and conceptuality is to hand in order to articulate a relationship that is *sui generis* and therefore beyond the scope of all such language and conceptuality: the relationship between Jesus Christ and those who are in Christ. This is an asymmetrical relationship in which one partner is acknowledged by the other as 'Lord', and the then-current conception of marriage as an asymmetrical relationship is therefore integral to the imagery. The woman is said to be *hypandros*, under man's authority (v. 2). Yet there is no intention to affirm a particular conception of marriage, for it is not the marriage of man and woman but the relation of Christ and the Christian that is at issue.[6]

As in marriage, Christian life is centred on *personal relationship*. The naïve pietistic emphasis on 'personal relationship with Jesus' is no doubt open to various criticisms. It is important that 'Jesus' here should really be 'Jesus Christ of Nazareth' (Acts 3.6), and not a fantasy figure whose pure contemporaneity is detached from a fleshly, historical existence. It is important that the relationship with Jesus should be located within a trinitarian and communal framework. With these qualifications, however, talk of a 'personal relationship with Jesus' comes much closer to the truth than a supposedly more sophisticated description of Christian existence in primarily sociological categories, which would in effect deny to the Christian community its foundation and dwelling-place within the divine life. The life of the risen Jesus is not the secret preserve of himself and his Father, as

---

[6] Elizabeth Castelli argues that in Rom. 7.1–6 Paul 'uses a recognized hierarchical relationship to illuminate his point about another hierarchical relationship . . . By using women to think with, Paul (like other authors who use gender and social roles as metaphors and analogies) helps to underwrite the understanding of women's roles on which his argument depends' ('Romans', in E. Schüssler Fiorenza (ed.), *Searching the Scriptures*, vol. II: *A Feminist Commentary*, New York: Crossroad, 1994; London, SCM Press, 1995, 272–300; 283). Castelli later makes a similar point about the use of the image of slavery (e.g. in Rom. 6.22): 'While this passage is clearly not *about* slavery (neither for it nor against it), it depends on the reality of slavery to convey its meanings and therefore reinscribes the relation of slavery' (294). But when in 1 Cor. 7.23 Paul writes, 'You were bought with a price; do not become slaves of humans', the image of the Christian as Christ's slave (cf. v. 22b) sets the metaphorical sense *in opposition to* the literal one; a similar disjunction also underlies the qualified argument against marriage in 1 Cor. 7.32–5 (cf. 6.13–17). A critique of 'metaphors of domination' (295), even where the metaphorical application is detached from the original social relation and is perhaps critical of it, presupposes the possibility and desirability of a pure, anarchic, utopian language – a language without *archē*, without imperatives, and without opposites (feminist emphasis on multiplicity is 'inimical to' that is, *opposed to*, 'binary opposition' or 'dualism' (286)). In substance, Castelli's objection to the Pauline text is that it is written not in the language of an imagined utopia but in *koine* Greek.

though the human Jesus had somehow ceased to represent humankind in his relationship to the Father. It is a *shared* life that arises out of the promise, 'I am with you always, to the close of the age' (Matt. 28.20).

As in marriage, the relationship of Christ and the Christian is an affair of the *body*. It is the death of 'the body of Christ' that makes it possible; and in his resurrection Jesus resumes his body, rather than finally casting it off. The attempt in 1 Corinthians 15 to articulate the difference between the present, frail body of flesh and blood and the glorified body that Jesus already possesses is so tortuous precisely because Paul will not concede that the word 'body' is more appropriately applied to empirical human reality than to eschatological destiny. Without his body, the risen Christ would not still be Jesus. But if there is no disembodied humanity in the case of Jesus Christ, the same must be true of those who are in Christ. It is in their bodies that they are one with him – in the concreteness, materiality and wholeness of their existence.

As in marriage, the existence of each of the partners is *oriented towards the other* rather than centred in the self. Indeed, marriage gives only an inadequate picture of this other-orientation. The terms 'husband' and 'wife' do not exhaustively identify the man and woman who are united in marriage, for each of them is more than the spouse of the other. In the case of Christ and the Christian, however, that qualification does not apply. Jesus would not be Christ without his relation to those who are 'in Christ'; he would not be himself. Similarly, the term 'Christian' denotes not just the most important among a number of relationships in which one is involved, but the relationship that comprehends all other relationships – a relationship of absolute belonging. 'If we live, we live to the Lord; if we die, we die to the Lord; and so, whether we live or whether we die, we are the Lord's' (Rom. 14.8).

It follows that, as in marriage, the relationship of Christ and the Christian is *exclusive*, and indeed that this is a bodily exclusiveness. 'The body is not for *porneia* but for the Lord, and the Lord is for the body' (1 Cor. 6.13). For a man and a woman to join together in *porneia*, becoming 'one body' and 'one flesh', would be to subvert the union with Christ, with whom one is 'one spirit' (6.16–17). It would be a sin against Christ and against one's own body, which, as the temple of the Holy Spirit, is Christ's (6.18–19). Even marriage itself may detract, in some respects, from the exclusiveness of the relationship with the Lord (7.32–5). Marriage, however, is not a sin. On the contrary, 'it was ordained for a remedy against sin, and to avoid fornication' – as the Book of Common Prayer puts it, following 1 Corinthians 7.2. In marriage the body of each partner is oriented towards the other (7.4), in a parable of the relationship of Christ and the Christian that differs fundamentally from the destructive caricature that occurs in *porneia*.

As in marriage, the relationship of Christ and the Christian is intended to be *fruitful*. Belonging to another has as its goal 'that we might bear fruit for God' (Rom. 7.4). Marriage 'was ordained for the procreation of children, to be brought up in the fear and nurture of the Lord, and to the praise of his holy Name' (Book of Common Prayer). This fruitfulness might be identified with the 'fruit of the Spirit', which is 'love, joy, peace, patience, kindness, goodness, gentleness, faithfulness, self-control'; a life that is fruitful along these lines will have no place for 'the works of the flesh' or for gratifying 'the desire of the flesh' (Gal. 5.16–24). This true fruitfulness is independent of marriage, or of fertility within marriage. It may well be that it is the single man or woman who is most 'anxious about the affairs of the Lord' (1 Cor. 7.32, 34) and who is therefore most 'fruitful'. Where there is marriage and family life, however, this will be one of the primary communal contexts in which love, joy, peace, patience and kindness must come to fruition. It is in the midst of intimate human relations of one kind or another that the testing implied in the statement, 'You shall know them by their fruits' (Matt. 7.16) is carried out. The source of this fruitfulness is Christ himself, through the Spirit: 'It is the one who abides in me, and I in him, who bears much fruit; for apart from me you can do nothing' (Jn. 15.5).

For when we were in the flesh, the passions of sins were through the law at work in our members, to bear fruit for death. (v. 5) The present state, in

which there is fruit-bearing for God (v. 4), is now contrasted
with a past state in which there was fruit-bearing for death – the
death that is disclosed but also overcome in Christ's death and
our participation in it. The vocabulary – flesh, sin, members,
fruit, death – continues to echo chapter 6; what is new in
chapter 7 is the emphasis on 'law'. In chapter 6 it was said that
'sin will not rule over you, for you are not under law but under
grace' (v. 14, cf. v. 15), yet the implied claim that the law furthers
the dominion of sin was not clarified – despite the obvious
objection that the law actually hinders and limits sin's dominion, rather than furthering it. The role of the law within the
drama of sin and salvation is the theme of chapter 7, although it
is introduced only indirectly in the opening verses. The chapter
is addressed 'to those who know the law', and it opens with an
assertion about the law: that it rules over a man only during his
lifetime (v. 1). In the example of the married woman whose
husband dies, the emphasis lies on her change of status in
relation to the law: once bound by 'the law of the husband', she
is now free from this law (vv. 2, 3). The 'dying to sin' that is the
theme of 6.1–11 becomes in 7.4 a 'dying to the law'. As in 6.14,
the law is apparently assigned a negative role, but as yet without
explanation. In the law–grace contrast and in the image of the
married woman, 'law' and 'Christ' are related antithetically to
one another – even though the rest of chapter 7 will emphasize
that 'law' remains 'the law of God', the same God as the God
and Father of our Lord Jesus Christ. Paul does not intend to be
a Marcionite – although it is his law–grace antithesis that
enables Marcion to understand himself as a Paulinist.

If Paul's aim is merely to legitimate the non-practice of
Judaism in the Gentile communities that he has founded, the
antithesis is not the best or most obvious way of achieving this.
Although there are antithetical elements in Galatians (for
example, in the contrast between the curse of the law and the
blessing of Abraham (3.8–14)), the dominant model presents the
law as a preliminary stage in the divine 'education of the
human race'. The law was our *paidagōgos* – our 'schoolmaster',
in the Authorized Version's free but vivid rendering – whose
task was to discipline our childish follies and prepare us for the

adult life which is now ours through Christ (3.21–4.11). We are free from the law in the same way as we are free from the preliminary disciplines of childhood. Although in the Pauline version of this theme the law is only indirectly of divine origin (3.19, 4.1–3, 8–9), this 'educational' model later made it possible for Irenaeus to emphasize the coherence of the unfolding divine dealings with humankind, in opposition both to Marcionite antithesis and, indirectly, to Judaism.[7] Yet in Romans, supposedly a more considered and mature text than Galatians, there is no trace of the 'educational' model, and antithesis predominates.[8] Having established the antithesis in Romans 6.14 and 7.1–4, Paul begins in 7.5 to explain why it is necessary. The law is associated with the rule of sin because our sinful passions were at work in us *through the law*. It is not said that the law simply proved powerless to restrain our sinful passions, like a schoolmaster unable to control an unruly class. It is said that the law actively provoked and incited the sinful passions that rule over the flesh. The law is part of the problem. Yet, as Paul will immediately emphasize, it remains the law of God and its requirements are holy, just and good. The problem must lie not in the law as such but in its human addressees.

Two narratives help to shed light on these cryptic Pauline statements. One is the story of Israel's experiences in the

---

[7] Direct use of relevant texts from Galatians is found in Irenaeus, *Adversus haereses*, iv. 2.7 (Gal. 3.24, the Pauline image of the law as *paidagōgos*) and iii.16.7 (Gal. 4.4, the sending of the Son 'in the fullness of time').

[8] In developmental accounts of Pauline theology, Paul is said to have reached a 'balanced' view of the law in Romans that contrasts with and corrects the extremism of the earlier Galatian letter. 'Whereas in Galatians Paul sees scarcely any value at all in the Old Testament Law, which did not even have God as its author (Gal. 3.19), in Romans, "the law is holy and the commandment is just and good" (7.12)' (J. W. Drane, *Paul: Libertine or Legalist? A Study in the Theology of the Major Pauline Epistles*, London: SPCK, 1975, 73). H. Hübner too argues that Paul in Romans modifies the negative verdict on the law he had pronounced in Galatians, suggesting that 'it was perhaps the very fact of Galatians becoming known in Jerusalem that occasioned the posing of critical questions to the author – which the latter then also, contrary to all expectations, began to ask himself . . . [T]he difference between Galatians and Romans is best explained if we assume that there was a far from trivial theological development on the part of Paul between the two letters' (*Law in Paul's Thought*, ET Edinburgh: T. & T. Clark, 1984, 55). Developmental accounts will tend to overlook both the independent significance of Galatians, which is reduced to a moment in a process of development, and the presence in Romans of elements that are more radical than anything in Galatians.

wilderness; this will be treated in connection with verses 8–10. The other is Augustine's well-known account of an act of youthful folly, in which an act of theft was provoked not by the desirability of the object but simply by the law's prohibition.[9] Augustine writes:

I wanted to steal, and steal I did, although I was not compelled by any lack – unless it were the lack of a sense of justice, or a distaste for what was right and a love of wickedness. For of what I stole I already had plenty, and much better at that, and I had no wish to enjoy the things I sought to steal, but only to enjoy the theft itself and the sin. There was a pear-tree near our vineyard, laden with fruit that was tempting neither for its colour nor for its flavour. To shake the fruit off the tree and carry off the pears, I and a gang of dissolute boys set off late at night – for we had continued our games in the streets till then, as was our disreputable habit – and removed an enormous quantity, not to eat them ourselves but simply to throw to the pigs. Perhaps we ate some of them, but our pleasure consisted in doing what was forbidden. (*Confessions*, ii.4.9)

This apparently trivial incident is significant because it enables Augustine to identify and isolate an element in the act of sin that is normally concealed. On one definition, sin is the choice of a lesser good in preference to a higher one. All the good gifts of creation 'can be occasions of sin because, good though they are, they are of the lowest order of good, and if we are too much tempted by them we abandon those higher and better things: you yourself, O Lord our God, your truth and your law' (ii.5.10). This account of the nature of sin recalls the analysis of the confusion of the creature with the creator in Wisdom of Solomon 13, echoed by Paul in Romans 1. The good gifts of creation serve only to conceal the creator: humans 'were unable from the good things that are seen to know the one who is, nor did they recognize the maker while attending to his works . . . If through delight in the beauty of these things they assumed them to be gods, let them know how much better than these is their

---

[9] The Augustine passage is cited by C. H. Dodd, in connection with Rom. 7.7–8: Augustine, 'a master of introspective psychology, as well as the greatest interpreter of Paul', articulates here what is actually 'quite a common experience' (*The Epistle of Paul to the Romans* [1932], London: Collins, 1959, 127). Here, Augustine interprets Paul *as* he engages in 'introspective psychology'; Augustine's narrative tacitly presupposes the Pauline passage.

Lord, for the author of beauty created them' (Wis. 13.1, 3). According to Augustine, this substitution of a lesser, created good for the higher, uncreated good is characteristic of sin in general; sin is, as it were, parasitic on the goodness of creation. The problem is that this does not explain why he stole the pears. It is true that even these poor-quality pears were God's creatures and therefore 'good'. But that was not why he stole them. He did not want the pears, he wanted only to steal; there was no trace even of a distorted beauty or goodness in that act. An alternative definition of sin is therefore needed. Sin, we might say, is that human pride which pursues what belongs to God alone:

All who desert you and exalt themselves against you are perversely imitating you . . . What was it then that pleased me in that act of theft? And in what did I corruptly and perversely imitate my Lord? Did I wish to act contrary to your law by deceit because I had not the power to do so by force? Did I, like a prisoner with restricted liberty, do with impunity what is not permitted so as to acquire a faint resemblance of your omnipotence? (*Confessions*, ii.6.14)

It was the divine prohibition of theft that incited the sixteen-year-old Augustine to steal the pears. In Pauline language, his 'sinful passions' were at work in him 'through the law'. Human pride, aspiring to omnipotence, cannot endure the restriction of its freedom that the law represents; and so the law unwittingly provokes the very actions that it prohibits. It proves to be counterproductive.

Transgression is a defiant claim to freedom. In the act of transgression it is therefore transgression itself that is loved, as well as or even in place of the forbidden object. The theft of the pears is a 'pure' example of this love of transgression for its own sake, independent of its object, and it suggests that this same assertion of freedom may still be found in those transgressive acts where, unlike the pears, the object *is* desired. The story of the theft of the pears occurs in the context of an account of the adolescent Augustine's first sexual experiences. At this time it was his mother who represented for him the voice of the divine law. 'Whose words were they but yours which you were chanting in my ears through your mother, your faithful servant?

. . . Her concern (and in the secret of my conscience I recall the memory of her admonition, delivered with vehement anxiety) was that I should not fall into fornication, and above all that I should not commit adultery with someone else's wife' (ii.3.7). But the young Augustine is influenced more by a peer group in which 'the greater the sin the more they gloried in it – so that I took pleasure in the same vices not only for the pleasure's sake but also for the praise' (ii.3.7). In the case of the theft, it is only the presence of others that makes the sinful action pleasurable: 'Had I been alone, it would have given me absolutely no pleasure, nor would I have committed it' (ii.9.17). The object of the theft gives none of the pleasure that is found in sexual objects, but in both cases there is the pleasure of transgression itself, in which one's knowledge of oneself as a transgressor is confirmed by the admiration of one's peers.

Augustine's searching analysis of his adolescent follies recalls the Pauline description of those who, 'knowing the decree of God that those who practise such things are worthy of death, not only do them but also approve those who practise them' (Rom. 1.32). In itself, to do what is forbidden means only that the prohibition is ignored (as in the case of Monica's warning to the young Augustine); the law proves powerless to secure the obedience it seeks. But where transgression is not only practised but also approved in principle, transgression itself belongs to the object of the act. For those who are 'in the flesh' (7.5), the decree of God is a provocation that incites resistance in both deed and word. 'The mind of the flesh is hostile to God' (8.7): it does not and cannot submit to the law of God, but finds occasion in the law of God to express its hostility to God. Thus (according to Augustine's reading of the Pauline text) our 'sinful passions' are at work in us 'through the law'. Adolescent rebellion becomes a parable of human alienation from God. Using an image that recurs in Freud,[10] Augustine later argues that the law,

---

[10] Freud speaks of the construction during childhood of 'mental forces which are later to impede the course of the sexual drive and, like dams, restrict its flow – disgust, feelings of shame and the claims of aesthetic and moral ideals' (*Three Essays on Sexuality*, Penguin Freud Library 7.93). As in Augustine, libido or concupiscence is compared to the flow of a stream, which morality or law attempts to control.

however good in itself, only augments the evil desire by forbidding it – just as the rush of water which flows incessantly in a particular direction becomes more violent when it meets with any impediment, and when it has overcome the obstacle falls in greater volume, and with increased impetuosity rushes on in its downward course. In some strange way the very object which we covet becomes all the more desirable when it is forbidden [*quod concupiscitur fit iocondius dum vetatur*]. And this is the sin which by the commandment deceives and by it kills, whenever transgression is actually added, which does not occur where there is no law. (*De spir. et litt.*, 6)

Apart from the law, concupiscence would simply be a morally neutral natural force. It is 'through the law' that it is present in us in the form of 'sinful passions' for which transgression is not only a means to an end but also an end in itself.

But now we are freed from the law, having died to that which held us bound, so that we may serve in newness of the Spirit and not in oldness of the letter. (v. 6) 'The letter' draws attention to the fact that the law is a written text (cf. 2 Cor. 3.6). The writing is that of Moses, but at its heart is the divine writing of the Decalogue, 'written' [*eggegrammenē*] or 'engraved' [*entetupōmenē*] in tablets of stone by the finger of God. As Moses himself says of the Decalogue: 'These words the Lord spoke to all your assembly at the mountain out of the midst of the fire, the cloud and the thick darkness, with a loud voice, and he added no more. And he wrote them upon two tables of stone and gave them to me' (Deut. 5.22).[11] To hear the divine voice was Israel's unique privilege: 'Did any people ever hear the voice of God speaking out of the midst of the fire, as you have heard, and still live?'

---

[11] In Exodus, it is less clear than in Deuteronomy exactly what was written on the stone tablets. In Ex. 24.4, it is said that 'Moses wrote all the words of the Lord' – referring presumably both to the ten commandments (20.1–17) and to the extensive additional material in 20.22–23.33. This initial literary production is the 'book of the covenant' which Moses read 'in the hearing of the people' (24.7). Subsequently Moses is commanded to climb Mount Sinai so as to receive 'the tablets of stone, with the law and the commandment, which I have written for your instruction' (24.12); these are handed over (31.18), broken (32.15–19) and replaced (34.1–4, 29), although it is now Moses – and no longer 'the finger of God' (31.18) – who writes the 'ten words' on the stone tablets (34.27–8). If the reference is to the divine commandments of 34.10–26 (as v. 27 seems to indicate; cf. v. 10a), then the content of these stone tablets is not the decalogue of Ex. 20.

(4.33). For Paul, however, this is an event of worldwide significance. The coming of the law was an event no less universal in its scope than Adam's sin (Rom. 5.12–14, 20–1); the Gentile Christians addressed in Romans 7 are therefore 'not under law . . .' (6.14) in the sense that they are *no longer* under law. No less than Jews, they 'know the law' (7.1). Even in their pre-Christian days, they 'knew the decree of God . . .' (1.32): for 'from early generations Moses has had in every city those who preach him, for he is read every sabbath in the synagogues' (Acts 15.21). Those who were beyond the range of this preaching still had 'nature' to instruct them in the law of God (Rom. 2.14–15). Israel under the law of God discloses the situation of the entire world.

As Augustine rightly argued, the antithesis between 'letter' and 'Spirit' does not involve a contrast between the particularity of the one and the universality of the other:

Now carefully consider this entire passage, and see whether it says anything about circumcision or the sabbath or anything else relating to a foreshadowing sacrament. Does not its whole scope amount to this, that the letter which forbids sin fails to give humans life, but rather 'kills' by increasing concupiscence and by aggravating sinfulness by transgression – unless indeed grace liberates us by the law of faith, which is in Christ Jesus, when his love is shed abroad in our hearts by the Holy Spirit who is given to us? The apostle, having used these words: 'That we should serve in newness of the Spirit and not in oldness of the letter', goes on to inquire: 'What shall we say then? Is the law sin? God forbid! But I would not have known sin except by the law; I would not have known lust [*concupiscentiam nesciebam*] if the law had not said, Thou shalt not lust [*non concupisces*]. But sin, taking occasion by the commandment, wrought in me all manner of concupiscence . . .' (*De spir. et litt.*, 25)

The point here is that the law's prohibition of concupiscence (Rom. 7.7–8) is as universal in scope as the concupiscence that it unwittingly serves to generate. As Augustine points out, the same is true of the commandments, Thou shalt not commit adultery, Thou shalt not kill, Thou shalt not steal, summarized in the commandment to love our neighbour as ourself (13.8–9). 'Love is the fulfilling of the law' (13.10), and this love – the *caritas Dei* – is 'shed abroad in our hearts [*diffunditur in cordibus nostris*] by the Holy Spirit who was given to us' (5.5). 'There it was on tablets of stone that the finger of God operated; here it was on human hearts' (*De spir. et litt.*, 29). At Sinai there was fear, at Pentecost, freedom: 'The people on the earlier occasion were deterred by a terrible fear from approaching the place where the law was given, whereas in the other case the Holy Spirit came upon those who were gathered together in expectation of his promised gift' (29).

Paul's language about a service of God 'in newness of the Spirit and not in oldness of the letter' says nothing about the content of that service. Yet the idea that 'the letter' requires one set of actions and 'the Spirit' another is alien to this context, in which it is the universal heart of the law that is at issue rather than the distinctive practices of Judaism – although it is within Judaism that this universal heart of the law is disclosed. Since Paul himself will later cite commandments from the Decalogue as still binding on Christians, and then reduce them to love of neighbour (Rom. 13.8–10), it seems that Augustine's reading is correct: the letter–Spirit antithesis assumes a single *content* to the divine will for humankind and contrasts instead the *manner* in which this single content is promulgated. The law and its content remain 'holy and just and good' (7.12) for Christians, but the question is how its commandments can be fulfilled if their immediate result is simply to arouse *ta pathēmata tōn hamartiōn* and evoke resistance (7.5). The answer – Paul's and Augustine's answer – is that human fulfilment of the divine will can occur only through the Spirit (7.6, cf. 8.4), in whom 'the love of God' that is the fulfilment of the law is 'shed abroad in our hearts' (5.5). 'The fruit of the Spirit is love, joy, peace', and so on, and 'against such things there is no law' (Gal. 5.22–3): for the love of neighbour that is the fruit of the Spirit is also the fulfilment of 'the whole law' (5.14). Freedom from the law is freedom *for* the fulfilment of the law through the Spirit, and so freedom *from* the law in its absolute, abstract form as a demand that merely discloses sin and evokes resistance.

In this freedom, the law that is 'holy and just and good' and that discloses the divine will for humankind is itself freed from human arbitrariness and taken up into a new, comprehensive, trinitarian context. The 'newness of the Spirit' in which we now serve (Rom. 7.6) can also be described as our belonging 'to the one who has been raised from the dead, so that we may bear fruit for God' (7.4). In this new context, the law – which in itself is 'weak through the flesh' (8.3) – becomes the law of freedom, 'the law of the Spirit of life in Christ Jesus' (8.2); the fulfilment in us of the law's decree occurs through the Spirit and on the basis of God's sending his only Son in the likeness of sinful flesh (8.3–4). Such language indicates that the Spirit is not an independent agent but 'the Holy Spirit of the Father and the Son' (*De spir. et litt.*, 59). 'The Holy Spirit, according to the holy scriptures, is neither of the Father alone, nor of the Son alone, but of both; and so discloses to us the mutual love [*caritatem communem*] with which the Father and the Son love one another' (*De trinitate*, xv. 27). Indeed, the Holy Spirit *is* that love: 'The Holy Spirit, of whom [God] has given us, causes us to abide in God and him in us; and this it is that love does' (xv. 31). If the Holy Spirit is the mutual love of Father and Son, then we are comprehended within that love when the love of God is shed abroad in our hearts through the Holy Spirit (xv.31).

This trinitarian context of the 'newness of the Spirit' which has replaced the 'oldness of the letter' must be understood christologically, that is, in terms of the human life of Jesus: for the law is fulfilled in us through the Spirit only insofar as it is first fulfilled in him. It is true that the 'obedience' of Jesus is an 'obedience unto death, even the death of the cross' (Phil. 2.8) – an obedience to a specific, unique divine vocation. But in his obedience to this vocation Jesus also loves his neighbour and so fulfils the law: it was 'for our sake' [*di' humas*] that 'though he was rich he became poor' (2 Cor. 8.9). If, although he was 'born under the law' (Gal. 4.4), he 'knew no sin' (2 Cor. 5.21), then his sinlessness consists in his fulfilment of the law. Although Paul does not explicitly make this point, we may say that it is through the Spirit that the human Jesus fulfils the law and loves his neighbour. According to Augustine, the creative role of the Holy Spirit in Jesus' conception

is intended as a manifestation of the grace of God. For it was by this grace that a human, without any prior merit, was at the very beginning of his existence as human so united in one person with the Word of God that the very person who was Son of man was at the same time Son of God, and the very person who was Son of God was at the same time Son of man. In the adoption of his human nature into the divine, grace itself became in a way so natural to the man as to leave no room for the entrance of sin. It is this grace that is signified by the Holy Spirit; for he, though in his own nature God, may also be called the gift of God. (*Enchiridion*, 40)

Human freedom to fulfil the law and to love one's neighbour is, in the first instance, *Jesus'* freedom. This freedom of divine grace comes naturally to Jesus because grace is the origin of his being – the grace of the Spirit which in him unites a human nature that is in itself unworthy of grace with the divine nature, as the Son of man is identified with the Son of God. The mutual love of the Father and the Son, which is the Spirit, is thus identified with the mutual love of the Father and the human Jesus. Through the Spirit, the intradivine love is extended into the human realm and assumes the new form of a divine–*human* relationship of mutual love. In and through this relationship, the *telos* of human existence – which is to answer the prior divine love with love of God and of neighbour – is fulfilled. To be 'in Christ Jesus' is to participate, through the Spirit, in that *telos*.

This attempt to reconstruct a trinitarian and christological logic from the Pauline reference to the 'newness of the Spirit' set out from the fact that the new state that is ascribed to the Spirit in Romans 7.6 is also ascribed to the crucified and risen Christ and, indirectly, to God in verse 4. Through the action of the triune God, a new mode of human existence has been brought into being whose 'newness' is that of a 'new creation' (2 Cor. 5.17, Gal. 6.15). Reconstructing the logic of this divine action requires one to fill out the fragmentary although still coherent Pauline account with material from elsewhere – especially from the synoptic emphasis on the role of the Spirit in the life of Jesus. To an exegesis concerned only with the surface of texts, this may seem a questionable procedure. But a theological exegesis, concerned with the texts in their relation to their subject matter, must on occasion pursue their logic beyond what they explicitly say. 'The language of the Word of God, in order to exercise us, has caused those things to be sought into with the greater zeal which do not lie on the surface [*in promptu*] but are to be found only in the hidden depths [*in abdito*], and drawn out from there' (*De trin.*, xv.27).

A new mode of human existence, a new creation originating in the being-in-action of the triune God: this is the only possible framework for Christian ethics, and, more specifically, for our particular theme, a Christian understanding of sexuality. In retracing the Pauline argument up to this point, nothing has been said that is not directly and immediately relevant to that theme. It is this account of the divine being-in-action that is the context of Paul's reflection on the anomalies of 'desire' – concupiscence, libido – in the verses that follow.

DESIRE IN THE DESERT (VERSES 7–9)

What then shall we say? Is the law sin? Certainly not! But I would not have known sin except through the law. I would not have known desire if the law had not said, You shall not desire. (v. 7) With the death of her husband, the married woman is freed from the law; and we too have died to the law and are freed from it, so as to belong to Christ within the new life of the Spirit, bearing fruit for God. The new life contrasts with the old, in which 'the passions of sins' were at work within our bodies 'through the law'. The intimate relation of sin and law means that freedom from sin (Rom. 6) must also be freedom from the law (7.1–6). 'Sin will no longer rule over you', when 'you are not under law' (6.14). If sin and law are so intimately related, are they to be identified? Does the law provoke sin in the sense that the actions and abstentions it enjoins are actually sinful? The suggestion is absurd, but it does enable Paul to show how it is that the law can be both the holy, just and good law of God and incapable of securing for humans the 'life' that it intends. In the background here is the question why, contrary to all the expectations of Paul the Pharisee and persecutor of the church, the glory of the law has now been eclipsed by the surpassing glory of Christ (2 Cor. 3.10).

The law is not sin, but it provokes sin. The 'knowledge of sin' that it gives is a first-hand knowledge. Without the law I would not have known the sin of 'desire'; through the law sin worked in me 'every kind of desire': what would not have been known without the law is this *activity* of sin. A law that merely disclosed sin by defining it would not be a problem but would be positively beneficial; a law that in defining sin actually provokes it is another matter. The particular sin that it provokes is 'desire' (*epithumia*) – the desire prohibited by the tenth commandment. In the Masoretic form of Exodus 20.17, what is prohibited is desire for one's neighbour's property, of which a number of examples are given:

You shall not desire your neighbour's house. You shall not desire your neighbour's wife, his male or his female servant, his ox, his ass, or anything that belongs to your neighbour.

Here, the repetition of 'you shall not desire' appears to be redundant. In the parallel passage in Deut. 5.21, the order is different:

You shall not desire your neighbour's wife. And you shall not desire your neighbour's house, his field, his male or female servant, his ox, his ass, or anything that belongs to your neighbour.

In the Exodus version of the tenth commandment, the emphasis is on property, and the sexual element, present in the reference to the neighbour's wife and his female slave, is not emphasized. In the Deuteronomy version, the reversal of 'house' and 'wife' has the effect of making the sexual element much more prominent. It is because there is no difference in principle between desiring one's neighbour's house and desiring his ox that the second 'you shall not desire' is redundant in Exodus 20.17. But desiring one's neighbour's wife is quite different to desiring his house or his ox, and the effect here of the repeated 'you shall not desire' is to differentiate the desire for adultery from other kinds of desire for one's neighbour's property, thus linking the tenth commandment to the seventh as well as the eighth. As the most powerful and dangerous of all desires, sexual desire for a prohibited object is distinguished from other desires. Desire for prohibited objects may take various forms, but the sexual form is the first and most obvious of these, a paradigm for the others.

In the Septuagint version quoted by Paul in Romans 7.7, Exodus 20.17 is identical in wording to Deuteronomy 5.21. In both cases, the tenth commandment opens by prohibiting the desire for adultery (*ouk epithumēseis tēn gunaika tou plēsion sou*), and continues with a separate prohibition of desire for the neighbour's house, field, and so on, again introduced by 'you shall not desire' (*ouk epithumēseis*).[12] The result is that sexual desire is presented as paradigmatic of all desires for prohibited objects. Thus in Paul too 'desire' (*epithumia*) is not exclusively sexual, but it is primarily and paradigmatically sexual. Desire is associated with *flesh*. We are to 'put on the Lord Jesus Christ and make no provision for the desires [*eis epithumias*] of the flesh' (Rom. 13.14). Of the six prohibited practices named in the previous verse, two – *koitai*, 'beds', a euphemism for sexual intercourse, and *aselgeiai*, 'debauchery' or 'licentiousness' – are explicitly sexual, and the other four ('revelry', 'drunkenness', 'quarrelling' and 'jealousy') appear to relate not to discrete 'desires of the flesh' but to the type of social context within which illicit sexual activity takes place. 'The desires of the flesh' do not consist in a series of separate orientations, one relating to sex, another to alcohol, and so on, but to a complex of interrelated and inseparable drives which express themselves in the type of situation to which the list of prohibited practices refers. Similarly, in Galatians 5.16–17 it is said that those who walk by the Spirit 'will not fulfil the desire of the flesh [*epithumian sarkos*]', and that 'the flesh desires [*epithumei*] against the Spirit, and the Spirit against the flesh'; in Galatians 5.24 it is said that those who belong to Christ 'have crucified the flesh with its passions and desires [*sun tais pathēmasin kai tais epithumiais*]'. Once again, sexual desire is

---

[12] The significance for Paul's argument of the Septuagintal form of the tenth commandment is noted by Daniel Boyarin, in his *A Radical Jew: Paul and the Politics of Identity*, Berkeley, Los Angeles, London: University of California Press, 163. According to Boyarin, the law 'directly and necessarily stirs the passions' in the sense that, in Gen. 1.28, it 'enjoins the procreation of children' (169). The problem for this interpretation is that the specific commandment which 'worked in me every kind of desire' (7.8) is not 'Be fruitful and multiply' but 'You shall not desire' (7.7). Reading the tenth commandment back into Gen. 2–3 is possible, but does not resolve this problem.

paradigmatic here of desire in general: for 'the works of the flesh' are, first, 'fornication, uncleanness, debauchery [*porneia, akatharsia, aselgeia*]', although they also take non-sexual forms in 'idolatry, magic, enmity, quarrelling, jealousy, anger' and so on (Gal. 5.19–21). Like the English 'lust', *epithumia* can on occasion stand for sexual desire without the need to specify its object. The Thessalonians are warned to abstain from *porneia*, to keep their body (*to heautou skeuos*) in holiness and honour and not to act 'in the passion of desire [*mē en pathei epithumias*] like the Gentiles who do not know God' (1 Thes. 4.3–5). In this context, *epithumia* is closely related to the first part of the tenth commandment, 'You shall not desire [*ouk epithumēseis*] your neighbour's wife'; for in the following verse Paul warns his readers not to 'transgress and cheat one's brother in this matter' (v. 6), with obvious reference to adultery.[13]

The desire that the tenth commandment prohibits is primarily but not exclusively sexual, and the prohibition even of the desire for prohibited objects sets this commandment apart from the others by tracing the actions prohibited by the other negative commandments back to the motivation in which they originate. The tenth commandment is for Paul not just one commandment among many; like the commandment to love one's neighbour, it is a summary of the entire law. The whole law is fulfilled in the single statement: you shall not desire . . . In tracing all sin back to desire, Paul is at one with James: 'Desire

---

[13] That the tenth commandment is concerned primarily but not exclusively with sexual desire is also acknowledged by the author of 4 Maccabees, for whom the commandment, 'You shall not desire your neighbour's wife or anything else that is your neighbour's' means that 'not only is reason proved to rule over the frenzied urge of sexual desire [*tēs hēdupatheias*], but also over every desire [*pasēs epithumias*]' (4 Macc. 2.5). 'Not only' refers back to the example of Joseph that has just been cited. There is also evidence in this Hellenistic Jewish text of a negative view of *epithumia* itself, irrespective of its object. 'Self-control [*sōphrosunē*]' is dominance over the desires [*epikrateia tōn epithumiōn*]' (1.31). David on one occasion 'opposed reason to desire [*tē epithumia ton logismon*]' (3.16); for desire is in itself irrational (*alogistos epithumia*, 3.11). Thus, as in Rom. 7.7, the tenth commandment can be seen as prohibiting desire itself: the law told us 'not to desire [*mē epithumein*]' (4 Macc. 2.6). This negative sense is also present in Philo, according to whom 'the last commandment opposes desire, for he [Moses] knew desire [*tēn epithumian*] to be resourceful and insidious. For all the passions of the soul which stir and shake it against its proper nature [*para phusin*] and do not let it continue in sound health are hard to deal with, but desire is hardest of all' (*de decalogo*, 142).

[*epithumia*] when it has conceived gives birth to sin; and sin when it is full-grown brings forth death' (Jas. 1.15). If *agapē* is the positive content of the law, as 'you shall love [*agapēseis*] your neighbour as yourself' suggests (Gal. 5.14, Rom. 13.9–10), then its negative content is summarized in the prohibition even of the desire for prohibited objects. Positive and negative belong together: loving one's neighbour as oneself is incompatible with desire for his wife, or rather, with desire for the neighbour who is herself the wife of another. For the sake of *agapē*, *erōs* must be subjected to severe restrictions, so as to eliminate not just the erotic act but even the desire for it. Jesus' saying makes the same point: 'I say to you that everyone who looks at a woman to desire her [*pros to epithumēsai autēn*] has already committed adultery with her in his heart [*en tē kardia autou*]' (Matt. 5.28). This drastic restriction of 'normal' male sexual conduct is a negative consequence of the 'great commandment', which enjoins the love of God, and its corollary, the love of neighbour (Matt. 22.36–40). We do not 'love the Lord our God with all our heart [*kardia*] . . .' when that 'heart' is filled with the fantasy of sexual intercourse with the object of the erotic gaze. We do not 'love our neighbour as ourselves' when we make her (or him) the object of that fantasy. The prohibition of the desire and the fantasy is intended to create space for *agapē*.

For Augustine too, the tenth commandment is a summary of the entire law. The apostle 'purposely selected this general precept, in which he included everything, as if this were the voice of the law prohibiting us from all sin, when he says, "Thou shalt not covet" [*non concupisces*] ; for there is no sin committed except by evil concupiscence [*concupiscentia*]' (*De spir. et litt.*, 6). Here, 'concupiscence' does not refer exclusively to sexual desire. But because desire for prohibited sexual objects is the paradigmatic form of the tenth commandment, Augustine elsewhere identifies concupiscence specifically with sexual desire. When Paul confesses that 'I do not do what I want, but I do the very thing that I hate' (Rom. 7.15), it is the specifically sexual instance of concupiscence that he has in mind (*De nuptiis et concupiscentia*, i.30). 'The law too wills not that which I also will not; for it wills not that I should have concupiscence, for it says:

"Thou shalt not lust"; and I am no less unwilling to cherish so evil a desire' (i.30). The Pauline abbreviation of the tenth commandment enables Augustine to argue that concupiscence or 'lust' is itself sin, shifting the emphasis from desire for the illicit sexual object to the desire itself. Concupiscence does not belong to the original constitution of marriage; it derives from the Fall, where Adam and Eve's shame at their nakedness is symptomatic of their enslavement to a new power that has subjected the body to the primacy of genital union. The convention that nakedness, especially of the genitals, should be covered is an attempt to resist the imperative of concupiscence; and this is reinforced by the law's prohibition. Romans 7.7–25 is read as commentary on Genesis 3.

The claim that concupiscence does not belong to the original constitution of marriage will be greeted with incredulity by Pelagian or semi-Pelagian readers; but Augustine insists that the phenomenon of *shame* marks a fundamental reordering and distortion of the sexuality that belongs to the creation of humans as male and female. Challenged by his Pelagian opponent to show how there can be bodily marriage without sexual connection, Augustine replies:

I do not show him any bodily marriage without sexual connection; but then, neither does he show me any case of sexual connection which is without shame. In paradise, however, if sin had not preceded, there would indeed have been no procreation without sexual union, but this union would have been without shame; for in the sexual union there would have been a quiet acquiescence of the members, not a lust of the flesh [*concupiscentia carnis*] resulting in shame. (*De nupt. et conc.*, ii.37)

Marriage was instituted, first, for the procreation of children in accordance with the divine command, 'Be fruitful and multiply' (Gen. 1.29). 'For accomplishing this good work, various members were created, suited to each sex; these members were of course in existence before sin, but they were not objects of shame' (*De nupt. et conc.*, i.23). Marriage was instituted, second, for the maintenance of fidelity and chastity, and third, for the creation of a sacramental bond. It is said of marriage as originally created: 'A man shall leave his father and his mother,

and shall cleave to his wife, and the two shall become one flesh'
(Gen. 2.24): 'This the apostle applies to the case of Christ and
the Church, and calls it then a "great sacrament" [*sacramentum
magnum*, Eph. 5.32]. What then in Christ and the Church is
"great" is in the case of each married couple very small, but
even then it is the sacrament of an inseparable union' (v. 32).
Marriage is good, but concupiscence is evil – for the law tells us,
'Thou shalt not lust' (*non concupisces*). If sexual union was
originally accompanied by desire for pleasure, this was a desire
subject to the will which 'would arise at the summons of will just
at the time when chaste prudence would have perceived before-
hand that intercourse was necessary', quite different to the
disorderly, immoderate concupiscence to which we are now
subject and which causes us shame (*Contra duas epistolas Pelagianorum*, i.34).

Concupiscence as we now know it is inseparable from shame.
If this *concupiscentia carnis* be asked

how it is that acts now bring shame which once were free from shame,
will not her answer be that she only took up residence in the human
body after sin? And, therefore, that the apostle described her influence
as the 'law of sin', since she subjected humans to herself when they
were unwilling to remain subject to their God; and that it was she who
made the first married pair ashamed at that moment when they
covered their loins; just as everyone is still ashamed, and seeks privacy
for the sexual act, not daring even to allow children, whom they have
begotten in just this manner, to witness what they do. It was against
this modesty of natural shame that the Cynic philosophers, in the
error of their astonishing shamelessness, struggled so hard: they
thought that the intercourse of husband and wife, since it was lawful
and honourable, should therefore be performed in public. Such bare-
faced obscenity deserved to receive the name of dogs; and so they
went by the title of 'Cynics'. (*De nupt. et conc.*, i.24)

The concealment of sexual intercourse even within marriage is
a sign of the shame that is integral to concupiscence. In one
sense, the Cynics were right to think that the association
between sexual union and shame is unnatural, the product of
secondary conventions that are at odds with the law of nature;
they were right to imagine an original, shame-free sexuality.
They went wrong in failing to see the irreversible necessity of

the secondary conventions in a distorted, corrupted state in which the original state remains inaccessible. Believing the conventions to be merely arbitrary and reformable, they did not notice that the way back to paradise was barred by the cherubim and the flaming sword.

Concupiscence is thus an anonymous, impersonal power that permeates human life and penetrates into the heart even of marriage. As Paul argues, husbands and wives are not to deprive one another of sexual union – 'lest Satan tempt you through lack of self-control [*dia tēn akrasian humōn*]' (1 Cor. 7.5). This is precisely the temptation which, in a fallen world, constitutes a further reason for marriage: 'Because of the temptation to immorality [*dia de tas porneias*] each man should have his own wife and each woman her own husband' (7.2). Quite apart from the question of procreation, sexual intercourse within marriage is pragmatically necessary – although this necessity is more that of a 'permission' than of a 'command' (7.6) – since its purpose is to *contain* the concupiscence of both man and woman, which might otherwise express itself in acts of *porneia*. 'To escape this evil, even those embraces of husband and wife that do not have procreation as their object, but serve an overbearing concupiscence, are permitted, so far as to be within range of forgiveness, though not prescribed by way of commandment . . . Now in a case where permission [*venia*] must be given, it certainly cannot be argued that there is not some amount of sin' (*De nupt. et conc.*, i.16). Augustine's intention here is to underline the continuity between the concupiscence which finds expression in acts of *porneia* and that which occurs in marriage. If marital intercourse is in part a substitute for *porneia*, and if, in its absence, *porneia* may in turn be a substitute for marital intercourse, then something of the character of *porneia* must be present even within marital intercourse. The happily married couple, whose sexual fidelity to one another is never seriously tested, is perhaps not in a position to cast the first stone at the less fortunate. Yet marriage is indeed the divinely ordained context in which the evil of concupiscence is restrained and indeed put to good use.

According to Augustine, it is permissible to seek the pleasure of sexual union rather than procreation so long as there is no attempt actually to prevent conception. This qualification is not directed against the modern concept of 'family planning'. Augustine's criticism is directed against those (he assumes them to be legally married) who detach the divine permission from the divine command by practising sexual intercourse in the context of a settled intention not to have children. This intention is expressed in a variety of practices, contraceptive and otherwise:

Having proceeded thus far, they are betrayed into exposing their children, which were born against their will. They hate to nourish and retain those whom they were afraid they would beget. This infliction of cruelty on their offspring, so reluctantly begotten, unmasks the sin which they had practised in darkness and drags it clearly into the light of day. The open cruelty reproves the concealed sin. Sometimes, indeed, this lustful cruelty, or cruel lust, resorts to such extravagant methods as to use poisonous drugs to secure barrenness; or else, if unsuccessful in this, to destroy the conceived seed by some means previous to birth, preferring that its offspring should rather perish than receive vitality; or if it was advancing in life within the womb, should be slain before it was born. (*De nupt. et conc.*, i.17)

Contraception is linked with abortion and exposure insofar as it is practised as a means not of 'family planning' but of family prevention or family destruction. In this context, it serves as a first line of defence against the disaster of the 'unwanted pregnancy', that is, of the unwanted child. If this fails, a second line of defence is available: the child in the womb may be surgically removed. (If that is its appointed destiny, it is described as a 'foetus'.) If this too fails or is omitted, the child may be abandoned after birth. The disadvantage of this method in comparison to the others lies in its 'open cruelty'. The secret shame of concupiscence, which in a marriage open to procreation is restrained and put to good use, issues here in the public shame of abandoning a fellow human being to the mercy of the fates and the elements. It is understandable that public opinion should favour the destruction of unwanted children at an earlier stage, when concealment is still possible; but even where the third line of defence is abandoned, the defensive strategy to which it belonged remains intact. Contraception and abortion together preserve the hegemony of sex. They protect the integrity of paradise by promising that the couple who become one flesh there will not have to face any undesirable consequences. Although the concupiscence that rules this paradise is also present in the sphere of marital fidelity and the family ('planned' or otherwise), it does not rule there. Within the sphere of its hegemony, concupiscence 'plays the king in the foul indulgences of adultery, fornication, lasciviousness and uncleanness, whereas in the indisputable duties of the married state it shows the docility of the slave' (*De nupt. et conc.*, i.13).

The prohibition, 'Thou shalt not lust' (*non concupisces*) is the basis for Augustine's depiction of *concupiscentia* as a corruption of the human nature that was created male and female. But, as Paul argues, the problem about this prohibition is that it is counterproductive (Rom. 7.7–9). Despite its own intentions, it serves only to promote the *concupiscentia* it prohibits. It is integral to the paradise-like hegemony of sex to be *illicit*. Like the serpent in Genesis 3, sin can use even the holy, just and good commandment of God to further its own ends.

But sin, finding its opportunity through the commandment, worked in me every kind of desire. Apart from the law sin lies dead. I was once alive apart from the law; but when the commandment came sin sprang to life and I died. (vv. 8–9) Sin used the commandment to produce in me every kind of desire (v. 8). Here the claim of verse 5 is repeated, that 'the passions of sins were *through the law* at work in our members . . .' But although the law is instrumental in the genesis of sin, it is not the active agent in this process. The law is indeed 'counterproductive', but it does not 'produce' the sin it defines and condemns by itself. It is sin itself, the orientation towards sin that is latent before the law, that makes itself manifest in sinful desires or actions provoked by the law. The law's prohibition awakens a previously dormant rebellion or resentment, which expresses itself in a desire for the illicit not because it is necessarily desirable in itself but simply because it is illicit. The young Augustine and his friends steal the forbidden fruit because it is forbidden; their latent adolescent resistance to authority is aroused not by the fruit in itself but by the fact that it is prohibited. The sin that is merely latent apart from the commandment becomes manifest through the commandment.

Sin is like the serpent in the Garden of Eden, who uses the commandment prohibiting the fruit of the tree of the knowledge of good and evil to evoke desire for that fruit. But in the Garden of Eden it is eating that was prohibited, not desiring. The commandment, 'You shall not desire', was promulgated not in Eden but at Sinai. It was 'when the commandment came' (*elthousēs de tēs entolēs*) that 'sin revived and I died . . .' (vv. 9–10), and the coming of the commandment can only be that event in which 'law came in [*pareisēlthen*] so that the trespass [*to paraptōma*] might increase' (5.20). Sin was dead 'apart from law' (7.8), and I was once alive 'apart from law' (7.9). There was therefore a time before the coming of the commandment, the time 'from Adam to Moses' (5.14) during which, in the absence of law, sin was 'not counted' (5.13). In Eden, there was no such time before the commandment. It is true that the coming of the commandment brought death to one who previously lived (7.9–11), whereas from Adam to Moses 'death reigned' even though sin was not counted (5.14). But in both passages the point is that the law made the situation of humanity after Adam worse rather than better. In the earlier passage, the situation becomes worse because through the law 'the trespass' – Adam's trespass – 'increased'. Before Moses, people did not sin 'in the likeness of Adam's transgression [*parabasis*]' (5.14); after Moses they did so, in the sense that they now sinned in conscious defiance of an explicit divine commandment. The coming of the law can therefore be seen as a re-enactment of the story of the Fall, a second transition from life to death. If the ministry of Moses is a 'ministry [*diakonia*] of death' (2 Cor. 3.7), and if 'the letter kills' (v. 6), then the people of Israel who received this 'letter' in the form of 'stone tablets' (v. 7) must have been 'alive' before the glorious ministry of Moses brought death to them.[14]

---

[14] The significance of Adam for the interpretation of this passage is often exaggerated. According to Käsemann, 'a story is told in vv. 9–11 and . . . the event depicted can refer strictly only to Adam' (*Commentary on Romans* [1973], ET London: SCM Press,

According to Romans 7, 'the letter' brought death to the people of Israel because it provoked the very sin it prohibited. The coming of the commandment, 'You shall not desire', aroused every kind of desire for forbidden objects, and sin led to death (*dia tēs hamartias ho thanatos*, 5.12). We shall in due course answer the question why the first person singular is used in this passage. The first task is to show in more detail how it can credibly be understood as a reflection on Israel's experience in the wilderness.[15]

At Sinai, the commandment came: 'You shall not desire' (*ouk

<hr>

1980, 196); so too H. Schlier, *Der Römerbrief*, Herders theologischer Kommentar zum Neuen Testament, Freiburg im Breisgau: Herder, 1977, 223 ('Dieses Geschehen ist die Geschichte Adams, den jeder Mensch in seiner Existenz im Nachvollzug der Sünde präsent macht'); U. Wilckens, *Der Brief an die Römer*, Evangelisch-katholischer Kommentar zum Neuen Testament, Zürich, Einsiedeln, Cologne: Benziger/Neukirchener Verlag, 1980, 2.79 ('in der Geschichte des "Ich" wird Adams Geschichte je existentiell konkret'). In opposition to this, N. T. Wright rightly argues that 'the primary emphasis of the argument is on Israel, not Adam: what is being asserted about Israel is that when the Torah arrived it had the same effect on her as God's commandment in the Garden had on Adam' (*The Climax of the Covenant: Christ and the Law in Pauline Theology*, Edinburgh: T. & T. Clark, 1991, 197). See also D. J. Moo, 'Israel and Paul in Rom. 7.7–12', *NTS* 32 (1986), 122–35. The shortcomings of the 'Adamic' reading of this passage are also noted by R. H. Gundry, 'The Moral Frustration of Paul before his Conversion: Sexual Lust in Romans 7:7–25', in *Pauline Studies: Essays presented to F. F. Bruce*, ed. D. A. Hagner and M. J. Harris, Exeter: Paternoster, 1980, 228–45; 230–2.

15 Does Paul in Rom. 7.7–13 consciously 'intend' the intertextual links with passages in the Psalms and the Pentateuch that are explored in what follows, and does he 'intend' to communicate these links to his readers? Richard Hays identifies five possible explanations for the phenomenon of the textual 'echo', the hermeneutical event of a textual fusion: the event occurs in the mind of the author, in the original readers, in the text itself, in the act of reading, in a community of interpretation (*Echoes of Scripture in the Letters of Paul*, New Haven and London: Yale University Press, 1989, 26). Rather than aligning himself with any one of these hermeneutical options, Hays wishes to 'hold them all together in creative tension' (27). 'The hermeneutical event occurs in my reading of the text, but my reading always proceeds within a community of interpretation, whose hermeneutical conventions inform my reading. Prominent among these conventions are the convictions that a proposed interpretation must be justified with reference to evidence provided both by the text's rhetorical structure and by what can be known through critical investigation about the author and original readers. Any interpretation must respect these constraints in order to be persuasive within my reading community' (28). My own claim is that Rom. 7.7–13 can be read, credibly and naturally, against the background of narrative texts in the Pentateuch and the Psalter. Beyond that, we are in the realm of supposition: I assume that this intertextual matrix was not far from Paul's mind as he wrote, and that the more perceptive among his first readers might have recognized this.

epithumēseis). Did it really provoke 'every kind of desire' (*pasan epithumian*)? Israel's experience in the wilderness was indeed an experience of desire. According to Psalms 105.14–15, 'They desired [with] desire in the wilderness [*kai epethumēsan epithumian en tē erēmō*], and they tested God in the desert. And he gave them what they asked, and sent fullness [*plēsmonēn*] into their souls.' The reference is to Numbers 11, where it is said that

> the rabble that was among them desired [with] desire [*epethumēsan epithumian*], and seating themselves the sons of Israel wept and said, Who will give us meat to eat? We remember [*emnēsthēmen*] the fish that we ate in Egypt for nothing, and the cucumbers, melons, leeks, onions and garlic; but now our soul is dried up, and there is nothing but manna before our eyes. (vv. 4–6)

In response, the Lord promises to provide the people with meat every day for a month, until they are sick of it – 'because they disobeyed [*ēpeithēsate*] the Lord who is among you' (vv. 18–20). A wind from the Lord brings a glut of quails, which the people gather (vv. 31–2). But

> while the meat was still between their teeth, before it was consumed, the Lord was angry with the people and the Lord smote the people with a very great plague. And the name of that place was called Tombs-of-Desire [*Mnēmata tēs Epithumias*], because there they buried the people who had desired [*ton laon ton epithumētēn*]. From Tombs-of-Desire [*apo Mnēmatōn Epithumias*] the people journeyed to Aseroth, and the people were in Aseroth. (vv. 33–5)

The memorials to desire are mentioned again in Numbers 33.16–17, in the context of an itinerary that takes the people of Israel from Egypt to the plains of Moab (vv. 1–49), and in Deuteronomy 9.22, where Moses reminds the people how 'at Conflagration [*en tō Empurismō*] and at Testing [*en tō Peirasmō*] and at Tombs-of-Desire [*en tois Mnēmasin tēs Epithumias*] you angered the Lord your God'. ('Conflagration' is 'Taberah', so called because there 'a fire from the Lord' [*pur para kuriou*] burned among the people (Num. 11.3). 'Testing' (cf. Deut. 6.16) is 'Massah', where the people of Israel put the Lord to the test by demanding water; its full name is Testing-and-Abuse [*Peirasmos kai Loidorēsis*], 'because of the abuse [*loidorian*] of the sons of Israel and because they tested the Lord [*dia to peirazein kurion*], saying, Is the Lord among us or not?' (Ex. 17.7).) The brief reference to these ill-fated places in Deuteronomy 9.22 occurs in the context of the claim that the people will inherit the promised land not on account of their righteousness but in spite of their stubborn and rebellious heart (Deut. 9.1–10.11); the incident of the Golden Calf is narrated here at length. Thus 'desire' takes its place in a narrative of rebellion against God that is also characterized by idolatry and by 'testing'. As in Romans 7.9–11, desire leads to death – a fact that is commemorated in the place-name, 'Tombs-of-Desire'. The people who desired remembered the rich food of Egypt, but they themselves were remembered only in the form of the warning embedded in the place-name. The link between desire and death is especially clear in Psalms 77.26–31:

He caused an east wind to blow from heaven, and led out the south wind by his power. And he rained upon them flesh like dust, winged birds like the sand of the seas, and made them fall in the midst of their camp, around their tents. And they ate and were well satisfied, for he brought them their desire [*ten epithumian autōn*]. They were not rid of their desire [*apo tēs epithumias autōn*], their food was still in their mouths, when the wrath of God [*hē orgē tou theou*] fell upon them; he killed [*apekteinen*] as they drank, as the elect [*tous eklektous*] of Israel danced together.

Even for the elect of Israel, desire leads to death. As in Romans 7.7–11, the desire that leads to death is rebellion against God.

In 1 Corinthians 10.6–11, Paul himself describes Israel's experience in the wilderness in terms of desire and death. Here, 'desire' is no longer tied to the single incident of the quails. A number of incidents of rebellion and death in the wilderness substantiate the warning that we are not to be 'desirers of evil things [*epithumētas kakōn*], as they desired [*epethumēsan*]' (v. 6). Desire issues, first, in idolatry, the making of the Golden Calf together with the revelry that accompanied it: 'The people sat to eat and drink and rose to play' (v. 7, quoting Ex. 32.6). Desire issues, second, in *porneia*. 'We must not commit fornication, as some of them committed fornication, and twenty-three thousand fell in one day' (v. 8). The reference is to another instance of idolatry, when 'the people profaned itself by committing fornication [*ekporneusai*] with the daughters of Moab. They invited them to the sacrifices of their idols, and the people ate of their sacrifices and worshipped their idols' (Num. 25.1–2). Twenty-four thousand people died in the ensuing plague (v. 9), which was halted by the zeal of Phinehas, who pierced an Israelite man and a Moabite woman through the body with a single thrust of his spear, as they engaged in the sexual act (vv. 6–8). Desire issues, third, in 'putting the Lord [or, the Christ] to the test, as some of them put him to the test and were destroyed by snakes' (1 Cor. 10.9). On this occasion, 'the people spoke against God and against Moses, saying, Why did you bring us out from Egypt, to kill us in the wilderness? For there is no bread or water, and our soul is tired of this worthless food' (Num. 21.5). The plague of snakes that followed was halted by the setting up of a bronze snake on a pole, which brought healing to those who looked at it (v. 9). It is not explicitly said here that those who spoke against God and Moses 'put the Lord to the test'. But in Numbers 14.22 it is said that the people 'have put me to the test these ten times, and have not listened to my voice' – indicating that 'putting the Lord to the test' by making demands of him is a constant theme of these narratives. 'They tested him again and again, and provoked the Holy One of Israel' (Ps. 78(77).4). Finally, desire issues in complaining: 'Do not complain, as some of them complained and were destroyed by the destroyer' (1 Cor. 10.10). Shortly after their deliverance at the Red Sea, the people begin to 'complain' about their lot (Ex. 15.24, 16.7–12); Exodus 17.2–3 indicates that 'complaining' against Moses cannot be sharply distinguished from 'putting the Lord to the test'. But it is only after the giving of the law at Sinai that this tendency to complain leads to destruction. In Numbers 14, the complaints that follow the report of the spies (v. 2) lead to the divine proclamation that the present generation of Israelites will, with just two exceptions, perish in the wilderness (vv. 26–35). In Numbers 16, the Levites' complaints against Aaron's priestly prerogatives (v. 11) result in the destruction of Korah, Dathan and Abiram and their company. When the people complain that 'you have killed the people of the Lord' (v. 41), the killing continues as a plague destroys many more people. In each of these incidents of idolatry, immorality, testing and complaining, the people of Israel show themselves to be 'desirers of evil' (1 Cor. 10.6). All of these narratives are 'memorials of desire' (*Mnēmata tēs Epithumias*). They warn their readers not to desire the evil that the Israelites once desired.

According to Romans 7.7–9, 'I was once alive apart from the commandment'; at that time, 'sin lay dead'. But then 'the commandment came' – the commandment, 'You shall not desire' – with the result that 'sin, taking opportunity through the commandment, worked in me every kind of desire'. Initially, I was alive and sin was dead; but through the law, sin came to life and I died. We have seen that in 1 Corinthians 10 Paul presents Israel's experience in the wilderness as a history of evil desire – extending a theme that in the Pentateuch is confined to the single incident in Numbers 11. Although in 1 Corinthians 10 Paul does not imply that the law was instrumental in generating this desire, the reduction of the tenth commandment to a general prohibition of desire in Romans 7.7 creates a link with his earlier reading of the wilderness narratives as a history of desire. The examples of idolatry, *porneia*, testing and complaining that he selects all *follow* the giving of the law, for it is only from Sinai onwards that Israel's rebellious actions have the destructive consequences that Paul emphasizes. It is true that incidents of putting the Lord to the test and of complaining occur before as well as after the event at Sinai. But idolatry and *porneia* occur only afterwards; they are closely associated in the Pentateuchal stories (Ex. 32 and Num. 25), which tell of two occasions when the people transgress the first and second commandments, and when transgression leads to death. In these events, 'the letter kills'; the ministry of Moses turns out to be a 'ministry of death' (2 Cor. 3.6–7). But the law does not kill of itself. 'It was sin, working death in me through what was good . . .' (Rom. 7.13). 'Sin, finding opportunity in the commandment, deceived me and by it killed me' (7.11): it is this event that is commemorated in the place-name – in Latin, *Sepulchra Concupiscentiae*. The latent sin of the people, hardly a significant factor prior to the revelation at Sinai, expresses itself immediately afterwards in actions that wilfully transgress the

commandments. In Paul's reading of this history, the fact of the
divine prohibition has the effect of making idolatry and the
porneia that is associated with it *desirable*. In these acts, a latent
resistance to the God of the exodus and of the fathers, of which
the testing and complaining are already symptomatic, becomes
manifest and visible in crude acts of defiance. For Paul, it is the
law itself which, by prohibiting desire, actually provokes the
desire that comes to expression in the demand, 'Up, make us
gods who shall go before us; as for this man Moses, who
brought us out of Egypt, we do not know what has become of
him' (Ex. 32.1). The claim that sinful passions operate in our
members 'through the law' (Rom. 7.5) is an attempt to explain
how a people who at Sinai solemnly attest, 'All that the Lord
has spoken we will do and hear' (Ex. 24.7) are shortly afterwards
practising *porneia* and idolatry with the daughters of Moab
(Num. 25.1–2).

The law of God provokes a resistance in the sinful human
heart that issues in acts where what is desired is the transgression itself: that is the theme both of Augustine's autobiographical reading of the incident of the pear tree and of
Paul's autobiographical reading of the history of Israel in the
wilderness. This 'autobiographical' dimension of the Pauline
narrative now requires closer attention.

EGO AND ALTER EGO (VERSES 10–25)

*I found that the commandment that promised life brought me death. For
sin, finding its opportunity through the commandment, deceived me and
through it killed me.* (vv. 10–11) As in the preceding verses, motifs
from Genesis 2–3 are visible here. As the serpent in the Garden
of Eden found in the divine commandment the opportunity it
needed to deceive the first human couple and to bring about
their death, so in this first-person narrative the pattern of the
Fall is re-enacted. In confessing how sin 'deceived me' (*exēpatēsen
me*), the speaker identifies himself with Eve, who confessed that
'the serpent deceived me [*ēpatēsen me*]' (Gen. 3.13). 'As the
serpent deceived [*exēpatēsen*] Eve by his cunning' (2 Cor. 11.3), so
now sin has 'deceived me'. Yet, as we have seen, the nexus of

life, death, sin and the commandment relates primarily to the history of Israel in the wilderness. It cannot be said of the single commandment in the Garden of Eden that it promised life. It was a commandment 'unto life' (*eis zōēn*) only in the very general sense that observing it allowed Adam and Eve unhindered access to the tree of life. The commandment that is 'unto life' is the Law of Moses, for it is promised here that 'the person who observes these things will live by them [*zēsetai en autois*]' (Lev. 18.5, quoted in Rom. 10.5, Gal. 3.12). Thus the speaker's experience re-enacts the pattern of the Fall only insofar as this is projected onto the history of Israel in the wilderness. Motifs from Genesis help to interpret this history, in which Adam's transgression comes to fruition (Rom. 5.12–14, 20); but the first person narrative cannot be read simply as a retelling of the Genesis story. The speaker is identified with Eve or Adam only insofar as Israel is.

At the beginning of Romans 7, second person plural verbs are used in addressing predominantly Gentile readers (v. 1, 4ab). In verses 4c–6, Paul identifies himself with his readers by shifting to the first person plural. With the exception only of 'what then shall we say?' (v. 7) and 'we know that the law is spiritual' (v. 14), verses 7–25 are consistent in their use of the first person singular, which has previously occurred only in 'I speak to those who know the law' (v. 1) and in 'my brothers' (v. 4). If the speaker is in some sense Paul himself, then he must be speaking in a representative capacity; his first person discourse would have no bearing on his claim that 'we' are freed from 'the oldness of the letter' (v. 6) if he were speaking of a purely individual experience. Since it is the history of Israel in the wilderness that is retold in this first person narrative, Paul must be speaking as a representative of Israel. Elsewhere in this letter, he speaks of himself not only as a slave and apostle of Jesus Christ (1.1) but also as 'an Israelite, of the seed of Abraham and the tribe of Benjamin' (11.1). As such, he represents in his own person the fact that 'God has not rejected his people whom he foreknew' (11.2); for the 'Israelites', to whom belong 'the sonship and the glory and the covenants and the giving of the law and the worship and the promises', are 'my brethren' and 'my kinsmen according to the flesh' (9.3–4). In chapter 7, he can therefore speak as a representative Jew in whom Israel's initial highly ambivalent experience of the law is re-enacted.

Yet the event at Sinai is for Paul universal in its scope. The situation of Jews under the law discloses the situation of the world. In the first person story of the Jewish narrator in Romans 7, Gentiles such as Augustine can also read their own stories. The story that is told is a tragic story, the story of a catastrophe. It explains how it came about that one who is the privileged recipient of 'the words of God' (3.2) is nevertheless condemned as a transgressor by those same divine words, over and over again (3.9–20). The divine words that point the way to life have led only to death, because sin, finding its opportunity through the commandment, deceived me and worked in me sin and death. The Israelite who speaks here is closely related to the earlier figure of the Jew who zealously teaches the law to those who are in darkness and yet transgresses its commandments himself (2.17–24). But he is also related to the 'man' (whether Gentile or Jew) who judges another: 'For in passing judgment on him you condemn yourself, because you, the judge, are doing the very same things' (2.1). Every attempt to live right-eously in an unrighteous world is subverted by the fact that 'all have sinned' (3.23); this attempt and its failure become visible in the figure of a Jew such as Paul himself, but, once identified, the pattern can also be traced elsewhere. The Pharisee and the tax-collector in the temple are hardly exclusively Jewish figures.

The tragedy or catastrophe, presented so starkly on page after page of Jewish scripture, is embraced within a divine comedy: 'Where sin increased, grace abounded all the more' (Rom. 5.20). The speaker in chapter 7 is not only an Israelite who must tell how the divine gift led to his death; he is also an apostle called to proclaim a God who raises the dead. The Israelite and the apostle are one. The story-teller who narrates the divine comedy must also be capable of narrating the human tragedy, if he is to show how in Jesus (another Israelite) the divine grace and mercy have triumphed over human sin. In Jesus, the 'oldness of the letter' has been embraced and surpassed in the 'newness of the Spirit' (v. 6). As his sad story reaches its conclusion, the story-teller will therefore lament and give thanks as if in a single breath: 'Wretched man that I am! Who will deliver me from the body of this death? Thanks be to God through Jesus Christ our Lord!' (vv. 24–5).

So the law is holy and the commandment is holy and just and good. Did what is good bring death to me, then? Certainly not! It was sin, so that it might be exposed as sin, that worked death in me through what is good, so that sin might become exceedingly sinful through the commandment. (vv. 12–13) The law does not generate sin of itself. It is sin – latent sin – which uses the law to make itself manifest. Thus the law itself is good, and cannot be held responsible for its disastrous consequences, beginning with the cycle of rebellion and punishment that characterized Israel's experience in the wilderness. If, because of the sin latent in the human heart, the law provokes the sin that it forbids and is therefore the bringer of death rather than life, that does not detract from its divine glory. If it can be said that the glory of the law has now been eclipsed by a glory that surpasses it (2 Cor. 3.7–11), the reason is that the 'life' and 'righteousness' that the law intends are now fulfilled in the resurrection of Jesus Christ, so that the judgment pronounced by the law is not God's last word to humankind. The contrast between 'the oldness of the letter' and 'the newness of the Spirit' (Rom. 7.6) disparages not the law but the human sin that not only fails to obey the law but also uses it to further its own rebellious purposes. The law's inability of itself to place humankind on the way to life is the result not just of human weakness but of human malice. If 'the power of sin is the law' (1 Cor. 15.56), this is an indictment not of the law but of the sinful human heart. 'The heart is deceitful above all things, and desperately corrupt; who can understand it?' (Jer. 17.9). It is the deceitful human heart that uses even the divine gift of the law at Sinai as an occasion for sin, and that necessitates a 'new covenant' in which the intention of the old, that 'I will be their God and they shall be my people', is at last fulfilled (31.31–3). It is fulfilled through a death and a resurrection: 'You have died to the law through the body of Christ, so that you may belong to another, to the one who has been raised from the dead so that we may bear fruit for God' (Rom. 7.4). In Christ's death, the deceitful human heart is 'condemned' (Rom. 8.3). The new covenant is therefore 'the new covenant in my blood' (1 Cor. 11.25). In Christ's resurrection, we are incorporated through the Spirit into his own life of bearing fruit for God. The new covenant is therefore the work of the life-giving Spirit (2 Cor. 3.6). Jesus is the 'Israelite' in whom the promise that 'I will be your God and they shall be my people' is fulfilled; God is therefore 'the God and Father of our Lord Jesus Christ' (15.6) and Jesus is 'his Son' (1.3, 8.3). It is this covenantal relationship into which we are incorporated through the Spirit, so that we too address God as 'Abba, Father' (8.15).

In this covenantal relationship, the law is surpassed and superseded insofar as, in itself, it represents the 'ministry of death' (2 Cor. 3.7). But its commandment remains 'holy and just and good' (Rom. 7.12). It still identifies the pattern of human conduct that conforms to the will of God and that is 'good and acceptable and perfect' before God (12.2). Christian *agapē* is the love for the neighbour that fulfils the law and that is variously expressed in the individual commandments: You shall not commit adultery, you shall not kill, you shall not steal, you shall not desire (13.8–10). The idolatry and *porneia* that the law forbids but unwittingly provokes are also forbidden within the new covenant, where the imperatives are no less uncompromising. 'Flee from idolatry' (1 Cor. 10.14). 'Flee immorality' (6.18). In showing how the new covenant takes up this pattern of conduct, which in itself leads only to sin and death when exposed to the deceitful human heart, 'we affirm the law' rather than annulling it (3.31).

For we know that the law is spiritual, but I am carnal, sold under sin. For what I do I do not recognize; for I do not do what I want, but I do what I hate. If I do what I do not want, I accept that the law is good, and it is now no longer I that do it but sin dwelling within me. (vv. 14–17) Indwelling, latent sin has used what is good in order to manifest itself in sinful actions that lead to death (v. 13). This is a past event that occurred at Sinai and that has its correlate in the speaker's past life. The catastrophe at Sinai, where the deceitful human heart learned to further its own ends through the divine commandment, was not a matter for the wilderness generation alone; it is a paradigm of Israel's entire history with God as presented in the scriptural record, and the individual Israelite is therefore implicated in it. Since Israel's history with God represents human history with God, it can be said that what is disclosed at Sinai is simply 'human nature' – not the human nature that Adam and Eve received from God, but the human nature that they passed on to their descendants.

In the shift to the present tense, the narrator begins to speak of the life he now lives in the shadow of the catastrophe. This narrator is Paul, a Jew who confesses: 'I am an Israelite, of the seed of Abraham and the tribe of Benjamin' (11.1). The *ego eimi* of that confession is identical to the *ego eimi* of 7.14: 'I am carnal, sold under sin'. Paul is an Israelite who is also an apostle of Jesus Christ, but for the present the first aspect of his vocation is considered in abstraction from the second. He knows that he is carnal, sold under sin, because the law tells him so. He has heard the words of condemnation that the law addresses to 'those who are under the law', and he acknowledges the law's verdict on behalf of 'the whole world', 'all flesh' (3.19–20). He affirms the goodness of the law as embodying the divine will for humankind, he disowns the hostility and resistance to God that the law evoked in his corrupt heart – and yet he must also confess that traces of this hostility and resistance are everywhere evident in his own conduct. Having learned from the law about his true situation, he is in no position to 'establish a right-eousness of his own' (10.3) but echoes the confession of Daniel:

O Lord, the great and terrible God, who keepest covenant and steadfast love with those who love him and keep his commandments, we have sinned and done wrong and acted wickedly and rebelled, turning aside from thy commandments and ordinances. We have not listened to thy servants the prophets, who spoke in thy name to our kings, our princes and our fathers, and to all the people of the land. To thee, O Lord, belongs righteousness, but to us confusion of face . . . (Dn. 9.4–7)

In his confession, the Israelite represents a mid-point between the deceitful heart, in which the divine gift of the law serves

only to evoke resistance and hostility to God, and the new
covenant established in the death and resurrection of Jesus, who
is also an Israelite (Rom. 9.4). The confession is a confession of
what one *is* and of what human nature *is*, yet in the act of
confession what one *is* is relegated to the past; what one *is* is
now the person who confesses what one *was* but *is* no longer. 'I
do what I hate' (7.15): the 'I' that performs the evil action is
supplanted by the 'I' that hates this action because it contra-
venes the law which is acknowledged as holy and just and good.
From the standpoint of this confession, 'it is *now no longer I* that
do it but sin dwelling within me' (v. 17). The law provides no
escape from this dialectic of sin and repentance; yet, in the
retrospective light of the new covenant, it becomes clear that
the problematic self-knowledge expressed in it is integral to the
testimony of the law and the prophets to 'the righteousness of
God through the faith of Jesus Christ' (3.21–2).

For I know that nothing good dwells within me, that is, within my flesh.
For to will is possible for me, but to do what is good is not. For I do not do
the good I want, but the evil I do not want is what I do. If I do what I do
not want, it is no longer I that do it but sin dwelling within me.
(vv. 18–20) 'I know that nothing good dwells within me . . .' is
parallel to 'I am carnal, sold under sin' in v. 14, which opens
with a statement of what 'we know'. This is the knowledge of
human nature, exemplified in one's own person, that corresponds to the discovery that I do what I do not want. The
moment of discovery is the moment of confession, and in this
account willing is tied to that moment. 'The good I want' is the
good I want in the moment of confession. To confess that 'we
have left undone those things which we ought to have done and
done those things which we ought not to have done' is already
to will the good and to acknowledge the gulf between present
willing and past doing. But only in that moment of confession
does a willing arise that critically detaches itself from doing. It
cannot be the speaker's view that in the human person there
coexist in parallel an unwilled, involuntary action and an
impotent willing of a quite different action, as though the self
were trapped in a machine over which it has no control. Action

is always voluntary, willed action; involuntary responses to a stimulus are not 'action'. The willing that in confession detaches itself from action denies not that action was willed but that *I* – the *ego* that is now the subject of confession – willed it. In confession, the willing that accompanied the action that one now 'hates' is disowned and attributed to an *alter ego* that is not-I but 'sin dwelling within me'. Yet when I act I am the subject of my actions; I identify myself again with the *alter ego* I disowned, and I no longer hate my actions or myself as the subject of my actions.[16]

This dialectic of sin and repentance appears to arise from an original encounter with the law in which sin sprang to life and I died. The sin that once found its opportunity in the law and by it killed me is the sin that still dwells within me and subverts my willing of the good that the law intends. Despite the seamless continuity of the narrative, however, the view that it is distinctively *Christian* experience that is depicted in Rom. 7.14–25 has remained influential.[17] Augustine explains how he reached that conclusion:

It had once appeared to me too that the apostle was in this argument of his describing a man under the law. But afterwards I was compelled to give up the idea by those words where he says, 'Now then it is no longer I that do it' – for to this corresponds what he later says, 'There is therefore now no condemnation to those who are in Christ Jesus' – and also because I do not see how a man under the law could say, 'I delight in the law of God after the inward man', since this very delight in good . . . can only be attributed to grace. (*Con. duas epist.*, i.22)

Augustine maintains this view over against the Pelagian claim that the passage depicts the person under the law. In his *De*

---

[16] In Augustine's reading, willing the good and doing the evil are simultaneous because it is the tenth commandment, forbidding *concupiscentia*, that is at the same time affirmed and transgressed. Although I shall follow Augustine's reading of vv. 21–3 in terms of Gen. 3, I do not think that the conflict described in vv. 14–23 can be confined to *epithumia* and the tenth commandment if the text is read on its own terms.

[17] Cranfield approvingly cites Calvin's comment, that in this passage Paul 'is depicting in his own person the character and extent of the weakness of believers' (*Romans*, 1.356); see also A. Nygren, *Commentary on Romans* [1944], ET London: SCM Press, 1952, 284–303; John Murray, *The Epistle to the Romans*, New International Commentary on the New Testament, Grand Rapids: Eerdmans, 1959, where 7.14–25 is entitled 'the contradiction in the believer' (256).

gratia Christi, he quotes Pelagius' own interpretation of the passage, taken from a dialogue with an Augustinian opponent. Pelagius writes:

Now, that which you wish us to understand of the apostle himself, all church writers assert that he spoke in the person of the sinner, and of one who was still under the law – such a man as was, because vice had long been customary with him, held bound, as it were, by a certain necessity of sinning, and who although he desired good with his will in practice indeed was rushed headlong into evil. In the person, however, of one man, the apostle designates the people who still sinned under the ancient law. This nation he declares was to be delivered from this evil of custom through Christ, who first of all remits all sins in baptism to those who believe in him, and then urges them by an imitation of himself to perfect holiness, and by the example of his own virtues overcomes the evil custom of their sins. (*De grat. Chr.*, i.43)

On any reading, the passage is a problem for Pelagius, for whom the freedom originally bestowed on Adam must still survive unimpaired. Although Pelagius does not admit this, the 'man under the law' is on his view labouring under a misapprehension. This man believes that the habit of sin makes sin necessary, failing to recognize that he still retains the freedom to break with that habit. He is, in effect, an Augustinian. In other words, the passage opposes the Pelagian position whether the speaker is held to be a Christian or a Jew. The only advantage Pelagius derives from his claim that the apostle speaks here as a person under the law is that this makes it possible to contradict him.

Augustine's claim that 'delight in the law' is inconceivable for the 'man under law' is contradicted by Jewish scripture, where the hostility to the law that runs through the history of Israel is always presented from a standpoint of loyalty to the law as the law of God. Israel's ambivalence towards the law stems from its position on the boundary between the corrupted human nature of the 'deceitful heart' and the human nature renewed in and through the obedience of Jesus.

This is what I discover, then, about the law: that when I will the good, evil is present to me. For I delight in the law of God in my inner self, but I see

another law in my members, fighting against the law my mind acknowl-
edges, and making me captive to the law of sin that is in my members.
(vv. 21–3) The conflict between willing the good and doing the
evil is now redescribed as a conflict between the law of God
acknowledged by the mind and the law of sin acknowledged by
my members. This conflict is described as a discovery about the
law, which does not give me the capacity to resist those
imperatives of the body that it denounces as sinful.[18] The
earlier reflection on the law's involvement in the origins of sin is
here replaced by an emphasis on its *powerlessness*; the law was
'weak through the flesh' (8.3). Yet the law that proves to be both
counterproductive and ineffectual remains the holy, just and
good law of God, in which the mind delights. It is counterproductive and ineffectual only in abstraction from the new
covenant in which it attains its true *telos*.

The precise content of the good that is willed and the evil
that is done has been left vague in the preceding verses. In
vv. 7–12, however, the entire law is summarized in the single
commandment, 'You shall not desire'. Sexual desire – Augustine's *concupiscentia* – is for Paul the paradigmatic instance of the
desire the law prohibits. This makes it possible for Augustine to
assume that 'the law of sin that is in my members' is to be
identified with concupiscence – the concupiscence that Adam
and Eve first experienced when they knew themselves to be
naked:

When the first man transgressed the law of God, he began to have
another law in his members which was repugnant to the law of his
mind, and he felt the evil of his own disobedience when he experienced in the disobedience of his own flesh a most righteous retribution
recoiling on himself. (*De nupt. et conc.*, i.7)

The Pauline text is read here as a commentary on the events
narrated in Genesis 3, the function of which is to point out that
concupiscentia entails a loss of control over the body, in the form

---

[18] In 7.21, *ton nomon* is usually understood as 'the principle', for which appeal is made to
3.27 (so J. Fitzmyer, *Romans*, Anchor Bible, New York: Doubleday, 1993, 475). With
Dunn, (*Romans 1–8*, Word Biblical Commentary, Dallas: Word Books, 1988, 392–3),
I assume that this is a statement about the law itself; *heurisko ara ton nomon* (7.21) recalls
heurethē moi hē entolē (7.10).

of a reorganization of the body around the genitals. Thus the overtly sexual dimension of the Genesis narrative is interpreted along the lines of the Pauline text, which is accordingly interpreted as an analysis of sexuality. In this intertextual relationship, each text exercises a certain influence over the other as they are drawn into a problematic that arises not from their individual sense but from their fusion. The possibility of this fusion is suggested to Augustine by one small detail of the Genesis text – the fact that, when Adam and Eve knew themselves to be naked, they made themselves *perizōmata* (Gen. 3.7), that is, garments that concealed the genitals. This is an unexpected outcome of their transgression:

> If those members by which sin was committed were to be covered after the sin, they ought not indeed to have been clothed in loin-cloths [*in tunicis*] but to have covered their hand and mouth, because they sinned by taking and eating. What then is the meaning, when the prohibited food was taken and the transgression of the commandment had been committed, of the look turned towards those members? What unknown novelty is felt there and compels itself to be noticed? (*Con. duas epist.*, i.32)

The answer is that the law of sin was already at work in their members, opposing the law of their minds:

> Since they were suddenly so ashamed of their nakedness – which they had daily been in the habit of seeing, but were not confused by it – that they could now no longer bear those members naked, but immediately took care to cover them, did they not – he in the visible motion [*in motu aperto*], she in the hidden one [*in occulto*] – perceive those members to be disobedient to the choice of their will, which certainly they ought to have ruled like the rest by their voluntary command? And this they deservedly suffered, because they also were not obedient to their Lord. Therefore they blushed that they had so failed to serve their Creator that they should deserve to lose control over those members by which children were to be procreated. (i.32)

This lack of control is an anomaly within our bodily constitution:

> It is significant that the eyes, lips, tongue, hands and feet, the bending of the back, neck and sides, are all subject to our power – to be applied to such actions as are suitable to them, when we have a body free from physical handicaps and in a sound state of health; but when

it comes to man's great function in the procreation of children, the members which were expressly created for this purpose will not obey the direction of the will, but lust has to be awaited to set these members in motion, as if it had a legal right over them – so that sometimes it refuses to act when the mind wills, while more often it acts against its will. (*De nupt. et conc.*, i.7)

Whether through impotence or involuntary, unwelcome sexual arousal, the disobedient male genitals evoke *shame* (in which the female genitals, their object, are also implicated); and this shame is a symptom of the underlying cause of shame, the human failure to worship and serve the Creator. In involuntary sexual arousal, the 'mind' (*nous*) that 'delights in the law of God' may find itself at odds with the 'flesh' (unlike the 'mind [*phronēma*] of the flesh' (Rom. 8.7) that is hostile to the law of God and delights in the law of sin). At this point, the conflict between willing and doing (7.14–21) is traced back to a conflict that precedes action – the conflict between the mind's acquiescence in the commandment, 'You shall not desire', and the quasi-autonomous 'desire' through which the entire body is reoriented towards the genitals and so reveals its humiliating subjection to the 'law of sin'. It is this conflict that causes Adam and Eve to be, for the first time, ashamed of their nakedness and to hide the bodily parts on which that shame is focused. Augustine's phenomenology of sexuality shows that the link between sexuality and shame is basic. Symptoms of this may be traced across a range of phenomena: public conventions about 'decency' of clothing or speech; the uneasy pleasure of sexual innuendo or jokes; anxieties about sexual 'performance'; the excitement and hostility aroused by other people's sexual behaviour; the voyeuristic obsession with the 'sexually explicit' image or word; the guilt that often accompanies the practice of masturbation; the tensions that surround the sex education of children; the intense emotional ambivalences associated with the erect penis and female pubic hair. These and many other inexplicable phenomena of sexuality – culturally variable though they may be – are all symptoms of the Pauline and Augustinian 'law of sin which is in my members'.

Wretched man that I am! Who will deliver me from the body of this death? Thanks be to God through Jesus Christ our Lord! So then I myself serve the law of God with the mind, but with the flesh the law of sin. (vv. 24–5) We have seen that the apostle is speaking in this passage not as an apostle but as a 'man under the law' who has attained disturbing insights into the complex relationship of law and sin. But it is only as a Christian that he can impersonate this man. Gentiles as well as Jews may attain insights that resemble the position of this Pauline 'man under the law'. (Epictetus wishes to convince his pupil that 'he is not doing what he wishes and is doing what he does not wish [*ho thelei ou poiei kai ho mē thelei poiei*]' (*Discourses*, ii.26.4). Paul himself envisages Gentiles whose conscience bears witness that the work of the law is inscribed on their hearts, as it condemns or approves their conduct (Rom. 2.14–15).) But neither Jew nor Gentile has any reason to draw the radical Pauline conclusions about the law itself – that the divine law, holy and just and good though it is, is instrumental in establishing the possibility and actuality of sin, which it is powerless to prevent. A veil (Moses' veil) conceals these bitter truths when the law is read week by week in the synagogue (2 Cor. 3.14–15), and when its requirements are proclaimed by the Jewish teacher (Rom. 2.17–24) or the Gentile moralist (Rom. 2.1–5). It is 'when one turns to the Lord' that 'the veil is taken away' (2 Cor. 3.16), so that one sees for the first time what the corrupt human heart has made of the law – in the dawning light of the knowledge of what the God of the new covenant has made of the corrupt human heart, through Jesus and his Spirit.[19]

---

[19] This interpretation of the *ego* in Rom. 7.7–25 is only superficially similar to the position of W. G. Kümmel, in his *Römer 7 und die Bekehrung des Paulus* [1929], repr. Munich: Kaiser, 1974. According to Kümmel, the passage is a retrospective description of a non-Christian longing for redemption, but from a Christian standpoint (118); it is not a rendering of any particular autobiographical experience, and the use of the first person is a rhetorical device (87). On my view, the passage is a Christian rendering of the distinctively Jewish experience of the law, in which Israel under the law is representative of humankind; the speaker can therefore be identified as Paul himself, but speaking as a Jew. The theme of the passage is neither a general human 'longing for redemption' nor an experience from which non-Jews are excluded. Kümmel's position is anticipated by R. Bultmann, in his 'Das Problem der Ethik bei

Insight into 'the oldness of the letter' arises from knowledge of 'the newness of the Spirit' (Rom. 7.6) and of the one 'who has been raised from the dead in order that we may be fruitful for God' (7.4). Within the sphere of the *koinōnia* established by the action of the triune God, the 'law of sin' is not only unmasked but also overcome. The captive who in Romans 7 speaks from within the narrow confines of his prison cell must hear the proclamation of his liberation:

There is no condemnation now, for those who are in Christ Jesus: for the law of the Spirit of life in Christ Jesus has freed you [*se*] from the law of sin and death. For what was impossible for the law [*to adunaton tou nomou*], in that it was weak through the flesh, God has done: sending his own Son in the likeness of sinful flesh and as an offering for sin, he condemned sin in the flesh, so that the law's decree might be fulfilled in us, who walk not according to the flesh but according to the Spirit. (Rom. 8.1–4)

Freedom from the 'law of sin' that makes the body a 'body of death' is actualized through the Spirit, on the basis of the divine condemnation of sin that occurs in the human life, death and resurrection of Jesus. In his life, Jesus bears the *likeness* of sinful flesh, although he himself is 'without sin' (2 Cor. 5.21). His life already expresses his solidarity with the 'wretched man' of Romans 7. In his death, Jesus identifies himself so completely with the man or woman under the dominion of the law of sin that he himself endures the divine condemnation of that dominion: God 'made him to be sin for us' (2 Cor. 5.21). It is therefore 'you' – Christian readers, men or women, in Rome or elsewhere – who 'died to the law through the body of Christ' (Rom. 7.5), and who now participate in his risen life.

Paulus', *Zeitschrift für neutestamentliche Wissenschaft* 23 (1924), 123–40; 130 (see also Bultmann's later article, 'Romans 7 and the Anthropology of Paul' [1932], ET in *Existence and Faith*, ed. S. Ogden, London: Collins, 1964, 147–57). In opposition to an autobiographical reading and to the pietistic understanding of sin and guilt to which it gives rise, Bultmann argues that sin is not a perceptible entity in the empirical human life but the self-sufficient attempt, provoked by the law (cf. Rom. 7.7–8), to establish oneself in relationship with God – the attempt that is exposed and renounced in the event of faith (135–6). In analysing the various proposed identifications of the speaker in Rom. 7.7–25 (there are 'at least five' of these, according to J. Fitzmyer, *Romans*, 463–5), it is important to bear in mind that superficially similar solutions may differ from one another both exegetically and theologically.

This knowledge of the triune divine action breaks into the end of the lament, in the form of a thanksgiving: 'Thanks be to God through Jesus Christ our Lord!' (Rom. 7.25). It is true that, as Augustine says, the vestiges of *concupiscentia* will only finally be eliminated in the renewal of the human body at the resurrection of the dead. Until that day, the exhortation, 'Let not sin reign in your mortal bodies, to make you obey their passions' (6.12) will never be redundant. Yet the Christian community lives already on the basis of the divine act that has condemned the corrupt and deceitful human heart and brought a new creation into being. That is the reality acknowledged by the thanksgiving.

PART III

Sacramentum: *Ephesians 5*

A man leaves his father and his mother and is joined to his wife, so that the two become one flesh. This is not the only way in which man and woman belong together, nor is it the primary way. But among the various aspects of their belonging together, there is also this one: their becoming one flesh. Where this event participates in the love of Christ that reconciles the church and all things to himself, it may be said: *sacramentum hoc magnum est.* If the veil marks the limit of eros in order to preserve the space of agape, there is no corresponding limit of agape; for an agape deriving from the breadth and length and height and depth of the love of Christ knows no limit but must occupy this sphere too, the space of the eros of man and woman.

This space may appear to be self-contained and self-sufficient, withdrawn from the eyes of the profane – a sacred space within which sacrifices are performed that celebrate the divinity of the flesh. But the flesh is not divine, and neither is eros: these are creaturely realities, and their original goodness is that of the creature. The agape that overflows into this space too exposes the pretensions of pseudo-divinities and restores to them their proper creaturely status, bringing harmony and proportion where there was previously wilfulness and excess.

As Luce Irigaray argues, sexual ethics must show how the two remain two and indeed are constituted as two as they become one flesh. Their oneness is not the dissolution of their twoness but a third that embraces them; an undifferentiated oneness is a symptom of a male projection onto the other that denies her personhood and refashions her in the image of its own need. Unfortunately, Irigaray's sensitivity to the irreducibility of male–female difference is not matched by an awareness of the irreducibility of divine–human difference: in eros, it is assumed, humanity is divinized and divinity incarnated. Eros is transfigured, and male–female erotic oneness and difference assume metaphysical importance. Something similar occurs in theology itself, where the erotic relation is traced back to a gendered archetype in the relation of God to the world or Christ to the church (Barth, von Balthasar). But no such apotheosis of eros or gender occurs in the Pauline text to which appeal is made (Eph. 5). The eros of man and woman is at best a parable – one among many – of the divine–human agape disclosed in Jesus. Eros and gender remain purely creaturely realities, but they too participate in the assumption and transfiguration of the creature within the divine agape.

CHAPTER FIVE

Eros transfigured?

In order to secure the space of agape, within which the speech of men and women with each other corresponds to their speech to and from God, eros had to be limited. His limit was marked by the veil – a visible sign, bound to a particular cultural context and questionable even there, of the invisible reality of a boundary that must be established wherever there is *ekklesia*, in which woman is not apart from man nor man from woman. In the Lord, the belonging-together of man and woman is not an erotic relation. 'Man' and 'woman' are present here not as potential sexual partners, to be identified as such by way of the erotically charged look that seeks out the face and body that might provide an answer to its insistent question, but as called in Christ to be together in agape.

In the union of the Christian with Christ, there is a fruit-bearing for God that supersedes the fruit-bearing for death that occurs under the law. The law's prohibition of desire is sin's opportunity to generate every kind of prohibited desire; for the divine law is the place where the possibility of human autonomy is established. Yet the possibility of an autonomous desire subject only to its own law is excluded by a death and a resurrection, through which the intent of the law – a pattern of human conduct oriented towards life rather than death – is fulfilled. The commandment, 'You shall love your neighbour as yourself' is fulfilled as, in union with Christ and through the Spirit, there is fruit-bearing for God. But the commandment in which the whole law is summarized also has a negative counterpart: 'You shall not desire.' Space for agape is again ensured by the exclusion of eros. Sexual desire is an expression of a law of sin in my members that is at war with the law of my mind. This desire is, however, a corrupted derivative of that mutual desire of man and woman to belong to one another and, within this relationship, to fulfil the divine command and permission to be nothing less than co-creators. The corruption of this original goodness is not absolute, and in Christ the *telos* of this work of co-creation or pro-creation is disclosed as death and resurrection.

In these Pauline reflections, is eros the victim of slander and of caricature? Is there a malicious blindness here to the greatness of eros, despite the testimony of common human experience? What is at stake here is not a 'negative' view of eros but the distinction between its goodness as the creature of God and the claim to divinity that constitutes its corruption. As a creature of God, eros may serve as a parable of the divine–human relationship. In the union of man and woman as 'one flesh', the relationship of Christ and the *ekklēsia* may be prophetically foreshadowed (Eph. 5.31–2). The kingdom of God is like a sower going forth to sow, it is like a woman baking bread or searching for a lost coin, it is like a man who finds a pearl of great price – and it is like the erotic union that also belongs to human life as given by God. Sexual union is neither more nor less like the kingdom of God than sowing or baking. If there is a co-creation in the one case, there is equally a co-creation in the others. But in all these cases, this is a *creaturely* co-creation: sexual union does not divinize the human creature any more than sowing or baking does, nor does it bestow any participation in divinity. The celebration of eros as divine is no less a sign of its corruption than is the shame that celebration represses.

In the work of Luce Irigaray, an ethic of sexual difference is set within the horizon of a divine eros that bestows divinity on the man and woman who participate, as two and as one, in the sexual act. This ethic is opposed to an understanding of sexuality in which the female role is to 'satisfy' male 'needs' – which is a denial of 'difference' in the sense that woman becomes the projection of man's self-image and lacks a subjectivity and personhood of her own. In Irigaray's ethics, 'difference' is not mere heterogeneity or *in*difference: it is both the ground and the fruit of the belonging-together of man and woman that culminates in sexual union. In setting the ethical act of man and woman within the horizon of divinity, Irigaray has recourse to biblical and Christian terminology – understood in a self-consciously 'heterodox' manner. This makes it possible to reopen the question of the relation of agape and eros that her 'eroticism' forecloses.[1]

Following Irigaray's own intertextual practice, this inter-action with her philosophy of eros will take the form of a 'reading' of a chapter of one of her texts – the introductory reflections on 'Sexual Difference' in her *An Ethics of Sexual Difference*.[2]

THE DOMINION OF EROS

'Sexual difference is one of the major philosophical issues, if not the issue, of our age. According to Heidegger, each age has one issue to think through, and one only. Sexual difference is probably the issue in our time which could be our "salvation" if we thought it through'. (Ethics, 5)

[1] Reading Irigaray in terms of the agape–eros problematic means that I have little to say here about her so-called 'essentialist' account of gender, in its opposition to constructionist accounts. According to Margaret Whitford, interpretation of Irigaray has long been hindered by 'the deadlock produced by the terms of the essentialist/antiessentialist debate'; in opposition to this, 'the multiplicity for which she is celebrated should be a prescription for the reader as well' ('Reading Irigaray in the Nineties', in C. Burke, N. Schor, M. Whitford (eds.), *Engaging with Irigaray*, New York: Columbia University Press, 1994, 15–33, 15–16). However, Irigaray's advocacy of a feminism of difference, in opposition to a feminism of equality, is related to the essentialist–constructionist distinction and is one of a number of points at which her work diverges from most recent north American feminist theology: see her critique of Elisabeth Schüssler Fiorenza's *In Memory of Her*, 'Equal to Whom?', ET in *differences* 1 (1988), 59–76. Another such divergence may be seen in Irigaray's insistence that in their difference man and woman belong together: see her sharply critical comments on a purely 'between-women sociality' in *i love to you: Sketch of a Possible Felicity in History* (1992), ET London and New York: Routledge, 1996, 1–6.

[2] Works cited in the main text of this chapter are as follows: *An Ethics of Sexual Difference* (1984), ET London: Athlone Press, 1993; *This Sex which is Not One* (1977), ET New York: Cornell University Press, 1985; *Marine Lover of Friedrich Nietzsche* (1980), ET New York: Columbia University Press, 1991; 'Women-mothers: the silent substratum of the social order' (1981), ET in *The Irigaray Reader*, ed. Margaret Whitford, Oxford: Blackwell: 1991, 47–52; *Thinking the Difference: For a Peaceful Revolution* (1989), London: Athlone Press, 1994; *je, tu, nous: Toward a Culture of Difference* (1990), ET London and New York: Routledge, 1993.

Is Heidegger right when he pronounces that 'each age has one issue to think through', and adds, for still greater emphasis: 'and one only'? On that view, which is also Irigaray's, it is 'an age' that thinks and speaks in the person of the philosopher. At a particular moment in its unfolding, Spirit or *Geist* thinks itself, and at *this* moment – our moment – it must think itself not in its dialectical identity with itself but in the original, undialectical, irreducible *difference* that lies concealed behind every such claim to identity. Without detriment to its divinity, Spirit is the human spirit: it was the philosophical task of an earlier age to establish this identity. Building on this achievement, our age is called to recognize in 'the human spirit' itself a secondary abstraction from the original fact that 'spirit' is always qualified as male or female. Male and female are not secondary derivatives of spirit but its primary embodiments, and spirit is therefore twofold. The notion of a unitary spirit that embraces difference is (perhaps) the product of a Judaeo-Christian monotheistic prejudice; the apparent 'naturalness' of this monotheism in the development of human thought may be nothing other than the 'naturalness' of patriarchy, a sign of its success in banishing the old gods and goddesses and disguising the limited, male perspective of which it is the projection. The task of a post-Christian, post-monotheistic age, 'after the death of God', is to think through the twofoldness that has so long been concealed. If this twofoldness is the single issue of 'our' age, then – insofar as the possessive pronoun includes both women and men – the difference that is 'our' allotted subject matter will require a differential treatment. Woman and man will think through this difference from opposite sides of the boundary that divides them, and their thinking will never simply coincide. Yet it is 'one issue, and one only' that is given to them to think through, on behalf of the 'age' for which they speak. A unitary *Geist* continues to hover above the articulation of 'sexual difference', ensuring that the dialogical form issues in a monological content.

'Our age' articulates itself through its art and literature, but above all through its *philosophy*; only in philosophy is the issue imposed on us adequately 'thought through'. There is no place here for *theology*. The theme of theology is *theos*, 'God', and our age knows itself to be an age 'after the death of God'. Like Heidegger and Nietzsche, Irigaray sees in the death of God the necessary darkness that precedes the dawning of a new day in which the gods are reborn. Philosophy too speaks of *theos* – but not in such a way as to share a subject matter with theology. The death of God is the death of the *Christian* God; and yet this God remains the subject matter of theology. Here, in defiance of 'our age', this God is acknowledged still as 'the living God'. Our age cannot permit theology to play any part in its self-articulation, for theology is guilty of a great and fundamental *anachronism*, the sin against the age itself – however skilfully it contrives to mimic contemporaneity. The time for rational discourse (*logos*) about this *theos* has long since passed; but the time of the 'wisdom' (*sophia*) beloved by philosophy is always present. In the face of this exclusion order, theology can only appeal to the fact that, where the theme of 'sexual difference' has been announced, a dialogue between a 'masculine' *logos* and a 'feminine' *sophia* might be a more appropriate expression of this theme than a philosophical monologue. Whether or not 'our age' speaks in this dialogue is perhaps (*pace* Heidegger) not very important.

Setting aside the mythology of the age, its single issue and its philosophical mouthpiece, we acknowledge that 'sexual difference' is indeed an important contemporary issue. But what is this 'sexual difference'? The phrase is ambiguous. 'Sexual difference' is that difference that pertains to sex. But sex is twofold: sex is gender, and it is sexual intercourse. Sexual difference is either the difference that pertains to sexual intercourse or the difference that pertains to gender; it takes either a narrower or a broader form. In the first case, the man and woman whose sexual difference is to be investigated are naked together, in preparation for the sexual act. Their difference is displayed in the difference of their genital organs, normally concealed but here revealed; the concern will be to establish that the 'difference' in question is not that of an inversion, in which one becomes – in Irigaray's terms – the 'container' or 'envelope' for the other, but a genuine heterogeneity or otherness which must be respected if the act is to be ethical. In the second case – 'sexual difference' as gender difference – the man and woman (now clothed) are observed as they act and speak in the course of their 'everyday life'. Although they are clothed (perhaps very similarly), it cannot be said that their 'sexual difference' is concealed here and is uncovered only in their physical nakedness. Sexual difference is nowhere concealed and everywhere manifest; and, in this broad sense, sexual difference is one of the major issues of our age because, although ubiquitous and fundamental, it has until now rarely received the attention that it merits.

For Irigaray, 'sexual difference' embraces both gender difference in general and respect for otherness within the sexual act in particular. It is assumed that the sexual act is located at the *centre* of the relations between the sexes. In this act, everything that occurs between man and woman is gathered together and brought to light with a peculiar clarity and intensity; at this point, the fundamental quality of the entire relationship is disclosed. The sexual act has a representative function in relation to the other acts and speech-acts in which man and woman engage with one another. For Irigaray, the key to gender difference – in all its ramifications – lies in ethical sex. Sex (sexual intercourse) is the *telos* towards which the male–female relationship naturally gravitates, and if all is well here – if otherness is respected – then all will be well on the way that leads to it and from it. Since to be human is always to be human as male or female, sex as the key to the male–female relationship is also the key to our humanity. It is therefore in the act of sexual union and differentiation that we are most human and most ourselves as male or female: to eros is assigned a virtually unqualified dominion over human existence. Granted the fact of that dominion, the issue for our age is how this can be truly an *ethical* dominion.

Within the dominion of eros sex is compulsory, and this law creates great difficulties for Irigaray as a reader of the gospels. The women who encounter Christ do so merely as virgins or repentant sinners: 'Are they nothing but ears? With just a bit of mouth, eyes, and as much hand and leg as is needed to reach out and follow after Him. They seek Him, not He them. If He does occasionally take notice of them, it is out of his infinite benevolence, neither needed nor earned. Sex is virtually absent from their meetings, except for a few confessions or avowals of morbid symptoms. He listens, but does not marry/ make merry with women, for already he is bound to his heavenly Father' (*Marine Lover*, 165–6). 'Was he like that? Or has tradition made him like that? The place of his loves is rendered as virgin, or childlike, or adolescent. Must the Christic redemption mean that the advent of the divine has never taken place in the incarnation of a loving relation with the other? Must this messenger of life neglect or refuse the most elementary realities? Must he be a timid or morbid adolescent, too paralyzed to realize his desires, always attentive to his Father's edicts, executing the Father's wishes even to the point of accepting the passion and the Father's desertion as the price of such fidelity . . .? Who interpreted him in this way? Who abominated the body so much that he glorified the son of man for being abstinent, castrated?' (177). The Father is the deity who in his hatred for life forbids one passion – 'you shall not desire' – and commands another, in which the flesh of his own son is torn apart.

Outside the dominion of eros and the law of compulsory sex, one might read the gospels differently. Jesus, as rendered in the gospel narratives, might serve to expose the contemporary mythology which claims that humanity without sex (sexual intercourse) is defective, that we become fully human only in and through sex, that it is sex alone that establishes us as male or female, and that agape without eros is an expression of hatred of life and the body. On the other hand, if this mythology is held to be true, one might take up Irigaray's suggestion ('has tradition made him like that?') and postulate a sexually active Jesus (heterosexual or homosexual, according to taste) that tradition has sought to conceal. One might follow the lead of another writer, who reports that 'particularly in recent years there has been a passionate discussion of the question whether Jesus had intimate relationships with Mary Magdalene'. There is, after all, biblical evidence for this: in their Johannine post-resurrection encounter, 'there seems to be a delight, a happiness, an eroticism which transcend the teacher–pupil relationship'.[3] From a standpoint such as this, a Jesus portrayed as neither heterosexual nor homosexual, who commends those who castrate themselves for the sake of the kingdom of heaven, *cannot* be the real Jesus because he cannot truly 'love': the evangelists' apparent omission of sexuality from their rendering of Jesus' varied relations to others is a *skandalon* to contemporary piety. They appear to have believed that Jesus' 'sexuality' was as unimportant to his identity as the Christ as his physical appearance – about which they are also silent.

'Sexual difference would constitute the horizon of worlds more fecund than any known to date – at least in the West – and without reducing fecundity to the reproduction of bodies and flesh. For loving partners this would be a fecundity of birth and regeneration, but also the production of a new age of thought, art, poetry, and language: the creation of a new poetics'. (*Ethics,* 5)

'Sexual difference' is the difference presupposed in and established by the sexual act when it is performed ethically, in a manner respectful of the other. The sexual act may or may not lie at the centre of the relationship of man and woman, that whole manifold relationship may or may not gravitate towards it; but the ethical significance of the sexual act is clear even if its precise scope remains undetermined. It is significant that, among the various relationships derived from the twofoldness of human nature, there is this 'sexual' relationship – not simply a relationship in which, contingently, sexual acts occur, but a relationship *constituted* by this occurrence although not reducible to it. Can it be said that the sexual act lies at the centre of *this* form of the relationship of man and woman, that in this act they are most fully themselves at least in their relation to this particular other? Is this act truly a 'consummation', an act that perfects, completes and fulfils, spreading like a canopy over the entire relationship? 'This locus of my concentration and of his opening out without futile dispersion constitutes a possible

---

[3] E. Moltmann-Wendel, *The Women around Jesus,* ET New York: Crossroad, 1986, 87, 85.

habitation. Turning back on itself and protecting me until the next encounter. A kind of house that shelters without enclosing me, untying and tying me to the other, as one who helps me build and inhabit. Discharging me from a deadly fusion and uniting me through an acknowledgment of who is capable of building this place. My pleasure being, in a way, the material, one of the materials. Architects are needed. Architects of beauty who fashion jouissance – a very subtle material' (*Ethics*, 214). The dwelling-place is formed just *here*, on the site of the encounters that constitute the 'sexual relationship', because there occurs here, uniquely, a 'communion in the secret depths of the sensible realm' (211). (But might there not be *many* possibilities of such a communion? Does the sexual relationship hold a monopoly over the secret depths? Is the sexual act pure depth without banality or irony, a sacred rite performed in a temple? Does it establish itself as a dwelling-place *ex nihilo*, or does it find its natural habitat within an existing, material dwelling-place: a *home*, a place of settled co-habitation? Does this idealism of the flesh lack a material substructure?)[4]

The sexual act establishes sexual difference; it is not to be described simply as 'sexual union', for union means oneness and in the sexual act there are two as well as one. It is as an act of two that it is 'fecund' and fruitful. 'For loving partners this would be a fecundity of birth and regeneration . . .', and this fecundity is not to be reduced 'to the reproduction of bodies and flesh'. Each individually, and the two together, give birth to one another in and through the sexual act; in the act itself the command to be fruitful and multiply is *already* fulfilled. The act is complete in itself, it is consummation and perfection. It is an act of two not of one, but also not of three. It does not open out towards a third, an other who is as yet unknown and merely

---

[4] A similar criticism of Irigaray's idealism is made by Tina Beattie: 'In her near-wholesale rejection of social institutions such as marriage, the family and the church, she . . . risks sacrificing living worlds of value, joy and sexual love on the altar of a vision that she acknowledges is precarious and possibly unattainable' ('Carnal Love and Spiritual Imagination: Can Luce Irigaray and John Paul II Come Together?', in J. Davies and G. Loughlin (eds.), *Sex These Days: Essays on Theology, Sexuality and Society*, Sheffield: Sheffield Academic Press, 1997, 160–83, 182). The rejection of social institutions is characteristic of what I have called 'the discourse of sex'.

potential. The future onto which it opens out is its own future, the future in which the sexual encounter of two 'loving partners' will again be re-enacted as the architects resume their delicate labours. The fruitfulness of the encounter is not to be 'reduced' to 'reproduction', but there is no corresponding warning against reducing this fruitfulness to two, to the exclusion of the potential third. Is the exclusion or marginalizing of the potential third (a merely biological fruitfulness) a *necessary condition* of the true, spiritual fruitfulness? Granted that the two must face one another and not look away to the potential third, must the third be excluded from the communion of this mutual look? (That is not the case within the doctrine of the Trinity.) If so, the sexual act in its purest and most transparent form may require an *act* of exclusion, an act dependent no longer upon nature but upon technology. By one technique or another, male semen and female ovum must be kept apart, lest there should occur a 'deadly fusion' and the loss of their twofoldness. Where the fusion is allowed to occur this is an epiphenomenon of the act itself, in which the creation of sexual difference is already fruitful in and of itself. The potential third party has no part to play in the sexual relationship of these 'loving partners'. They have eyes only for each other. Erotic idealism envisages 'a new age of thought, art, poetry, and language', but it cannot encompass the flesh of the child.

A child will turn the 'loving partners' into a mother and a father, bound to one another anew, in and through the child. The potential third party will irrevocably *change* the loving partners; and according to Irigaray, he or she will thereby *endanger* them. The child is a threat to their spiritual fecundity.

In the breakthrough from sex into conception, pregnancy and birth, one of the loving partners is transformed into a mother. The ordeal of childbirth is an initiation into motherhood, and this is all too easily misunderstood as a transition into 'full' womanhood. Imperceptibly and without theoretical reflection, 'woman' comes to mean 'mother'. 'Most of the time women only make contact with each other in the context of discussions concerning their children . . . But is this definition, originally a male one, suitable for us? Or should we think about a different female identity, in which the sufferings and joys of motherhood are no longer the criteria for identification?' (*je, tu, nous,* 102, 103). The motherhood of the one partner turns the other into a father, and this transition too may be regressive in tendency. The loving partner may become a patriarch. If, for example, the potential mother freely chooses to terminate her pregnancy, her male partner may suddenly announce himself a devotee of the cult of 'the precious paternal seed', determined that 'the mother-mistress can and must suffer, or even die . . . in order to honour those chromosomes of the male race, that priceless *logos spermatikos*' (*Marine Lover,* 170). In the transition to parenthood there is an acute danger of forgetting that 'be fruitful and multiply' does not 'simply mean "make children" for the Father, but rather, create oneself and grow in the grace of fleshly fulfilment' (170). To create oneself, and not 'simply' to make a child: in ethical sex one excludes the potential third party, together with the threat to personal integrity that it entails. In this way one practises safe sex.

Parenthood poses yet another danger to the fecundity of sexual difference: the child displaces the sexual act from the centre of the partners' relationship. There is perhaps a grain of truth in Freud's largely false claim that for the mother the child serves as a substitute for the penis she has always envied. But this claim needs to be rewritten: for both parents, the child recentres a previously erotically focused relationship around itself. The child displaces eros from the centre of the relationship. The relationship is not *reducible* to the child, any more than it was previously reducible to eros, but if it can be said to have a 'centre' at all the child stands somewhere near that centre. Eros does not disappear when displaced by the child, but the sexual act will henceforth be the sexual act not simply of 'loving partners' but of parents. *If* the fecundity of eros is dependent on there being neither one nor three but two, then eros will never again be fecund. Eros is therefore the mortal enemy of the child. As in the *Symposium* (an older classic of erotic idealism), eros prefers a spiritual progeny to a fleshly one. Is an idealism that can speak disparagingly of 'the reproduction of bodies and flesh', as though this were a matter of little consequence, really a credible advocate of the human body, male and female? In its insistent celebration of the flesh, is there a silent drift towards an ambivalence, even a hostility, towards the flesh: the flesh of the child, maternal flesh, paternal flesh?[5]

There may indeed be personal loss as well as gain in parenthood, and especially in motherhood. A tacit identification of womanhood and motherhood is indeed oppressive and destructive. But what Irigaray gains in rejecting the law of compulsory motherhood she loses by insisting on the law of compulsory sex. Her attack on the Jesus of the gospels for flouting this law is an attack on everyone else, male or female, who rejects the dominion of eros. Jesus, we recall, 'neglects or refuses the most elementary realities' in his practice of sexual abstinence; he is 'a timid or morbid adolescent, too paralyzed to realize his desires'. Who was it that 'abominated the body so much' that he presented us with this pathetic, castrated figure? Here Irigaray speaks for a certain understanding of manhood, in which sexual experience – preferably extra-marital – is an initiation rite that establishes one as a 'real man'. Despite her critique of the concept of 'equality', this understanding of manhood is extended to womanhood in strictly egalitarian fashion. One can be a woman without motherhood, but can one be a real woman without sex? The women around Jesus are themselves implicated in his unfortunate sexual abstinence. 'Are they nothing but ears? With just a bit of mouth, eyes, and as much hand and leg as is needed to reach out and follow after Him.' Do they not possess the complete faces, arms, legs, breasts, and, in a word, *bodies* that would enable them to become his 'loving partners' rather than his servile 'followers'? Irigaray is in agreement with this man and these women when she insists that one can be woman or man without being mother or father. But she does not even notice this agreement. What she does notice in the gospels is the claim that one can be

---

[5] Irigaray's constant emphasis on the importance of the mother–daughter relationship might lead one to qualify this judgment (see for example 'The Bodily Encounter with the Mother' [1981], in *The Irigaray Reader*, 34–46). But her reflections on the 'genealogy of women' are concerned with the daughter's re-establishing the broken link with the mother, as an instance of the need for a genuine intersubjectivity among women. Even here, there is little reflection on the role of the mother *as a mother*.

man or woman without sex. How unethical! What a denial of the body! 'Is not the body more than clothing?' (Matt. 6.25). But the body is not more than sex. Sex is the secret source of all its fecundity. Without sex it withers and dies.

UNNATURAL LAW

'If traditionally, and as a mother, woman represents place *for man, such a limit means that she becomes a* thing, *with some possibility of change from one historical period to another. She finds herself delineated as a thing. Moreover, the maternal-feminine also serves as an* envelope, *a con-tainer, the starting point from which man limits his things . . . But, because he fails to leave her a subjective life, and to be on occasion her place and her thing in an intersubjective dynamic, man remains within a master–slave dialectic. The slave, ultimately, of a God on whom he bestows the characteristics of an absolute master. Secretly or obscurely, a slave to the power of the maternal-feminine which he diminishes or destroys. The maternal-feminine remains the* place *separated from "its" own place, deprived of "its" place. She is or ceaselessly becomes the place of the other who cannot separate himself from it. Without her knowing or willing it, she is then threatening because of what she lacks: a "proper" place'.* (*Ethics*, 10–11)

Whether or not human life is subjected to the unqualified dominion of eros, it remains the case that an ethic of the sexual act is needed – an ethic that goes beyond the question of the *dramatis personae*: who is to perform it, and with whom. In the sexual act one does not fall out of the ethical world into a primal, pre-ethical relation. But that is what happens when male desire construes woman as place but allows her no place of her own. She is place for him, but he is not place for her. She offers him a place where he is again enclosed and enveloped, a return to the original home in the womb and to the bliss of the maternal embrace. In the Freudian narrative, the original Oedipal ban on the maternal embrace is only temporary: the fulfilment of desire is to be deferred until the boy becomes a man and the time is ripe for the movement of return. But the temporary Oedipal ban is the work of the father – a point that is emphasized especially in Lacan's version of the Freudian narrative.[6] It is a prohibition imposed by the father on the son, and it is also a promise that the son will one day enjoy the father's access to the mother, or her substitute. The prohibition and the promise are exclusively the affair of father and son, they occur within an all-male relationship. The maternal object of the prohibition and the promise is construed as *place* – a particular place, *home*. In the Oedipal situation, two males negotiate a new relation to this place, and the outcome is that the younger of the two leaves home, in order to find it again by way of a detour. Home is passive; it does not move, and it does not itself initiate speech or action; it can hardly be said even to *wait*, it is simply *there*. When one leaves it, it closes up behind one and keeps itself in reserve so as to be intact for the moment when it receives one back. But access to it is the affair of fathers and sons. It is therefore not a person but a 'thing', infinitely precious because it marks one's place in the world by holding open the possibility of a return to the *archē*, the first home that relieves one of the fate of an eternal rootlessness and wandering. In sexual union, nostalgia is not compelled to remain wistfully outside, looking in through the window, but is miraculously reunited with the beloved object. It retains something of the bittersweet quality derived from the original ban, but only so that the pain may be taken up and transformed into the bliss of *comfort*. Father and son negotiate together about their deepest needs.

How is it that (according to Irigaray) woman has been changed into a place lacking a place of its own? Like man, she too has experienced the loss of the original maternal home. But here there has been no paternal prohibition; the loss occurs by way of *her own disillusion* with the mother. According to Freud, the daughter becomes disillusioned with a mother who had previously represented plenitude and abundance, the fulfilment

---

[6] As Juliet Mitchell shows, Lacan argues – in opposition to object-relations theory – that 'the relation of mother to child cannot be viewed outside the structure established by the position of the father . . . There can be nothing *human* that pre-exists or exists outside the law represented by the father' ('Introduction I', in J. Mitchell and J. Rose, *Feminine Sexuality: Jacques Lacan and the École Freudienne*, Basingstoke: Macmillan, 1982, 23).

of every desire, because she discovers a lack, a hole, at the very centre of this supposed plenitude. Unlike the father and the brother, the mother lacks a penis. So too does the daughter; and the mother is quite unable to give her one. The illusion of plenitude is dispelled, and the daughter's turn away from the mother towards the father is undertaken of her own volition and not in reluctant obedience to an alien authority. This turn does not mark the end of the Oedipal situation but the beginning. The father is now the promise of plenitude: he will bestow the longed-for penis, or rather, its equivalent, the child. This Oedipal dependence is perhaps never overcome, and there is a smooth transition when in marriage the woman is transferred from the custody of one male to that of another. If the child she now bears possesses the penis she lacks, then her joy will be complete: for it confirms her in the role she has adopted in relation to males (father, brothers, husband, son . . .), which is to be their dwelling-place – not to *have* a place but to *be* a place. Her satisfaction lies in their satisfaction. Thus she finally succeeds in occupying the space marked out for her by her own mother, whom she has forgotten. There is no genealogical connection with the mother to correspond to the genealogies of fathers and sons, and there is no going back on the decision – which was her own choice – to leave the original maternal home. It is her vocation not to *return* home but to *be* home.

Within this account of the genesis of masculine and feminine identity, the feminine exists only as the inverted, negative image of the masculine. What is true of the part is true of the whole: woman *is* 'a hole-envelope that serves to sheathe and massage the penis in intercourse: a non-sex, or a masculine organ turned back upon itself, self-embracing' (*This Sex which is not one*, 23). The hole is the whole: woman is the original home, the *archē*, but this is a place of absence and emptiness, an abyss into which one (the male 'one') *falls*. Woman is the blissful dream of the return to the first home, but she is also a chaotic void. And she is all this because this is what a 'primal male sexuality' has made of her: for 'limiting oneself to just one of the poles of sexual difference amounts to limiting oneself to the chaos of a primitive desire that preceded any human incarnation . . .

Urged by eros, man immerses himself in chaos because he refuses to make love *with* an other, to be *two* making love, to experience sexual attraction with tenderness and respect . . . This notion of love has led women to forget themselves, to submit childishly or slavishly to male sexuality, and to console themselves, through motherhood, for their fall and exile from themselves' (*Thinking the Difference*, 97, 99). The sexual relation is understood as a *pre-ethical* relation, and its premise is the fall or exile in which woman is permanently separated from her own first home in order that she should herself be home to another.

The Freudian story of an asymmetrical masculine and feminine becoming ends happily with the male return to the original maternal home and the female acquisition of the longed-for penis or child. How can it be said that woman is 'trapped in the role of she who satisfies need but has no access to desire' ('Women-mothers', 51) when she is herself so abundantly satisfied in satisfying the desire of the male other? What more does she want than what she already has? (A male suspicion: is she insatiable?) According to Irigaray, she is not satisfied because the desire that has been satisfied – the desire that takes up residence in her body and fills up her lack – is not in fact *her* desire but another's desire that has long since taken hold of her and reshaped her in its own image, the image of the phallus. So artfully was this done that the alien and alienating desire looks exactly as if it were truly her own. What could be more natural than that, on discovering the value of the phallus, woman should long to possess it for herself and turn away from one who merely mirrors her own lack? Where is the opening here through which an alien desire could enter, so as to pass itself off as her own? But the value of the phallus is not a natural value. The male organ becomes the desired, envied phallus because it has been *invested* with value by a social order which regards it as a passport to privileges from which those who lack it are excluded.[7] This inflationary investment in the phallus turns it into the ideal commodity – so seductive in its appeal to its consumers, so successfully marketed, that *everyone* desires it.

[7] 'Freud gave the moment when boy and girl child saw that they were different the status of a trauma in which the girl is seen to be lacking . . . But something can only

Those who possess it are fearful only of losing it, those who lack it long to acquire it. The marketing strategy is to make the desirability of this object appear inevitable, the natural outcome of an inherent value. Like all advertising, it seduces by making it difficult or impossible to interrogate the desire to which it appeals. How could one do anything other than to define oneself by one's possession or lack of such an infinitely desirable object? One already finds oneself defined as such. Mother and daughter will be united only negatively, in the desire for that which they both lack. The original positive relationship is permanently erased. There is no detour and no return home.

The Freudian story is retold by Irigaray as the true story of the genesis of patriarchy, founded as it is upon this act of erasure. The story is historically true – it describes what happens – but philosophically false, in assuming that what happens happens naturally and had to happen.[8] According to Aristotle, 'poetry is more philosophical and more worthy of serious attention than history; for while poetry is concerned with universal truths, history treats of particular facts' (*Poetics*, 9).[9] The Freudian history truthfully describes the particular facts of which it treats, but it is false insofar as it wishes also to be poetry, a rendering of what is universally and necessarily the case. A constantly re-enacted history that is neither universal nor necessary must be replaced by a new history in which the

---

be *seen* to be missing according to a pre-existing hierarchy of values' (Jacqueline Rose, 'Introduction II', *Feminine Sexuality*, 42).

8 'Does it go without saying that the little girl renounces her first object cathexes, the precociously cathected erogenous zones, in order to complete the itinerary that will enable her to satisfy man's lasting desire to make love with his mother, or an appropriate substitute? Why should a woman have to leave – and "hate" . . . – her own mother, leave her own house, abandon her own family, renounce the name of her own mother and father, in order to take man's genealogical desires upon herself?' (*This Sex which is Not One*, 65). Freud 'is describing an actual state of affairs', when he defines the feminine 'as the necessary complement to the operation of male sexuality, and, more often, as a negative image that provides male sexuality with an unfailingly phallic self-representation' (70). This actual state of affairs is the product of history, not nature; but it is disguised as the natural state of affairs where anatomy is seen as 'an irrefutable criterion of truth' (71). Women 'are deprived of the worth of their sex. The important thing, of course, is that no one should know who has deprived them, or why, and that "nature" be held accountable' (71).

9 Translation from *Aristotle, Horace, Longinus: Classical Literary Criticism*, Harmondsworth: Penguin Books, 1965.

mother–daughter relationship remains intact and female subjectivity is thereby assured: a subjectivity that is then taken
forward into the (hetero)sexual relation so as to ensure its
creativity. An old era, in which sexual difference was subsumed
into the project of male self-definition, would then be succeeded
by a new era in which the twofoldness of human nature comes
to full symbolic expression.

Irigaray's account of the loss of sexual difference may be
compared to the transition from the male/female distinction of
creation to the male hegemony established in the fall. 'Your
desire shall be for your husband, and he shall rule over you'
(Gen. 3.16).[10] After eating the forbidden fruit, Adam and Eve
conceal their genitals as a sign of the shame of a new, disordered
sexual desire. According to Augustine, the involuntary erection
of the penis is the outward and visible sign of this desire. But it
is also the sign of the desire (*teshuqah*) of the woman for her
husband: it signifies his desire for her, but it also signifies her
responsive desire for him. Why should her desire be signified by
that which she herself lacks? How has sexual difference become
an order in which one is characterized by possession, the other
by lack, so that the twofoldness of human being is reduced to
the polarity of plus and minus? Within an order in which 'your
desire shall be for your husband and he shall rule over you', it is
the man who possesses the signifier of desire: of *his* desire, but
also of *her* desire as one who lacks but who desires to incorporate
the signifier of her desire within her own body, even at the cost
of subjection to the dominance of the possessor. May she not
subject herself to the one who fills her lack with his plenitude?
May he not assume authority over the one whose lack is so
clearly intended by nature as the place at which his needs are
satisfied? As the phallus, the penis is now invested with a new
role that causes it to stand out from the other bodily members.
It will of course perform the reproductive function for which it
was created. ('Adam knew Eve his wife, and she conceived . . .'

---

[10] In what follows, I develop further the interpretation of Gen. 3.16 in my *Text, Church
and World: Biblical Interpretation in Theological Perspective*, Edinburgh: T. & T. Clark;
Grand Rapids: Eerdmans, 1994, 191–5: Gen. 3.16 is an assertion of the secondary,
non-original nature of patriarchy.

(Gen. 4.1).) But it will also incarnate an order of dominance and subjection that is, apparently, desired by both parties. This is not simply an order imposed on the weak by the strong. 'Your desire will be for your husband': those who lack will willingly subject themselves to those who possess, so as to gain a share in their possession in the union of flesh. Upheld by the desire of both parties, the rule of the phallus will be indistinguishable from the order of nature.

In which case Freud is perhaps right and Irigaray wrong? Perhaps human existence as male and female *is* human existence plus and minus? If, according to the Genesis text, human existence *becomes* this existence plus and minus (although 'from the beginning it was not so'), might this not be understood as an inevitable, necessary process in which the ungendered innocence of an infancy in which one knows nothing of good and evil is succeeded by the order of desire as naturally as night follows day? The (so-called) 'fall' is perhaps a pictorial rendering of the dawning of sexual self-consciousness, as the concealment of the genitals indicates, and the asymmetrical desire signified by the phallus would then be nothing other than the reverse side of this concealment, a phenomenon as natural as the child's discovery of itself as male or female, as possessing or not-possessing. If the Genesis story is truly a story of human genesis, then what is portrayed here is surely a natural development, an initiation into the rule of the phallus as the law of nature? What scope is there here for any other law?[11]

But in the garden Adam and Eve are not infants. They are created as man and woman; and the rule of the phallus is not

---

11 According to Freud, Paradise 'is no more than a group fantasy of the childhood of the individual. That is why mankind were naked in Paradise and were without shame in one another's presence; till a moment arrived when shame and anxiety awoke, expulsion followed, and sexual life and the tasks of cultural activity began' (*The Interpretation of Dreams* [1900], *Penguin Freud Library* 4.343). At the same time as Freud, H. Gunkel interpreted the story similarly: the knowledge that Adam and Eve lack is that of the difference of the sexes, and it is this that enables them to be naked and unashamed. 'The model for these elements is clearly the state of children who are not yet ashamed . . . [The narrator] understands "knowledge" as that which adults possess to a greater degree than children – insight, reason, including the knowledge of the difference between the sexes' (*Genesis* [1901], ET Macon, Georgia: Mercer University Press, 1997, 14).

the *telos* of a natural development but an accident that befalls their manhood and womanhood as the result of their own contingent action. Irigaray's assumption that the reign of the phallus is an unnatural reign is therefore fundamentally right. The woman who desires her husband as the plenitude that fills her lack has been overtaken by an alien desire that does not belong to her created nature. The man who desires as one possessing the signifier of desire has been similarly overtaken. The created twofoldness of human nature is not a human nature plus and minus: male and female alike are 'created in the image of God' (Gen. 1.27), and the original difference can hardly have been that of a plenitude and a lack. Human nature plus and minus is *superimposed* onto this original difference, as an expression of the alienation of the creature from the creator. A tragic narrative that culminates in the barring of access to the tree of life can hardly be the rendering of a 'natural development'.

The phallus itself acknowledges, unwillingly, that its reign is not original. As Augustine argues, the physiological possibility of the erection of the penis is assumed in the original command and vocation to be fruitful and multiply. Through the fall, a voluntary bodily movement becomes an involuntary bodily occurrence that generates such shame in the man and the woman that their immediate reaction is to conceal the sites of 'plenitude' and 'lack'. The signifier of desire, which one possesses and the other lacks and which thereby establishes an order of lordship and subjection, is the signifier of an *alien* desire which has already subjected man himself to its own lordship. He possesses the signifier of desire, but he does not control it. It controls him. He is not in full possession of that which he possesses. The garments of fig-leaves are an attempt to contain and conceal a desire so overwhelmingly powerful that it will 'normally' be aroused not just by voluntary sexual activity but by the mere involuntary sight of the unclothed body of the other. The erection of the signifier of desire is at the same time an occasion for shame that never escapes the imperative of concealment. Only when carefully screened from public view does it allow itself to be seen by its possessor and, perhaps, by his sexual partner. This strange symbol of male dominance behaves almost like a furtive nocturnal animal that can be glimpsed only occasionally and in passing. It can assert its claim to dominance only by way of *surrogates* – forms of male self-display which *stand in for* that which is unavoidably absent, concealed behind screens far more effective than the original fig-leaves; surrogates that signify a supreme signifier that is present only on the margins of discourse and practice. These surrogates will be careful not to allow their relation to the supreme signifier to become too visible and obvious. They must visibly signify only themselves, so as to have an alibi to hand if the issue of a relation to the supreme signifier is raised. Modes of dress and deportment, displays of wealth and power, control of discourse, various forms of technological mastery . . . Are these what they appear to be, and no more? Or are they signs of the reign of the phallus? To interpret them as surrogates of the supreme signifier is, however, to subvert them and expose them to ridicule. If they are expressions of the reign of the phallus, they are so only so long as that relationship is kept secret. But what kind of a signifier of male dominance is it that can never openly appear but must always hide itself, even in its surrogates? Why is it that the surrogates themselves must deny all know-ledge of their master and of their own role as his deputies? If this is the strategy of a power that can penetrate everywhere only so long as it remains invisible, *why* must the condition of universal penetration be this strict incognito? The emperor may hide himself away to preserve the aura of divinity, but his deputies do not feign ignorance of his very existence. Is the incognito more plausibly understood as the product of *shame*, and thus as an admission that the reign of the phallus is non-original and contingent, a corruption of the relation between man and woman given in creation? And, if the reign of the phallus cannot be sustained but is – like the house built on sand – liable to sudden collapse, might it be possible to divest the bodily organ of some of its symbolic pretensions and to restore it to the male body as one member among many? A 'circum-cision performed without hands', a participation in 'the circum-cision of Christ' (Col. 2.11)? A non-being of male and female and a oneness in Christ Jesus that is actually the *fulfilment* of the sexual difference given in creation, and not its erasure (Gal. 3.28)?

If there is any truth in this Pauline-Augustinian rewriting of Freud and Irigaray, the ethics of sexual difference must be grounded in being itself. In identifying, analysing and explaining the unethical or sub-ethical forms of the male–female relation, one implicitly or explicitly appeals to a true ethical relation as the ground both of critique and of hope. Only so can the naturalness of the order of the phallus be shown to be unnatural.

THE DIVINE LIFE AND THE CREATURE

'What we need is to discover how two *can be made which one day could become a* one *in that third which is love . . . No more dissociation of love and eroticism. This very often correlates with the division and hierarchy of parental functions. This way love becomes a perpetual tragedy, a sad charity, or a greedy devotion (a form of* agape *without* eros, *perhaps?)'* (*Ethics*, 66–7)

No dissociation of love and eroticism, no agape without eros; no assigning of eros to man and agape to woman, no difference without union or union without difference. If eros is a male prerogative, then woman will be the place where that prerogative is exercised: difference will be dissolved into a oneness in which the distinctive being of the second is lost. If agape is a female prerogative, then man will be the object of a love that he cannot reciprocate: he will become the place where this love is invested, and will himself be threatened with the loss of his own distinctive being. The two are to become one in such a way that they are two precisely in becoming one. If they establish their twoness in their oneness, the oneness of their shared love can be understood as a third, standing alongside their twoness rather than dissolving it, but also ensuring that they are two not as pure individuals or units but in the oneness of the relation with the other. The presence of the third indicates that difference is not engulfed in an ultimate, undifferentiated oneness; for there can be talk of a third only where there is not one alone but also two. Yet, in doubling back on the two, the third also indicates that their difference is not heterogeneity but is constituted by their oneness. The triune structure of the relationship of man and woman is to be distinguished from a 'monotheism' in which difference is dissolved and a 'polytheism' in which difference is absolutized. Both monotheism and polytheism are attempts to escape the trinitarian dialectic in which oneness and threeness are mutually constitutive and therefore equally irreducible to the other. In establishing the difference in the oneness and the oneness in the difference, the third is integral to the relational structure. Three is two plus one, neither two alone nor one alone but two together with their oneness. The oneness of two is more like an addition to two than a subtraction. 'There is neither male nor female, for you are all one in Christ Jesus' (Gal. 3.28): a subtraction, a dissolution of two into one? But it is also said that 'woman is not apart from man nor man from woman, in the Lord' (1 Cor. 11.11). In the Lord, in the oneness of being in Christ Jesus, man is established as man and woman as woman; they are established in their difference. But in their difference they are also established as belonging together. Woman and man are not apart from one another, as pure individuals or units, for they are what they are – woman and man – only in relation to the other. For Irigaray, the love in which man and woman are both two and one is the concrete expression of their being. In the love that unites them and differentiates them, they find themselves. It is within this trinitarian interrelatedness that we 'discover how *two* can be made which . . . become a *one* in that third which is love'.

Is there in all this a *vestigium trinitatis*, a sign of the ultimacy of a triune relationality in which difference is not dissolved into oneness but established by it? If the love of man and woman is erotic love, is eros the closest human analogue to the divine life? But the oneness of male and female in Christ Jesus is not the oneness of erotic union as one flesh. The belonging-together of woman and man is not confined to the sexual relationship, nor is that even its primary expression. The veil is interposed in order to confine eros to his limits, excluding him from the

ekklēsia, the place in which the belonging-together of man and
woman is disclosed, and differentiating him from the *agapē*
which is the mode of that belonging-together. 'A form of agape
without eros, perhaps?' An infringement of the rule, 'No more
dissociation of love and eroticism'? The *ekklēsia* includes unmarried people whose calling is not to become 'one flesh' in
marriage but to the discipline of celibacy, and – at least from
one point of view – this can even be seen as the higher of the
two vocations:

> The unmarried man [*ho agamos*] is concerned about the affairs of the
> Lord, how to please the Lord; but the married man [*ho gamēsas*] is
> concerned about worldly affairs [*ta tou kosmou*], how to please his wife,
> and his interests are divided. And the unmarried woman [*hē gunē hē
> agamos*] or girl [*parthenos*] is concerned about the affairs of the Lord,
> how to be holy in body and spirit; but the married woman [*hē
> gamēsasa*] is concerned about worldly affairs, how to please her
> husband. (1 Cor. 7.32b–34)

According to this Pauline teaching, the unmarried state is not to
be seen as a negation, a deprivation, a failure to achieve what
must be achieved to be truly man or woman, but a divine
vocation. In living the single life one follows the example of
Paul (1 Cor. 7.7–8), who himself follows the example of Jesus
(11.1). In these single lives, the place of eros is marked by
egkrateia, 'self-control' (7.9). But in these lives too it is the case
that 'woman is not apart from man nor man from woman, in
the Lord' (11.10): for the primary belonging-together of man
and woman occurs not in sexual union or marriage but in the
agape that establishes the community as the body of Christ,
without obliterating the difference between its various
'members' (12.12–26). Within the *ekklēsia* there is indeed 'a form
of agape without eros', in defiance of the law that prohibits the
'dissociation of love and eroticism'. (On what authority is it
asserted that man and woman become two and one primarily,
or even exclusively, in the sexual act? Must sexual experience be
seen as a compulsory rite of passage into 'real' manhood or
womanhood, without which they are deficient? Must this
manhood and womanhood be sustained in being by an ongoing
'sex life', within a single relationship or – preferably? – a

plurality of relationships? Must manhood and womanhood necessarily wither and die without the nourishment of sex?) The belonging-together of man and woman in the *ekklēsia* is a sign of the primacy of agape over eros.

If the eros of man and woman is seen as a *vestigium trinitatis*, and perhaps as a participation in the trinitarian divine life, the concrete form of that divine life will almost inevitably be undermined. The concrete form of the divine life is the reciprocal love of the Father and the Son in the Holy Spirit. It is in the descent of the Spirit in the form of a dove that Jesus knows himself to be addressed as 'my beloved Son', and it is in that same Spirit that he responds: 'Abba, Father'. If heterosexual eros is elevated to the status of *vestigium trinitatis*, then the absence both of the feminine and of eros itself within the concrete form of the divine life will immediately seem problematic. The father–son relationship is, ostensibly, all-male and non-erotic – and thus, from the standpoint of Irigaray's religious philosophy of eros, alienating and offensive. From that perspective, it appears that 'the perfection of love between son and Father, with its completion in a Trinity' makes the Christ-symbol 'eternally captive to the lure of a (male) Same' (*Marine Lover*, 186). The figure of the Christ is worth re-evaluating 'only if he goes beyond the Father–son relationship. If he announces – beyond Christianity? – that only through difference can the incarnation unfold without murderous or suicidal passion' (188). As things stand, however, 'the other has yet to enlighten him. To tell him something. Even to appear to him in her irreducibility . . . And if, to the whole of himself, he says "yes" and also asks her to say "yes" again, did it ever occur to him to say "yes" to her? Did he ever open himself to that other world?' Can we create from the Christ-symbol 'a marriage that has never been consummated and that the spirit, in Mary, would renew?' – a spirit that is no longer 'the product of the love between Father and son' but rather 'the universe already made flesh or capable of becoming flesh, and remaining in excess to the existing world' (190). If heterosexual eros is image of and participation in the divine life, then the concrete form of the inner-trinitarian life will have to be radically reinterpreted.

If we take the way from eros into the divine life, the Father, the Son and the Holy Spirit will be at best an irrelevance.

But if the agape of the inner-trinitarian life is opened up to human participation in the incarnation and through the Spirit, then the way from the human sphere into the divine is preceded by and grounded in the prior way from the divine sphere into the human. The point at which the divine way downwards and the human way upwards intersect is the moment in which the one who descended from heaven 'lifted up his eyes to heaven and said, Father, the hour has come; glorify thy Son that the Son may glorify thee' (Jn. 17.1). Does this represent an all-male divine relationality that excludes the feminine, the apotheosis of patriarchy? But the one addressed as 'Father' is not the oppressive heavenly patriarch of contemporary imagining. 'Abba' is functionally equivalent to a proper name, and the one so addressed is therefore a particular father who cannot be assimilated to an abstract fatherhood-in-general. Fathers, and even Father-Gods, are not necessarily all alike. If the one Jesus addresses as 'Abba' is diametrically opposed to every other Father-God, exposing them as idolatrous projections, this is not just another of patriarchy's in-house conflicts. And, although eros is indeed excluded from the inner-trinitarian life, being (like gender) a purely creaturely reality, it is not the case that the relationship of Father and Son is 'all male'. Considered as an inner-divine relation, the absence of a feminine other – a Mother, a Daughter – is an indication not of an apotheosis of male gender but of its absence. Male and female are male and female in relation to each other; where the female is absent, there is no male. (The gendering of the Holy Spirit as female would therefore bestow a maleness on the Father and the Son that was not previously there. It would also open up various possibilities of heterosexual eros within the triune life.)[12] While the terms 'father' and 'son' normally denote male humans in a peculiarly sharply defined and irreversible relationship to one another, they lose certain of their normal concomitants – temporal separation, bodiliness, maleness – when metaphori-

---

[12] For these reasons, I no longer find the use of feminine pronouns in connection with the Spirit to be appropriate (compare *Text, Church and World*, 215–17).

cally applied to the first and second persons of the divine Trinity. This is no more an all-male relationship than it is a temporal or bodily relationship.[13]

The question of maleness only arises when, in the incarnation, the inner-trinitarian agape is extended into the human sphere in and through a particular man – and not a woman. But the relation of Jesus to the heavenly Father is an *inclusive* relation. In Christ there is neither Jew nor Greek, slave nor free, male nor female, in the sense that no one is excluded from the *koinōnia* of this relation. That Jesus is 'born of the virgin Mary' is already an anticipation of this *koinōnia*. It is true of him as of all other males that 'man is now born of woman' (1 Cor. 11.12) and that the belonging-together of man and woman must initially take the form of the relationship of mother and son. 'Did it ever occur to him to say "yes" to her?' His birth was his 'yes' to Mary, who became his mother as he became her son. His 'yes' to his mother is constitutive of his human existence. To reject this form of the belonging-together of man and woman, to wish to replace it with a relationship centred on sexual union, is indeed to go 'beyond Christianity'. Eros demands the movement 'beyond Christianity' because he cannot endure the limit imposed on him by the divine-human agape.

In the *koinōnia* woman and man belong together not in eros but in this agape. But the *koinōnia* comprehends the whole of life – a life in which there is also marrying and giving in marriage, in accordance with the will of the Creator. Marriage bears witness to agape as a reciprocal love in which there is unreserved and enduring commitment to the other; and where there is marriage within the *koinōnia* of the church, the basis of marriage within the divine agape is known and acknowledged. The fact that man and woman belong together in Christ within the 'one body' is quite compatible with their belonging-together

[13] Gregory of Nazianzus argues similarly that the use of the term 'Son' does not entail the transference to the Godhead of all of its denotations and connotations in ordinary usage ('Theological Orations', v. 8, ET in *Christology of the Later Fathers*, London: SCM Press, 1954, 198). Otherwise we would have to 'consider our God to be a male, according to the same argument, because he is called God and Father, and deity to be feminine, from the gender of the word, and Spirit neuter'. But the triune God is not 'the hermaphrodite god of Marcion [*sic*] and Valentinus'.

as 'one flesh', within marriage. Agape does not need eros; there could be a church without eros, but there could not be a church without agape. Agape marks the limit of eros's presence within the church. But agape is not opposed to eros. Agape limits eros, but it also sanctifies it; that is, it sets it in the sphere of the eternal divine commitment to humankind, of which marriage is the *sacramentum* (Eph. 5.32). As the divine grace justifies the ungodly, so the divine agape sanctifies eros. And we may expect to find traces of this divine action in the belonging-together of man and woman inside and outside the church.

It is this belonging-together of man and woman in agape, in their difference and their oneness, their twoness and the third that is their oneness, that is the true *vestigium trinitatis* – originating as it does in the being-in-action of the triune God. Sanctified by agape, eros too may participate in its trinitarian structure.

'Who or what the other is, I never know. But the other who is forever unknowable is the one who differs from me sexually. This feeling of surprise, astonishment, and wonder in the face of the unknowable ought to be returned to its locus: that of sexual difference . . . Sometimes a space for wonder is left to works of art. But it is never found to reside in this locus: between man and woman. *Into this place came attraction, greed, possession, consummation, disgust, and so on. But not that wonder which beholds what it sees always as if for the first time, never taking hold of the other as its object. It does not try to seize, possess, or reduce this object, but leaves it subjective, still free.' (Ethics, 13)*

Does this speak of eros as a divinity who claims to mediate between the human and divine spheres and to bestow a participation in the divine life manifested in the face of the other? Or does it speak of eros as sanctified by the divine agape – although perhaps unaware of this basis within God's being and action? If this eros sanctified by agape is a reality at all, it is the reality of man and woman as such: the twofold human being created in the image and likeness of God, male and female. It is not the reality merely of a Christian man and Christian woman; for the new creation does not destroy the old, replacing it with something qualitatively different, but fulfils the *telos* of the old in the face of the disruption and confusion brought about by human sin. Even where the basis of the eros of man and woman in the divine agape is unacknowledged, even where eros is consequently distorted, this basis is real and cannot be ineffectual. Irigaray's supposedly 'post-Christian' ethics of sexual difference questions and denies this reality in its quest for an alternative, wholly future reality. But this reality is capable of making its presence felt even in the midst of questions and denials; perhaps more so here than in bland theological affirmations unmarked by any struggle with the temptation to question and deny.

'Who or what the other is, I never know.' This is the not-knowing not of indifference but of *wonder* – 'that wonder which beholds what it sees always as if for the first time, never taking hold of the other as its object'. Wonder is 'a mourning for the self as an autarchic entity', it is 'the advent or the event of the other', 'the beginning of a new story' (75). In the advent or event of the other, the other is seen *as if* for the first time: the strangeness that evokes wonder is therefore the strangeness of the familiar, the partial disclosure of that which lies concealed behind the veil of the everyday; a disclosure not of divinity but of the original goodness of the creature, and of the specific goodness of the human creature whose free subjectivity corresponds to one's own, across the boundary of sexual difference. Without this correspondence human existence would be solitary and 'not good' (Gen. 2.18); its goodness lies in the correspondence disclosed in the advent of the other, of Eve to Adam and of Adam to Eve. Wonder is evoked by the advent not of an alien other such as the animals brought to Adam to name, but of an other who is other precisely in the correspondence of reciprocal recognition across the boundary of difference. This advent is always the divine gift, as Eve is gift to Adam and Adam to Eve, and wonder is therefore always also *gratitude* – gratitude to being and, however indirectly, to God as the ground of being. The advent of the other across the boundary of sexual difference does not *only* occur in the context of eros. But it *may* occur in that context. Eros is certainly not closed to the advent of the other and the wonder that this evokes, and indeed it has its own particular mode of openness to that advent. Where eros is closed to the other – where it is characterized merely by 'attraction, greed, possession, consummation, disgust, and so on' – this occurs in defiance of the openness to the other that is originally proper to eros.

How may eros's distinctive mode of openness to the other be characterized? No adequate answer to this question is possible, since to 'wonder' is precisely to be conscious of the inadequacy of what can be said to what is felt. Experience is not always reducible to language, any more than its possibility is always pre-given in language; experience is always in excess of language. This excess is especially clear in the case of erotic experience, which may even be said to *resist* language. The sexual act requires speech if it is to be a reciprocal, communicative act, human rather than inhuman, but it does not in itself require *much* speech, nor does it require to be *much spoken about*. It is true that discourse circulates incessantly around the sexual act, infiltrating even what seem to be its most secret recesses for the sake of the pleasure of 'speaking openly' about it. But the pleasure of speaking, hearing or reading of eros is distinct from the pleasure of eros itself. The former pleasure is not a preparation for the latter, or an enhancement of it; there is no necessary relationship between the two, and it may be that any reducibility of eros to speech indicates a drift away from its basis in agape. It seems that eros is resistant to speech, whether in the form of conversation or of commentary. At this point, words fail. Even a word such as 'pleasure', long associated with the sexual act, is inadequate to eros: not simply because this word is lacking in depth, but because it appears to assimilate an experience which is *sui generis* to other experiences of pleasure, from which it differs totally. The failure of words is not in itself a sign of a mystery beyond words, as though words could only be concerned with the surface of life and not with its mysteries and depths. Words may be lacking on the surface too, and they may on occasion give profound articulation to the depths. Speechlessness may characterize banality as well as mystery, and the resistance of eros to speech does not in itself guarantee the presence even of a creaturely *mysterium tremendum*, let alone a divine one. Yet this reticence is at least compatible with the presence of a creaturely *mysterium tremendum*, with the 'feeling of surprise, astonishment, and wonder in the face of the unknowable' evoked by 'the advent or the event of the other'. The creaturely mystery that may be encountered here – although normally crowded out by 'attraction, greed, possession, consummation, disgust, and so on' – is that of the original goodness of the human creature, as male and female and always concretely as *this* male and *this* female, unique in their specific difference and togetherness.[14]

'So as not to remain fixed on a rare object, it is appropriate to turn voluntarily toward several objects. So as not to be attached to one unique woman, is it desirable to scatter oneself among several?' (Ethics, 79)

If in the sexual act – as in other encounters between man and woman – one *may* indirectly, fleetingly experience something of the original goodness of the human creature, one is surely at liberty to *maximize* this experience? To seek it wherever it may be found, beyond the exclusive commitment to one that characterizes conventional marriage? The original goodness of the other, and of oneself in union with the other, is unique to that particular other, male or female, and to that particular

---

[14] The assertion here that the original goodness of the human creature remains its ultimate truth derives from Karl Barth. According to Barth, we are to reject 'the common theological practice of depreciating human nature as much as possible in order to oppose to it the more effectively what may be made of man by divine grace . . . It is not by nature but by its denial and misuse that man is as alien and opposed to the grace of God as we see him to be in fact. But rightly to appreciate this corruption brought about by man, and therefore the sin of man, we must quietly consider what it is that is corrupted, and calmly maintain that all the corruption of man cannot make evil by nature the good work of God . . . But this enables us to see and understand why the mercy of God to man is not an act of caprice but has its sure basis in the fact that man is not a stranger or lost to his Creator even as a sinner, but in respect of his nature, of the secret of his humanity, still confronts him as he was created . . . And as God makes himself his Deliverer, he merely exercises his faithfulness as the Creator to his creature, which has not become different or been lost to him by its fall into sin' (Karl Barth, *Church Dogmatics*, III/2 [1948], ET Edinburgh: T. & T. Clark, 1960, 274–5). The 'secret of humanity', unerased by sin, is the fact that human existence is constituted by 'the mutual relationship of I and Thou' (267), of which the male/female distinction is paradigmatic (286).

relationship. It cannot be found elsewhere, and if it is not found here it will be lost forever. If wonder 'sees always as if for the first time', if it marks 'the beginning of a new story', why should one not initiate a number of new stories? Is it mere prejudice and timidity that can see in such ventures nothing more than 'adultery' or 'promiscuity'?

This is the logic of an eros without agape. The divine agape is an unreserved, eternal commitment to the human creature, and therefore to the *particular* human creature; and marriage is a divinely appointed analogue or *sacramentum* of the divine agape. If, in eros, there has occurred 'the advent of the other', this is not a transitory event that is immediately overtaken by other events, but a sign pointing to the unreserved, eternal commitment of the divine agape to the particular human other. To turn from that other to a third party is to destroy the sign by imposing a limitation on commitment and therefore on agape. To change the object of commitment in accordance with inclination and opportunity, drawn from one to another by the allure of the new, is precisely what agape *cannot* do. It is only faithfulness to one that corresponds to the divine faithfulness; the jealousy and anger evoked by the turning away of a husband or wife to a third party are symptoms of the rupturing of this correspondence. In this turning away, it is assumed that the former possibility of a 'wonder' that 'sees always as if for the first time' is now exhausted, that it has degenerated into irreconcilable conflict or routinized monotony. Yet the original goodness of the human creature does not degenerate in this way. It is eternally affirmed by the divine agape, and to turn away from this disclosure in quest of another is to show that the content of this disclosure has been forgotten or was never properly grasped. The original goodness of the particular human creature is now considered apart from the Creator, as contingent not on the eternal divine judgment but on the successive, perhaps shifting judgments of its human partner. The other to whom I am at present joined is good only insofar as I continue to regard her as good. She is thereby deprived of the eternal place accorded to her by the divine affirmation, to which my commitment to her should correspond, and her being is annexed and made dependent on my own. My own being thereby falls out of its relation to the divine affirmation, as I set myself in the place of the Creator as the ultimate judge of good and evil. I find, perhaps, that what once seemed good now seems evil, and I therefore turn away from it to seek the good elsewhere. But the good I appear to find will in no way correspond to the original goodness of the human creature as eternally affirmed by its Creator. I will find only an eros without agape: sin.

'The consequences of the nonfulfillment of the sexual act remain, and there are many. To take up only the most beautiful, as yet to be made manifest in the realm of time and space, there are angels. *These messengers who never remain enclosed in a place, who are also never immobile. Between God, as the perfectly immobile act, man, who is surrounded and enclosed by the world of his work, and woman, whose task would be to take care of nature and procreation,* angels *would circulate as mediators of that which has not yet happened, of what is still going to happen, of what is on the horizon. Endlessly reopening the enclosure of the universe, of universes, identities, the unfolding of actions, of history . . . They are not unrelated to sex. There is of course Gabriel, the angel of the annunciation. But other angels announce the consummation of marriage, notably all the angels in the Apocalypse and many in the Old Testament. As if the angel were a representation of a sexuality that has never been incarnated.' (Ethics,* 15–16)

'All' the angels of the Apocalypse, 'many' in the Old Testament, announce the consummation of a marriage and the incarnation of a new sexuality in which sexual union gives birth to sexual difference, set now within a cosmic context. 'The link uniting or reuniting masculine and feminine must be horizontal and vertical, terrestrial and heavenly . . . [I]t must forge a covenant between the divine and the mortal, such that the sexual encounter would be a festive celebration . . . ' (17). It is this future event that the angels announce – an event beyond the Father and the Son. 'The third era of the West might, at last, be the era of the *couple*: of the Spirit and the Bride?' After the coming of the Father that is inscribed in the Old Testament, after the coming of the Son in the New Testament, we would

see the beginning of the era of the Spirit and the Bride . . . The
Spirit and the Bride invite beyond genealogical destiny to the
era of the wedding and the festival of the world' (148–9). *Which*
apocalypse is here paraphrased? In the canonical one, it is
written: 'The Spirit and the Bride say, Come . . . And let the
one who is thirsty come, let the one who desires take the water
of life without price' (Rev. 22.17). This water of life flows 'from
the throne of God and of the Lamb through the middle of the
street of the city' (22.1–2). The Spirit and the Bride direct us to
God and to the Lamb as the source of living water; they do not
proclaim a third age in which God and the Lamb are superseded. The angels announce a future consummation – but it is
'the marriage supper of the Lamb' (19.19), and the Bride is 'the
wife of the Lamb' (20.9). A new sexuality, or the new Jerusalem,
the eternal dwelling-place of the people of God in God and of
God in his people? In the new Jerusalem, the cube-shaped holy
of holies built of gold and precious stones, the promise is fulfilled
and the dwelling of God is with humans: 'He will dwell with
them, and they shall be his people, and God himself will be with
them' (21.3). Within this dwelling-place of God among humans
and of humans in God, this meeting of heaven and earth, is
there a place for a new sexuality? Why should this be excluded?
Uncleanness and fornication are excluded from the heavenly
city (21.27, 22.15), but eros sanctified by agape is not uncleanness
or fornication. On the other hand, the Lamb's one hundred
and forty four thousand followers are described as 'virgins' –
male virgins, apparently, who 'have not defiled themselves with
women' (14.4). An obscure, one-sided allusion to a time in
which 'they neither marry nor are given in marriage, but are
like angels in heaven' (Matt. 22.30)? A time in which eros is no
more? Would it be so terrible if it were *eros* – and not the Father
or the Son – who was superseded in the age of the resurrection
of the flesh?

And yet, sexual difference is preserved in the image of the
Lamb and the Bride. The end of eros is the end only of a sign,
superseded by the reality of the fulfilled, consummated divine–
human covenant to which – when sanctified by agape – it once
pointed.

CHAPTER SIX

Engendering agape

After many vicissitudes, Levin (Constantine Dmitrich Levin) and Kitty (Ekaterina Shcherbatskaya) finally arrive at the church for their wedding. Throughout Tolstoy's novel, their developing relationship serves as the positive counterpart of Anna Karenina's adulterous relationship with Count Vronsky, which offers her an escape from a loveless marriage but ends with her suicide. The wedding is the hinge on which the whole novel turns. Starting from the intense emotional experiences of the couple at the centre of the event, the narrator moves outwards into the concentric circles of relatives and friends and of interested spectators of this 'society wedding'. As the service proceeds, members of these inner and outer circles comment on the unfolding drama like a Greek chorus.

All Moscow was in the church – relatives, friends and acquaintances. During the ceremony of plighting troth, in the brilliantly lit church, among the throng of elegantly clad women and girls, and men in white ties, frock-coats or uniforms, conversation in decorously low tones never flagged. It was mostly kept up by the men, for the women were absorbed in watching every detail of the service, which is so close to their hearts. (*Anna Karenina*, 480)[1]

Yet the women have their say as well as the men. Like a roving microphone, the narrator picks up snatches of conversation. 'Why is Marie in lilac? It's almost as unsuitable at a wedding as black.' 'With her complexion it's her only salvation. I wonder why they're having the wedding in the evening, like shop-people?' (480). The bridegroom's brother jokingly explains to

---

[1] Quotations are taken from the translation by Rosemary Edmonds, Harmondsworth: Penguin Books, 1954.

the bride's sister 'that the custom of going away after the wedding was becoming common because newly-married couples always felt slightly embarrassed' (481). But the most important question is: how will this marriage turn out? 'Well, let's see which of them is the first to step on the carpet. I told Kitty to remember', remarks the unconventional Countess Nordston to the other of the bride's sisters. 'It won't make any difference', she replies; 'we all make obedient wives – it runs in the family.' 'Well, I stepped on the carpet before Vassily on purpose' (481). The 'carpet' is where the couple stand for the marriage ceremony itself, after the preliminary part of the service has been completed. According to the old saying, 'the one who steps first on the carpet will be the head of the house' (483). If the bride reaches the carpet first, by luck or design, she will be the dominant partner in the marriage – unless, of course, heredity and upbringing prove more effectual than the old tradition. ('We all make obedient wives – it runs in the family.') On this occasion, bride and bridegroom both forget the old tradition as they step together onto the carpet, and are unaware of 'the loud remarks and disputes that followed, some maintaining that Levin was first and the others insisting that they had both stepped on together' (483).

In the outer circle too, the issue of obedience is raised. 'Is that her sister in the white satin? Now listen how the deacon will roar: "Wife, obey thy husband"' (482). This expectation is fulfilled when, at the reading of the Epistle, 'the head-deacon thunder[s] out the last verse, awaited with such impatience by the outside public' (483). The reference is presumably to the last verse of Ephesians 5.22–33 – a passage already alluded to in the preceding prayers, during which bride and groom 'were reminded that God created woman from Adam's rib, and "for this cause shall a man leave his father and mother, and cleave unto his wife, and they twain shall be one flesh", and that "this is a great mystery"' (483). The conclusion of this passage is not quite, 'Wife, obey your husband', but it is, 'Let the wife see that she respects her husband' – in the context of a passage that has required her to submit to her husband's headship. The deacon's fortissimo rendering of this text is evidently a personal foible, well known to those who habitually attend wedding ceremonies in this fashionable Moscow church. No doubt it is intended as a forceful reminder to the bride and other wives present of a scriptural precept they often appear to overlook, but it succeeds only in introducing a crudely dissonant note into the perform- ance of the solemn rites – entertaining for uninvolved onlook- ers, although some of those in the inner circle may perhaps wince at it. Does the church (in the person of the head-deacon) really think that it can enforce its most offensive precepts merely by shouting?

The issue of obedience (the wife's obedience, or her lack of it) is raised both by scripture (the Epistle) and by tradition (the carpet). It is, in one sense, still a 'live issue'; real tensions and sensitivities underlie the humour and the irony ('it runs in the family'). And yet in another sense it is irrelevant. Some main- tained that Levin was first onto the carpet, others that they stepped onto it together: they were so close that it was impos- sible to tell. If Levin is to be the head of this particular house, his headship will in practice be almost imperceptible. Indeed, 'headship' and 'subjection' – the terms used in the Epistle – are simply inappropriate to the complex dynamics of this particular relationship. Much of what is said during the service seems to be both beautiful and true – so far as Levin and Kitty are aware of it through the haze of joyful emotion that envelops them. But the two moments when the question of obedience is raised pass them by, unnoticed. Where there is love, why should there be talk of obedience? In spite of the deacon's best efforts, the Epistle falls on deaf ears. Perhaps at another time and place its words were beautiful and true, but they are so no longer. They are the empty shell of what may once have been a living communicative act, preserved like a fossil in a museum when the life has long since departed.

'Can these bones live?' What if one were to read this passage not fortissimo but sotto voce? Emphasizing that the subjection required of the wife is not to a tyrant but to a 'head' who is himself enjoined to love as Christ loves the church; hinting that this asymmetry may after all correspond to woman's own nature; indicating, tactfully, a few of the typical feminine shortcomings – wilfulness, indecision, petty-mindedness, and so on – from which she will be saved through submission to her appointed masculine head; noting with quiet satisfaction the superiority of scriptural wisdom over current secular opinion? But the male commentator's love of the woman he finds encoded in this text may well have little to do with the love of Christ for the church. The love of Christ for the church is not a patronizing love, nor is it a thinly veiled self-satisfaction.

Or are we to adopt the manner of the contemporary 'hermeneutics of suspicion' and denounce the text as an ideological construct, a building no longer fit for human habitation? But textual nihilism is an inadequate response to textual optimism, unless one is committed from the outset to the demolition of the concept of 'holy scripture'. In an attempt to find a way beyond textual optimism and textual nihilism, we begin with the modest observation that the selected passage (Eph. 5.22–33) begins in the middle of a sentence.

MUTUALITY AND SUBJECTION (VERSES 22–23)

. . . wives to your own husbands as to the Lord. (v. 22) 'Woman' and 'man' (*gunē* and *anēr*) are here presented in the roles of 'wife' and 'husband'. Marriage is not the only way that woman and man belong together in the Lord, but it is one such way; and this way is the theme of the passage as a whole (Eph. 5.22–33). However, in extracting the passage from its context we have already done violence to it, as the lack of a verb in the first clause indicates. This is not a self-contained set-piece, capable of independent life outside its context (as in the case of 1 Cor. 13). It is not a new chapter or paragraph, opening with the exhortation: 'Wives, be subject to your husbands . . .'[2] There is no dividing-line or

---

[2] There is, however, a textual problem in Eph. 5.22. After *hai gunaikes tois idiois andrasin*, many manuscripts insert either the third plural imperative *hupotassesthōsan* or the second plural *hupotassesthe* (the majority reading). The verse would then be translated, 'Let wives be subject to their own husbands', or, 'Wives, be subject to your own husbands.' Either way, the exhortation is detached from v. 21. The harder reading is undoubtedly the one that omits the imperative, and it is found in the earliest extant manuscript of the Pauline collection, 𝔓[46], and in Codex Vaticanus. The second plural imperative may be explained as an assimilation to Col. 3.18 and to the other

interval between this passage and that which precedes it, no conclusion followed by a new start. The address to women or wives arises from the preceding exhortations with hardly a pause for breath. Where it is forgotten that this passage is an integral part of the text known as 'the Epistle of Paul to the Ephesians', its interpretation will be seriously impaired.[3] The damage done to the passage by excising it from its context can only be repaired by grafting it back in again: by restoring the exhortation to wives and husbands to its immediate context, but above all by allowing the richness and complexity of the letter

imperatives in the 'household code' (Eph. 5.25, 6.1, 4, 5, 9) – although its position in the sentence is unusual. The third plural recalls 1 Cor. 14.34.

[3] Was the author of this letter really Paul, and was it originally addressed to the Ephesians? In 1.1, 'in Ephesus' is omitted by $\mathfrak{P}^{46}$ and by the original form of Codex Sinaiticus and Codex Alexandrinus. Marcion believed it to have been addressed to the Laodiceans – a deduction from Col. 4.16. The letter was 'perhaps intended as an encyclical, copies being sent to various churches, of which that at Ephesus was chief' (B. M. Metzger, *A Textual Commentary on the Greek New Testament*, London and New York: United Bible Societies, 2nd edn 1975, 601). As for the authorship question, it is widely agreed that if the author was not Paul he nevertheless shows a deep knowledge of Pauline theology (unlike the author of the Pastoral Epistles). But in that case, why should he not *be* Paul? (Is it any harder to think of Paul as the author of 1 Thessalonians, 1 Corinthians and Ephesians than it is to think of Beethoven as the composer of the String Quartets Op. 18, 59 and 131?) How far is the present consensus against Pauline authorship simply a matter of scholarly *fashion*? The consensus may derive in part from Ernst Käsemann's influential 'early catholicism' thesis, according to which later New Testament writings such as Ephesians and Acts betray a drift away from the Pauline gospel of the justification of the ungodly towards a 'catholic' interest in the church as a topic in its own right. 'A shift of emphasis is disclosed by the fact that for him [the author of Ephesians] the body of Christ grows not only into the open world but also . . . into the heights of heaven. The theme of the church dominates him to such an extent that the church is no longer mentioned as part of a continuing contrast to the world. The church has become an independent theme in relation to cosmology, just as it became one with respect to Christology' (E. Käsemann, 'Ephesians and Acts', in L. E. Keck and J. L. Martyn (eds.), *Studies in Luke–Acts*, Nashville: Abingdon Press, 1966, 288–97, 296). If one discounts these impressionistic and inaccurate statements, there is also the question whether the 'meditative-doxological style of Ephesians' is conceivable from an author whose preferred mode is argument and dialectic (289). But Paul does not always argue (compare Eph. 1.3–14 with Rom. 5.1–11). The defence of Pauline authorship in G. B. Caird's *Paul's Letters from Prison* (Oxford: Clarendon Press, 1976, 11–17) still seems to me to be valid. The issue is of some significance, and should not be evaded by too easy a recourse to a 'canonical perspective'. One position makes it possible to see this text as 'the crown of St Paul's writings', while the other can only recommend that it 'should not be wholly disregarded' in an account of Pauline theology (respectively, J. A. Robinson, *St Paul's Epistle to the Ephesians*, London: Macmillan, 2nd edn 1928, vii; J. D. G. Dunn, *The Theology of Paul the Apostle*, Grand Rapids: Eerdmans, 1998, 13n).

as a whole to inform our reading of this part of it. The theme of the letter is 'the many-sided wisdom of God' (Eph. 3.10), and something of this many-sidedness may perhaps be discernible beneath the surface even of an apparently one-sided text that counsels female submission to male headship.

In Eph. 5.18–21, two interrelated imperatives ('Do not be drunk with wine . . . , but be filled with the Spirit' (v. 18)) are followed by four participial clauses that give content to the exhortation to be filled with the Spirit (vv. 19–21): . . . *addressing one another in psalms and hymns and spiritual songs, singing and making melody to the Lord with your heart, always and for everything giving thanks to God the Father in the name of our Lord Jesus Christ, being subject to one another in the fear of Christ* . . . This is the context in which wives and husbands are now singled out: . . . *wives to your own husbands as to the Lord.* Of the four participial exhortations, the second and third speak of a practice directed towards the Lord or God (singing and making melody to the Lord, giving thanks to God the Father), whereas the first and fourth speak of a practice directed towards one another (addressing one another (*heautois*), being subject to one another (*allēlois*)). As in the entire letter up to this point, the addressees are simply 'the saints at Ephesus, who are faithful in Christ Jesus' (1.1). They are men and women, parents and children, slave-owners and slaves, but prior to the 'household code' of 5.22–6.9 they are not addressed *as* men or women, parents or children, slave-owners or slaves.[4] Thus, the exhortations to thankfulness and to mutual subjection are addressed to all, irrespective of gender, age or socio-economic status. It is irrelevant to the exhortation, 'being subject to one another . . . ', that one is a male householder or a female slave, a female householder or a male slave. The various groups do not have to be addressed separately; indeed *they must not be.* 'There is one body and one Spirit, just as you were called in the one hope of your calling; one Lord, one faith, one baptism, one God and Father of all . . . ' (4.4–6). In the one baptism into the one body, distinctions and categories do not

---

[4] The term 'slave-owners' acknowledges that in Eph. 6.9 *kurioi* ('masters') must presumably include *kuriai* ('mistresses').

cease to exist, but they are subordinated to a new, common identity. They are relegated to the background.

This new identity has a history; it has come into being. Although the addressees have always been conscious of themselves as men or women, slaves or free, a consciousness of themselves as 'Gentiles', non-Jews, may not previously have been a significant factor in their identity. Their new identity retrospectively constitutes them as 'Gentiles', only to declare that in the death of Jesus the Jew–Gentile divide has been removed. 'There is neither Jew nor Greek': one new humanity (*hena kainon anthrōpon*, 2.16) has arisen in place of the division, in such a way that Gentiles enter into the heritage of the apostles and prophets which is also the heritage of Israel (2.11–22). An expression of the former hostility may be seen in the offensive way that each group once expressed its abhorrence of the other. To Jews, Gentiles are, collectively, 'the foreskin' (*hē akrobustia*); to Gentiles, Jews are 'the circumcision' (2.11). Women as well as men are included in these designations, since the male reproductive organ is the concern of women as well as men. This hostility was a symptom of an underlying reality: Gentiles really were 'without Christ, alienated from the commonwealth of Israel and strangers to the covenants of promise' (2.12). But now, in Christ, Gentile and Jew are one. They do not simply cease to be Gentile or Jew. Paul continues to distinguish 'we who first hoped in Christ' from 'you also' who heard the gospel and believed it (1.12–13). Nor does the removal of the distinction issue in a 'third race', without antecedents. Insofar as Gentiles are now admitted to the heritage of Christ and of Israel, the 'one new humanity' is still a Jewish humanity (no less Jewish for being universal), and Gentile identity within it is a proselyte-identity. Difference is not erased, and there are moments when it is important to remember it (*mnēmoneuete*, 2.11). Yet difference has been relativized by the one baptism into the one body. That is true of the difference between Jew and Gentile, but it is also true of the difference between male and female, parent and child, slave and free. The fact that the letter as a whole is addressed to all Christians at Ephesus, irrespective of gender, age or socioeconomic status, is an indication that the new, common identity is not just an idea but a genuine social reality, reflecting the theological reality of the eternal divine *oikonomia* whose goal is the summing up (*anakephalaiōsis*) of all things in Christ (1.10).

In the 'household code' (5.22–6.9), it is acknowledged that differences persist within the 'one body' which has hitherto been addressed without differentiation. The new, common identity relativizes differences, but it does not erase them. Within the one body, there are still men and women, parents and children, slave-owners and slaves. They are one but they are also different, just as members of the body differ from one another within the body's comprehensive unity (4.7, 16, 25). Although they participate in Christ's exaltation into the heavenly realms (2.6), they do so while remaining on earth. They remain human, they have not been transformed into angels: indeed, their full humanity is precisely the goal of the divine *oikonomia* (4.13), which comprehends things on earth as well as things in heaven (1.10, cf. 3.15). The differences that are so integral to human life on earth are not obliterated within the one body, for the one body is not a gnostic denial of reality but the divinely ordained context within which human social reality is comprehended and transformed. Thus, an address to 'the saints at Ephesus, who are faithful in Christ Jesus' (1.1) can in the 'household code' acknowledge the differences within the one body by addressing particular groups – wives, husbands, children, parents, slaves, slave-owners – before again subsuming the differences into unity in the general exhortation, 'Be strong in the Lord . . . ' (6.10). The address to particular groups remains relevant to the body as a whole, for the way that wives and husbands, children and parents, slaves and slave-owners relate to one another is not a private concern but the concern of the whole body. If, within the one body, the relationship between a husband and wife is impaired, this is a threat to 'the unity of the Spirit' and 'the bond of peace' that bind together the body as a whole. Within the body there are no purely private concerns; 'for we are members one of another' (4.25).

'Being subject to one another in the fear of Christ, wives to your own husbands . . . ' (5.21–2). The difference between woman and man, wife and husband, is neither eradicated by the new identity nor absolutized. If it had been eradicated, there could be no specific address to wives and husbands; the general, undifferentiated relationship implied by 'one another' would be the only possibility. As the text stands, however, the mutuality of 'one another' does indicate that, although the gender difference is important, it is not all-important. Man and woman may be addressed *as* man or *as* woman, but they may also be addressed together, as humans who participate in the new humanity and who all alike share responsibility for the form of life in which it is expressed. If this new humanity is a true disclosure of 'human nature', it cannot be said of the latter 'that neither man nor woman can manifest nor experience its totality', since 'each gender possesses or represents only one part of it' (Irigaray).[5] Man and woman alike participate in the totality of human nature, and they do so *as* man and woman but also *as* human. Human nature is no more an unmediated 'two' than it is an undifferentiated 'one', and the basis for this assertion is the fact that Jesus establishes peace by 'making the two one' (Eph. 2.14). One does not eradicate two (there are still Jews and Gentiles, men and women); it is a third that mediates between them and thus establishes the peace that is their original *telos*. In the summing up of all things in Christ, the two are one without ceasing to be two; and Jesus' ability to comprehend the two derives not from any absolutizing of a limited (male) experience but from his divine vocation as the bringer of peace. The oneness that he establishes is not a oneness without difference but 'the oneness of the Spirit in the bond of peace' (4.3). It is again the doctrine of the immanent trinity that provides the conceptual model for this coinherence of unity and plurality.

This coinherence is formally illustrated by the exhortation to be 'subject to one another in the fear of Christ, wives to your own husbands . . .' (5.21–2), and it is also closely related to the

[5] Luce Irigaray, *i love to you: Sketch of a Possible Felicity in History*, ET London and New York: Routledge, 1996, 37–8. Other works of Irigaray cited in this chapter are *An Ethics of Sexual Difference* (1984), ET London: Athlone Press, 1993 and *Marine Lover of Friedrich Nietzsche* (1980), ET New York: Columbia University Press, 1991.

specific content of the exhortation. To be subject to another is to give precedence to the claim of the other over the claim one might otherwise advance on one's own behalf. Mutual subjection is the only possible form of life for those who are members of one another within the one body (4.4, 25). As Paul argues elsewhere, to refuse this subjection is to deny that one is part of the body. Yet 'the eye cannot say to the hand, "I have no need of you", nor again the head to the feet, "I have no need of you"' (1 Cor. 12.21). Rather than asserting an absurd claim to independence, we are to conform to a divinely appointed order in which 'the members have the same care for one another' (v. 25). Since this subjection is mutual rather than unilateral, the precedence given to the claim of the other also ensures that my own claim is attended to and is not forgotten – not as the result of my self-assertion but within the context of an inter-dependence in which my claim on another can never be detached from the other's claim on me. To say, 'Be subject to one another' is simply to say, 'We are members of one another.'

Because we are to be subject to one another, wives are to be subject to husbands. So closely is the address to wives bound to the preceding exhortation that there is no need to repeat the verb. The context of the subjection of wives to husbands is this *mutual* subjection to one another. Yet in singling out the subjection of wives without a corresponding appeal to husbands to be subject to their wives, there appears to be a shift from mutual to unilateral subjection. In the following verse (v. 23), the explanation that 'the husband is the head of the wife' confirms this shift: subjection is now a unilateral subjection to a superior who is merely the passive recipient of this subjection without the active response of subjecting himself to his wife. The address to wives has immediately brought us into the sphere of an understanding of marriage in which the male exercises authority over the female and in which the female is bound to submit to that authority. The text takes it for granted that marriage will take this form, just as it takes it for granted that the household will include not only parents and children but also slaves. The crucial question is whether, in the end, the text merely provides a new religious legitimation for the existing form or whether, taking the existing form as its starting-point, it nevertheless transforms it. If Jesus 'is our peace, who has made us both one' (2.14), is this a peace that affirms existing social structures by denying the legitimacy of conflict, or does it overcome a conflict endemic to the structures themselves?

Ideology or utopia: a familiar antithesis that will also determine the relation of the interpreter to the text – for an ideological text is a 'bad' text, whereas a utopian text is a 'good' one. These value judgments have their theological warrant in the assertion that Jesus came not to affirm what already exists but to transform it. But texts may prove recalcitrant when subjected to this critical antithesis. It is not always easy to determine exactly where complicity in an existent form ends and where subversion or transformation begins. Can it be said that the Christ of Ephesians 5 *either* 'functions as a legitimation of patriarchal marriage' *or* 'transforms patriarchal marriage by subjecting it to the criterion of love'?[6] Common to both positions is the assumption that the text is a simple entity with a single underlying tendency, either 'reactionary' or 'progressive', bad or good. In both of its forms, this assumption is itself 'reactionary': for the text is measured against the yardstick of a pre-existing criterion as to what is to count as good or bad, a criterion that it can only confirm (or 'legitimate'). Measured against the prior criterion, the text may be judged to be 'good' or 'bad'; but either way, the prior criterion judges itself to be 'good' and uses the text to reinforce and legitimate its positive self-image. The criterion is the *basis* for interpretation, the field upon which the interpretative game is played, and this excludes *a priori* not only the possibility that the criterion is simply wrong but also the more subtle possibility that it is not given in advance but can be adequately articulated only in and through

---

[6] Ben Witherington finds in this passage a 'new approach to marriage' which is 'Paul's deliberate attempt to reform the patriarchal structure of his day' (*Women and the Genesis of Christianity*, Cambridge: Cambridge University Press, 1990, 156). On the other hand, Sarah J. Tanzer argues that Eph. 5.22–6.9 (in contrast to 2.14) 'is clearly not about equals but about hierarchy; it does not break down dividing walls but rather establishes them and teaches one to live within those hierarchical bounds' ('Ephesians', in E. Schüssler Fiorenza (ed.), *Searching the Scriptures*, vol. II: *A Feminist Commentary*, New York: Crossroad, 1994, 325–48, 341). Both views simplify the passage by ignoring its anomalies.

critical dialogue with the text; that the criterion or criteria by which the text is to be assessed become clear only at the conclusion of the act of interpretation, not at the beginning. A nuanced hermeneutic along these lines is especially necessary in the case of a text as complex as Ephesians 5.22–33.

If one is forced to decide that this is either a 'good' text or a 'bad' one, the basic tendency of the present interpretation is to try to read it as a 'good' text (like 1 Cor. 11.2–16 – on which see chapter 2 – but unlike 1 Cor. 14.33–5 or 1 Tim. 2.11–15, which are clearly 'bad' texts). But whether or not it turns out to be a 'good' text, it is certainly a very *odd* one, and the first of its oddities has already become clear. An exhortation to mutual subjection, firmly grounded in Pauline ecclesiology, shows an unaccountable drift towards *unilateral* subjection when the exhortation is redirected specifically towards wives. The text is in contradiction to itself, and the question is how far it is capable of addressing and overcoming its own contradictions.

For the husband is head of the wife as Christ is head of the church, and is himself saviour of the body. (v. 23) An explanation is given of the subjection required of wives, and it appears to confirm that this subjection is unilateral. The subjection of wives is their recognition of the higher status of the husband, just as the church subjects itself to Christ in acknowledgment that he is its Lord.

The husband is head of the wife, Christ is head of the church: two male heads, exalted over two female subordinates? But maleness operates differently on the two sides of the equation. On the first side, maleness is integral to the argument. The husband–wife relationship is obviously a particular expression of the male–female relationship; an assertion about husband and wife is as such also an assertion about gender. But the relationship between Christ and the church is not so obviously a particular expression of the male–female relationship. Christ is the head of the church and Christ is male, but his maleness is only relevant if the Christ–church relation is located within the polarity of male and female. Christ is a male, but he is also a Galilean Jew who died in his early thirties: all of these facts are necessary for correct identification of the bearer of the name or title 'Christ', but they belong to the background of the assertion that 'Christ is head of the church' and not to its foreground. It is possible that, on the basis of the husband–wife relationship in the first half of the equation, gender is projected onto the Christ–church relationship in the second half; that question will be discussed in connection with the following verse. But as things stand here, it is not clear that the statement 'Christ is the head of the church' entails a maleness corresponding to the husband's. It is not said that the husband is suited to a role analogous to Christ's because Christ too is male.

Elsewhere in the New Testament, Christ's maleness is everywhere assumed but only rarely placed in the foreground. It comes briefly into sharp focus in the dialogue between Jesus and the Samaritan woman, especially at the point where the returning disciples 'were surprised that he was talking with a woman' (Jn. 4.27, in contrast to vv. 7–8, where the primary social boundary that Jesus crosses is the one between Jew and Samaritan, not male and female). The Pauline metaphor of Christ as 'head' is elsewhere not explicitly gendered – even in 1 Corinthians 11.3, where Christ is the head not of a feminine *ekklēsia* but of 'every man', a category which he himself seems here to transcend. The bridegroom-bride image, derived from Old Testament prophetic texts about the relation between Yahweh and Israel, occurs in its full form only in John 3.29, 2 Corinthians 12.2 and Revelation 19.7, 21.2, 9, 22.17 (where the marriage partners are a lamb and a city); elsewhere, the figure of the bridegroom consistently appears without the bride (Matt. 9.15, 22.2, 25.1–13). The maleness of Christ is theologically important only in the event of his circumcision as an eight-day-old child (Lk. 2.21, Col. 2.11), where it is correlated with his Jewishness and his bodiliness. The male–female polarity is less prominent here than the polarity of Jew and Gentile, partly because maleness is established here by the reference to the 'male member' and not by reference to the female.

The New Testament's lack of interest in Christ's maleness is consistent with the suggestion that the husband is not head of the wife because he is of the same sex as Christ, the head of the church. There is an analogy between the two headships, but no rationale for this analogy is provided. More significant is the question of what it means for the husband to be 'head of the wife as Christ is head of the church . . .' It is not said simply that he is head of the wife. If that were all, the assumption would be that to be 'head' is to fulfil a role whose duties and privileges are already well known. But the husband does not fill a well-known role. He is head of the wife *as* and *only as* Christ is head of the church. It is not said that his role is *the same* as Christ's, only that it is *like* Christ's (and, being 'like' rather than 'the same', also *unlike* Christ's). The unlikeness between Christ and the husband is so obvious that one wonders if the husband has here been promoted beyond his abilities. The husband is not 'head of the church', he is not 'saviour of the body', he is not saviour of his wife, he is not the object of her thanksgiving and song (cf. 5.18–19). But he is the object of her subjection, insofar as he is called to fulfil the role of a Christ-like headship. What is the nature of such a role?

As 'head over all things' (1.22), Christ has been exalted 'far above [*huperanō*] every rule and authority and power and lord-ship' (1.21). Is the husband exalted far above his wife? Yet all Christians – men, women, old, young, slaves, free – participate *together* in the exaltation of Christ. It is not said only of men that God has raised them with Christ and made them sit with him in the heavenly realms (2.6); nor is it men alone who in the strength of the Lord wage war against the world rulers of this present darkness (6.10–12). On the contrary, the exhortation to 'be strong in the Lord' (6.10) marks the closing up of the distinctions drawn in the 'household code' of 5.22–6.9. But the concept of exaltation or elevation alone does not adequately characterize Christ's headship. In Paul's interpretation of Psalms 68.19 (LXX), there is no ascent without a corresponding descent. 'What does "he ascended" mean, but that he also descended into the lower parts of the earth? He who descended is the same as he who ascended far above [*huperanō*] all the heavens, so that he might fill all things' (Eph. 4.9–10). If the one who descended is 'the same' as the one who ascended, the descent in question is the descent from heaven in the incarnation; a descent from the heights into the depths which is not simply cancelled out by the return from the depths into the heights, since otherwise Paul would hardly stress the identity of the one who descended with the one who ascended.[7] The headship of Christ over all things is not a matter of ascent alone; it is not only *compatible with* the movement of descent into the depths, it is *constituted* by it no less than by the corresponding movement of ascent into the heights. Headship over all things and over the church is the goal of the one who ascended into the heights because he descended into the depths; it discloses his nature as the one who descended and ascended. It is not the case that the depths are alien to him whereas the heights are his true home. He is truly himself in the depths as well as the heights – so much so that he would not be himself were he (by some impossibility) to be debarred from the depths and confined to the heights.[8] Otherwise it could not be said that the

---

[7] If the 'descent' of Eph. 4.9 is the descent into Sheol or Hades – as J. A. Robinson argues, on the basis of verbal parallels to Pss. 62.10, 118.15 LXX (*Ephesians*, 180) – this must still be seen as the end-point of a descent that begins with the incarnation, if the descent is to match the ascent (cf. Phil. 2.6–8). But *ta katōtera [merē] tēs gēs* may mean no more than 'this lower earth', which is 'low' in contrast to heaven. More significant is the possibility that the descent is *subsequent* to the ascent, and refers to the coming of the Spirit as the giver of the gifts referred to in Eph. 4.11. 'This is the descent of Christ to His Church alluded to in ii.17, "came and preached"; [and] in iii.17, "that Christ may dwell in your hearts" . . .' (T. K. Abbott, *The Epistles to the Ephesians and to the Colossians*, ICC, Edinburgh: T. & T. Clark, 1897, 116). This would be ruled out by the insertion of *prōton* after *katebē* (the majority reading), but this appears to be secondary. (The majority reading does indicate that this text was generally *read* as a reference to the incarnation – and/or descent into Hades.) But a reference to the Spirit is in any case unlikely here: (1) The purpose of the descent that corresponds to the ascent is said to be 'that he might fill all things' (4.10), not that he might bestow gifts (4.11). (2) In the psalm quotation in 4.8, the giving of gifts is the prerogative of the *ascended* Christ (*edōken* in v. 11 refers back to the quotation). (3) An identification of Christ and Spirit is incompatible with the clear distinctions between the 'one Spirit', the 'one Lord' and the 'one God' in 4.4–6 (cf. 1 Cor. 12.4–6).

[8] As Barth argues, 'True Godhead in the New Testament is being in the absolute freedom of love, and therefore the being of the Most High who is high and almighty and eternal and righteous and glorious not also but precisely in his lowliness' (*Church Dogmatics* IV/1 (1953), ET Edinburgh: T. & T. Clark, 1956, 191). Thus, 'Jesus Christ is the Son of God and as such, in conformity with the divine nature, the Most High who humbles himself and in that way is exalted and very high' (192). The close correlation of descent and ascent in Eph. 4.9–10 is important for Barth's presentation of 'the way of the Son of God into the far country' (IV/1, §59.1) and 'the homecoming of the Son of man' (IV/2, §64.2) as two sides of a single divine action. As Eph. 4.9–10 confirms, 'It is not . . . a matter of two different and successive actions, but of a single action in

purpose of the movement of descent and ascent was 'that he might fill all things' (4.10) – making them his permanent dwelling-place, irrespective of whether they are high or low. Otherwise he would bring about no true gathering together or *anakephalaiōsis* of things in heaven and things on earth (1.10).

If the husband is to be head of the wife as Christ is head of the church, he must, like Christ, be familiar with the depths as well as the heights. If so, the wife's subjection to her husband as her head is anything but straightforward. His headship is no longer just an elevated status. Like Christ (but also very unlike him), he comes 'not to be served but to serve' (Mk. 10.45); not to receive subjection (as is the way of 'those who are supposed to rule over the Gentiles' (10.42)), but to subject himself. Starting from the conventional view that his wife is bound to subject herself to him as her head, he has learned from Christ that 'whoever would be great among you must be your servant, and whoever would be first among you must be slave of all' (10.43–4). The wife too starts from the conventional view, but must learn from the church's subjection to Christ what it is to subject oneself to one who has first subjected himself to her. The form of 'patriarchal marriage' is maintained: the wife must submit to the husband as to her head. But behind the facade, its substance is subverted and transformed. The bridging of the gulf between above and below by Christ the reconciler is, if not the abolition, at least the *deconstruction* of patriarchal marriage. The flat contradiction between the mutual submission of Ephesians 5.21 and the unilateral submission of v. 22 is already a sign of the deconstructive process in operation.

THE MYSTERY OF CHRIST (VERSES 24–27)

But as the church is subject to Christ, so also the wives to their husbands, in everything. (v. 24) The husband is the head of the wife 'as' (*hōs*)

---

which each of the two elements is related to the other and can be known and understood only in this relationship: the going out of God only as it aims at the coming in of man; the coming in of man only as the goal and outworking of the going out of God; and the whole in its original and proper form only as the being and history of the one Jesus Christ' (IV/2, 21).

Christ is head of the church; wives are therefore to be subject to their husbands 'as' (*hōs*) the church is subject to Christ. Even if the 'head' metaphor does not in itself give unqualified support to male supremacy, it is obvious that in this passage the relationship between Christ and the church is brought into close connection with the relationship of male and female. But what is entailed in the twofold 'as'? If the relation of Christ to the church legitimates the relation of husband and wife, what is the significance here of Christ's maleness and the feminine gender of *ekklēsia*? How far is there not only a grounding of the male–female relation in the Christ–church relation, but also a corresponding projection of the male–female relation onto the Christ–church relation? The result of this would be that the asymmetry of the male–female relation (in the form of the wife's subjection to the man as head) would be grounded in a Christ–church relation *itself now construed as a male–female relationship*. The Christ–church relation would then be the transcendental, original pattern of the human male–female relation; a kind of Platonic form. Corresponding to the headship of Christ over the church there would be a headship of man over woman, derived not from the fall (as Gen. 3.16 implies) but from creation itself and from the heavenly archetype that precedes creation. Gender inequality would then be grounded in transcendental ontology. Ephesians 5 is certainly open to a platonizing reading along these lines. The question is whether it *requires* it.

Towards the end of his 'theological aesthetics', *The Glory of the Lord* (*Herrlichkeit*, 1961–9), Hans Urs von Balthasar explores the relationship between the New Testament usage of 'glory' (*doxa*) and human sociality.[9] Following Barth, von Balthasar understands the relationship between man and woman as 'the basic form of human togetherness', and finds theological and exegetical warrant for this claim in the Genesis creation narratives and in the New Testament's appropriation of 'the metaphor of the nuptiality between God and Israel' (VII.473, citing Hos. 2.19, Is. 54.4–8, 61.10, 62.4, Ez. 16.7–63, to which might be added

---

[9] Hans Urs von Balthasar, *The Glory of the Lord: A Theological Aesthetics*, VII: *Theology: The New Covenant*, ET Edinburgh: T. & T. Clark, 1989.

the whole of Hos. 1–3, together with later recurrences of the prostitution-motif (4.10–15, 5.3–4); Jer. 3.1–20, 13.26–7, 31.2, Ez. 23.1–49). In Ephesians 5, the Old Testament themes of creation and 'covenantal nuptiality' are 'bound together into a New Testament synthesis' (*The Glory of the Lord* VII. 480). In this passage, it is clear that Paul begins 'by projecting his thought in advance from the creaturely, sexual sphere (which is the subject of his exhortation) to the soteriological sphere'. Thus the Church becomes a female person, 'a reality that is pre-existent in God's election of her', the bride of Christ. 'The relationship between Christ and the Church . . . goes far beyond the natural relationship of the sexes, which finds itself subsumed by the former relationship and given a point of reference utterly superior to itself' (480). But its superiority does not lie in any transcending of gender; in this relationship, the creaturely reality of gender finds its apotheosis. The divine election that precedes the creation of the world (Eph. 1.4–6) is the election of the bride of Christ, and the sexual relationship of man and woman must therefore be seen 'as fundamentally related over and above itself to an eternal, holy and spotless standing before God, in the love of the incarnate Christ for his bride, which is the Church . . .' (482). This marriage, eternally decreed by God, becomes a historical reality when the beloved Son 'shed[s] his blood as a human being and as a man for his bride – which is undeniably a human, feminine bride – in order to give her from himself the form that is to be hers for ever' (483). This form is that of a Marian submission: the existence of the redeemed person is transformed into 'the obedient *fiat* that the Church speaks to God, the perfect *hupotassesthai en panti*, "submission in everything" (Eph. 5.24)' (483). This uninhibited gendering of the church gives corresponding prominence to the maleness of Christ, the bridegroom – and also to that of the bridegroom's father. The feminine *ekklēsia* submits to the masculine Christ, in accordance with the divine decree that established this archetypal male–female relationship before the foundation of the world. As in the conjunction in the *Timaeus* between the paternal demiurge and the maternal receptacle, the relationship of gender contains all things and is itself contained by nothing. We find ourselves in a world in gendered relation to a gendered deity. Feminine submission to masculine headship is the basic principle of this relation.

In §45 of the *Church Dogmatics* ('Man [*Der Mensch*] in his Determination as the Covenant-Partner of God', III/2 [1948]),[10] Karl Barth develops an account of the male–female relationship as the basic and original form of the I–Thou relationship that establishes humanity as, essentially and from the first, co-humanity (*Mitmenschlichkeit*). The essential nature of the human creature is disclosed in the figure of Jesus, who is 'man for God' (§44.1) and 'man for others' (§45.1). 'From the first, in the very fact that he is human, Jesus is not without his fellow-humans, but to them and with them and for them' (209). Jesus' being for his fellow-humans corresponds to his being for God, and there is an *analogia relationis* between his human existence for God and for others and the relationality of the inner-trinitarian divine life: thus in Jesus it is disclosed that human being is being in the *imago Dei* (219–20). This disclosure underlies the phenomenological analysis of human being as co-humanity that follows (§45.2), where Barth analyses the phenomena of eye contact, mutual speech and hearing, mutual help, all willingly undertaken, in the light of the basic thesis that humanity is co-humanity. In sum:

> In its basic form humanity is co-humanity. Everything else which is to be described as human nature and essence stands under this sign to the extent that it is human. If it is not co-human, if it is not in some way an approximation to being in the encounter of I and Thou, it is not human . . . Man is in fact co-human [*Der Mensch ist mitmenschlich*]. He is in fact in the encounter of I and Thou. This is true even though he may contradict it both in theory and in practice; even though he may pretend to be human in isolation and produce anthropologies to match. In so doing he merely proves that he is contradicting himself, not that he can divest himself of this basic form [*Grundform*] of his humanity. He has no choice to be co-human or something else. His being has this basic form. (285–6)

[10] Karl Barth, *Church Dogmatics*, III: *The Doctrine of Creation, part 2*, ET Edinburgh: T. & T. Clark, 1960, 203–324. Quotations are from this part-volume unless otherwise indicated.

At this point (§45.3), Barth identifies the male–female relation as the primary form of the *Mitmenschlichkeit* that is human nature:

> In the whole reach of human life there is no abstractly human [*kein abstrakt Menschliches*] but only concretely masculine and feminine being, feeling, willing, thinking, speaking, conduct and action, and only concretely masculine and feminine co-existence and co-operation [*Zusammensein und Zusammenwirken*] in all these things . . . Man is to woman and woman to man supremely the Other, the fellow-human [*der andere Mensch, der* Mit*mensch*], to see and to be seen by whom, to speak with and to listen to whom, to receive from and to render assistance to whom is necessarily a supreme human need and problem and fulfilment, so that whatever may take place between man and man and woman and woman is only as it were a preliminary and accompaniment for this true encounter between human and fellow-human, for this true being in co-humanity. (286, 288)

As Barth notes, 1 Corinthians 11.11–12 might be regarded as the text for this whole section: 'Nevertheless neither is woman without man nor man without woman in the Lord . . . ' (309). Man and woman belong together. They exist as man and as woman only in relation to the other, and without this belonging together there is no humanity.

All this evokes echoes from previous chapters. 'What we need is to discover how *two* can be made which one day could become a *one* in that third which is love' (Irigaray, *An Ethics of Sexual Difference*, 66): and what is here presented as a project for the present and the future is also the reality of human nature, given in creation. Like Irigaray, Barth is aware of the pervasive tendency to *reduce* the two to one, rather than treating the one as a third; and he is also aware that this characteristically takes the form of the absolutizing of the male – as in the case of Nietzsche. According to Barth, individualistic anthropology reaches its most extreme form in *Ecce Homo*, with its claim that the human is supremely disclosed in Nietzsche himself. It is consistent with this that he has 'no use at all for women' but 'can only ignore them or heap upon them scorn and his choicest invective' (*CD* III/2, 234). In her *Marine Lover: Of Friedrich Nietzsche* (1980), Irigaray confronts precisely this problem, addressing the philosopher directly, in the second person singular.

Like Barth, she regards Nietzsche's misogynistic traits not as an isolated blemish but as a symptom of what is at stake in his entire philosophical project. 'Behold the man': here, *homo* is a man without woman, a man in isolation – and therefore, according to both Barth and Irigaray, a man in contradiction to the basic reality of human nature as the co-humanity of male and female. Nietzsche's *homo* is an extreme version of the much broader phenomenon of man-in-isolation, which (according to Barth) may be traced historically to the fact that 'for so many centuries the philosophical and theological study of the West was the cloister-cell, from whose distinctive I-speculation in the absence of the Thou it has been difficult to break free even outside the cloister' (290). Further back still, there lies the world of the Greeks and their eros – or rather, the world of Greek *males*. 'For all the eroticism of theory and practice, this was a man's world in which there was no real place for woman; and for this reason it was necessarily a world of the I without the Thou, and therefore a world of the I wandering without limit or object, a demonic and tyrannical world' (290). It is true that in the *Symposium*, it is a woman (Diotima) who initiates Socrates into the higher mysteries of eros. But as Irigaray points out, Diotima is not actually present at this all-male drinking-party. 'Diotima is not the only example of a woman whose wisdom, especially about love, is reported in her absence by a man' (*Ethics*, 20). As we have seen, Irigaray identifies a further form of the basic error of reducing two to one (a masculine one) in the tendency to assign to woman opposite and complementary qualities to the qualities that man assigns to himself. Man projects onto woman what he thinks he wants of her, thus recreating her in the image of his own need and depriving her of her own subjectivity. Barth is similarly critical of the notion of complementarity, although not quite for this reason. It may be said, for example, that man is more interested in the objective and the outer, woman in the subjective and inner; that man is inclined towards freedom, woman towards dependence; that man prefers to wander, woman to stay at home. 'Statements such as these may sometimes be ventured as hypotheses, but cannot be represented as knowledge or dogma because real

man and real woman are far too complex and contradictory to
be summed up in portrayals of this nature' (*CD* III/2, 287).
Irigaray too insists on the fact of *difference* but regards its content
as something that must be discovered in encounter and that
cannot be precisely specified in advance.

So far so good? Unfortunately, Barth does wish to say one
thing about the content of the difference, ignoring his own
caveat about the complexity of 'real man and real woman'.
Man has precedence over woman. He is first, she is second.
This is not (he thinks) 'inferiority': without woman man could
not be man, and he is as dependent on her for his manhood as
she is on him for her womanhood. But where there is a
'relationship of super- and subordination', can 'superiority' and
'inferiority' really be excluded? The nature and scope of man's
headship and woman's subordination to it cannot be defined
but must be 'constantly experienced in their mutual exchanges
and co-existence' (287). But what if one cannot find it in the
mutual exchanges of this co-existence (however hard one looks),
or if one finds it only in forms one cannot regard as normative?
Why does Barth insist on this understanding of difference as the
difference of *super* and *sub*, over and under, above and below, a
difference of *elevation*, although his analysis of the basic form of
the I–Thou relationship constitutive of human nature gives
absolutely no grounds for this? The answer is that, like von
Balthasar after him, Barth finds the exegetical key to his
theological anthropology in Ephesians 5. It is only because the
whole range of scriptural teaching on the male–female relation
is in this passage 'set before us so authoritatively and perspicu-
ously' that we find the 'courage' to consider questions that
might otherwise seem beyond us (313). In particular, there is the
question *why* humankind was created as male and female. In the
light of Ephesians 5, the answer is as follows:

Behind the relationship of man and woman as we meet it in the
picture of Genesis 2 and the Song of Songs there stands the control-
ling original of the relationship between the God Yahweh-Elohim and
his people Israel. Behind these passages there stands Old Testament
prophecy. And according to the insight which continually breaks
through, the sum of all truth and actuality, which is thus also the

beginning and end of all things, the secret of creation and its consummation, is the very different duality merely reflected in the nature of man – that of God and man in their co-existence in the concrete form of the covenant established by God between himself and his people Israel. This duality . . . is the original [*das Urbild*] of which the essence of the human as the being of man and woman can only be the reflection and copy [*Reflex und Abbild*]. Man is primarily and properly Yahweh, and woman primarily and properly Israel [*Der Mann heisst zuerst und eigentlich Jahwe und die Frau heisst zuerst und eigentlich Israel*]. (297)

How does the Old Testament know all this? The old hermeneutical principle holds good: *vetus testamentum in novo patet*.

The New Testament answers that the covenant between Jesus Christ and his community was in the beginning, the first and proper object of the divine will and plan and election, and the internal basis of creation. This covenant is the original of the Old Testament original, the relationship between Yahweh and Israel, and therefore the original of the relationship between man and woman. It is on the basis of this original that the intra-creaturely relationship has its dignity and necessity . . . (299)

Man is Yahweh, woman is Israel; or rather, man is Jesus Christ, woman is the church. Conversely, Christ is Man, the church is Woman, and the relationship between this Man and this Woman is the innermost content of the eternal divine decree and therefore 'the sum of all truth and actuality, . . . the beginning and end of all things, the secret of creation and its consummation'. As in von Balthasar, we find ourselves in a world (supposed to be the world of Eph. 5) in which the male–female relation is the container that contains all things and is contained by nothing. In this strikingly Platonic world, the human male–female relation is a 'copy' of a transcendental, heavenly 'original' *that is itself gendered*.[11]

---

[11] The issue of subordination is much more prominent in this section (§45.3) than in Barth's later, more extensive treatment of the male–female relation in CD III/4, 116–240 (§54.1). In the light of the latter section, it might be possible to regard *difference* rather than *order* as Barth's primary concern in this area – the 'difference' presupposed in 'co-humanity', rather than the difference of mere heterogeneity (as, sometimes, in Irigaray). This conception of difference does not entail any prior judgments about the roles appropriate and inappropriate to women: 'Life is richer, and above all the command of God is more manifold, than might appear from preconceived opinions' (III/4, 154). Although Barth (like Virginia Woolf) finds in the

There are several interrelated issues here. One is the absolutizing of gender. That is also present in Irigaray, at moments where her 'ethics of sexual difference' take a metaphysical turn towards a post-Christian neo-polytheism in which the banished gods and goddesses again walk the earth in human flesh. A second issue is the 'vertical' account of sexual difference (absent in Irigaray, present in Ephesians 5 – although by no means as unproblematically as Barth and von Balthasar assume). A third issue, the product of the first two, is the projection of this vertical difference onto the divine–human relation. Does this projection really occur in Ephesians 5? Wives are to submit to their husbands 'as' (*hōs*) the church submits to Christ (Eph. 5.24). Is the church a Wife and is Christ her Husband? Nothing compels one to read into this passage the bridal language of Revelation or the prophetic image of Israel as the adulterous wife.[12] 'As' does indeed imply an analogy, even an *analogia entis* if both divine and human *ens* are inherently relational. But 'as' also implies the dissimilarity or limit that is as integral to the structure of analogy as similarity. 'The kingdom of God is as [*hōs*] a man who casts seed upon the earth . . . ' (Mk. 4.26). The man does so in accordance with the divine decree that he should be a tiller of the ground (cf. Gen. 1.29, 2.5, 15, 3.17–19); and the parable suggests that there is an analogy between this divinely ordained human activity and the divine action signified

---

modern feminist movement a 'desire on the part of women to occupy the position and fulfil the function of men' (III/4, 155), he is also aware of its positive significance in freeing women from 'the uncalled-for illusions of man, and his attempts to dictate what is suitable for her and what is not' (*ibid.*). It would be wrong to regard the notion of the gendered heavenly archetype of the male–female relation as the sum and goal of Barth's treatment of gender.

12　The prophetic depiction of the covenant as the (unhappy) marriage of Yahweh and Israel is one among a number of images of the covenant, and should not be given the systematic status Barth attributes to it. Even in Hosea, the probable source of this image, Israel is to Yahweh not only an unfaithful wife but also a stubborn heifer (Hos. 4.16), an unturned cake (7.8), a dove (7.11), a treacherous bow (7.16), a wild ass (8.9), grapes (9.10), a luxuriant vine (10.1), a trained heifer (10.11), a child learning to walk (11.3–4), a child in the womb (13.13) and a lily (14.5); and Yahweh is to Israel not only a wronged husband but also a moth, dry rot (5.12), a fowler (7.12), a loving parent (11.3–4), a lion, a leopard and a bear (5.14, 13.7–8), dew (14.5) and an evergreen cypress (14.8). Although the husband-wife image is able to say more than these other images, it is not clear that its status is any different from, for example, the parent-child image of 11.3–4.

by 'the kingdom of God'. On this basis, would it be appropriate to find 'the beginning and end of all things, the secret of creation and its consummation' in human agricultural activity, as well as in marriage? If this is inappropriate in the one case, can it be appropriate in the other? 'As' denotes an analogy, and to push an analogy beyond its limit, in the hope that it will yield a metaphysic, is simply to destroy it.[13]

Husbands, love your wives, as Christ loved the church and gave himself up for it . . . (v. 25) The household code is concerned with three relationships: between wives and husbands, children and parents, slaves and their owners. Each of the six groups is addressed, and is exhorted to fulfil the task to which it is called in relation to its opposite number. Thus the subject of an obligation is always also the object of a corresponding obligation. I have a duty to the other, but the other also has a duty towards me. Wives are to be subject to their husbands, but they are also to be the objects of their husbands' love. Children are to obey their parents, but they are themselves to be treated fairly, without arbitrariness (Eph. 6.1–4). Slaves are to obey their masters and mistresses, since in doing so they serve Christ himself; but if their owners represent Christ passively, as the object of service, their own conduct towards their servants must be actively Christ-like in its refusal to resort to threats (6.5–9). The action required of all six groups is not the unilinear action of a subject towards a passive object that lies outside the scope of the address; it belongs in the context of *reciprocal* action. The wife is to be subject to the husband who loves her as Christ loved the church: the pairing of the addressees and the exhortations ensures that each of the exhortations is set within a dialogical movement in which each addressee is both subject

---

[13] The gendered heavenly archetype that Barth finds in Eph. 5 is absent from his collaborator Charlotte von Kirschbaum's treatment of this passage in *Die wirkliche Frau* (1949) – now available in English in *The Question of Woman: The Collected Writings of Charlotte von Kirschbaum*, ed. E. Jackson, Grand Rapids: Eerdmans, 1996. Von Kirschbaum rightly notes that the relationship of Christ and the church in this passage is fundamentally the (ungendered) relation of the head to its own body (65). In general, von Kirschbaum's views are closely parallel to Barth's (as Barth acknowledges in *CD* III/4, 172).

and object of exhortation, and is subject *as* object and object *as* subject. Beneath the surface of the formal symmetry, everything is in constant circular motion. Each of the six groups may impair the to-and-fro, dialogical movement with its opposite number, or even bring it to a halt. The wife may refuse to be subject, the husband may fail to love, the child or slave may disobey, the parent or slave-owner may resort to arbitrariness and violence. Is the exhortation still binding on the other party when its own being as the object of a corresponding obligation is overlooked? The problem is particularly acute for the subordinate partner in each pair (wives, children and slaves). But there can be no prescribing in advance for extreme situations in which the attempt to fulfil one's own obligation is rendered meaningless or damaging by the other's refusal to acknowledge that obligation is mutual. Even under 'normal' conditions, the appropriate form for the fulfilment of one's obligation will not always be easy to determine. All of the exhortations are therefore subject to the qualification: 'Do not be foolish, but understand what the will of the Lord is' (Eph. 5.17, cf. v. 10). Attempts to codify the living, active will and guidance of the risen Lord are necessary, but they can never adequately represent the content of that will and guidance, they can only point towards it.

Wives are to be subject, husbands are to love, children and slaves are to be obedient, fathers are to bring up children in the discipline and instruction of the Lord, slave-owners are no longer to threaten. But is it *only* husbands who love, and not wives, children and parents? If the love in question is Christian agape, can even slaves and slave-owners be exempted from the obligation to love one another? Agape comprehends Christian living in its entirety, and there is no relationship that lies outside its scope, as though at some point agape reached its limit. 'Love never ends' (1 Cor. 13.8): it is not subject to limit. 'The will of the Lord' that we are to 'understand', within our concrete circumstances, will never be anything other than love. We are therefore to 'walk in love, as Christ loved us and gave himself up for us, a fragrant offering and sacrifice to God' (5.1–2). The comprehensive pattern for Christian living is the 'obedience unto death' that is also a 'love unto death' that draws Jesus to Jerusalem, in order to undergo the sufferings of Gethsemane and Golgotha for our sake. Can this action of his really serve as the paradigm for Christian living in its entirety? To understand it as such, we (not on our own, but in the company of 'all the saints') must receive from the indwelling Spirit who is also the indwelling Christ the ability 'to comprehend what is the length and breadth and height and depth, and to know the love of Christ that surpasses knowledge', and thus to live as those who are 'rooted and grounded in love' (3.16–19). To understand Jesus' self-sacrifice in its full dimensions is to see it as the moment in which the divine plan 'to unite all things in him, things in heaven and things on earth' (1.10) comes to fruition – and thus to see one's own life and the relationships in which it is set no longer as the whole but as comprehended within the immeasurable divine love that embraces all things and that wills their reconciliation and peace (cf. Col. 1.20). Love does not call us to new ways of relating to our neighbour without first setting us within these incomparably broad horizons. To be 'rooted and grounded' in *this* love is therefore the bestowal of space and freedom even within the constraints of relationships that may appear to confine us within the narrowest of limits: the relationships of wives and husbands, children and parents, slaves and slave-owners. As the love of Christ embraces these relationships and the individuals held within them, so all alike – and not only husbands – are called to 'walk in love'. This love is present in the depths as well as the heights, and its reach extends to those who are far off as well as those who are near. It dissolves the sharp outlines of asymmetrical, hierarchical relationships liable to hostility and violence, in order that they may attain to 'the measure of the stature of the fullness of Christ' and so become *fully human* (Eph. 4.13: *andra teleion*). There could be no fully human relationships if love was the prerogative of husbands alone.

Husbands are to love their wives; but wives too share in the calling of God to be 'holy and blameless before him in love' (1.4) – a love that includes the husband. This love is what is intended in the exhortation to be subject. Despite the appearance of a unilateral subjection, Christian subjection is *reciprocal* (5.21), and reciprocal subjection is nothing other than reciprocal love. The exhortation to wives to be subject to their husbands and to husbands to love their wives constitutes a *single* exhortation to mutual subjection or love. That at least is its *substance*, behind the facade of an order in which one is still (nominally) above and the other below.

. . . so that he might sanctify it, having made it clean by the washing of water, in the word, so that he might present the church to himself in glory, having no stain or wrinkle or any such thing, so that it might be holy and blameless. (vv. 26–7) At the beginning of v. 26, the feminine pronoun *autēn* might be translated either 'it' or 'her'. (In the phrase translated, 'making *it* clean . . .', there is no pronoun in the Greek.) If gender is projected from the husband–wife relationship onto the Christ–church relationship, then the maleness that is everywhere a background attribute of Christ is here brought into the foreground as the church is feminized. This also affects the translation of v. 25, where a feminine pronoun again refers to the church: did Christ give himself up 'for it' or 'for her' (*huper autēs*)? In v. 27, similarly, the phrase 'so that *it* might be . . .' could also be rendered 'so that *she* might be . . .' Thus RSV translates the relevant passage: '. . . and gave himself up for *her*, that he might sanctify *her*, having cleansed *her* by the washing of water with the word, that he might present the church to himself in splendour, without spot or wrinkle or any such thing, that *she* might be holy and without blemish' (compare NRSV, NIV, JB). The church here is clearly the bride of Christ, prepared for her wedding by her future husband. The passage is then reminiscent of the prophetic image of Yahweh and Israel as husband and wife, and especially of Ezekiel 16.9, where Yahweh reminds his wife (here, Jerusalem) how 'I bathed you with water [*elousa se en hudati*] and washed [*apepluna*] your blood from you, and anointed you with oil'. On the other hand, REB translates the passage: '. . . and gave himself up for *it*, to consecrate and cleanse *it* by water and word, so that he might present the church to himself all

glorious, with no stain or wrinkle or anything of the sort, but holy and without blemish' (compare NEB, AV, RV). On this translation, there is no reference here to the figure of a 'holy and spotless bride' (von Balthasar, *The Glory of the Lord*, VII.480).

The church is to be 'without stain or wrinkle', and the term *rupis* ('wrinkle') might seem to favour the view that the church here is personified and feminized. If the reference is to a *facial* wrinkle, then the *spilos* might similarly refer not to a 'stain' but to some kind of facial blemish. In that case, we behold here the pure, clear complexion of the church; a feminine church, a radiant bride prepared for her wedding day. But the imagery is not consistent. Christ purifies the church 'by the washing of water, in the word' (that is, in the baptism that follows the preaching of the word). Any 'stains' or 'wrinkles' that are removed are removed *by washing in water*; they are not facial blemishes, as though Christ were presented here as a beautician or cosmetic surgeon. The language appears to stop short of personification; there is no clear reference to the face of Christ's partner.

More importantly, Paul has already indicated that the relation of Christ to the church is not that of a husband to his wife but that of the head to the body. Christ is 'the head of the church', and as such he is 'saviour of the body' (5.23); this correlation between the head and the church as his body has also occurred earlier in the letter (1.22–3, 4.15–16) and in Colossians (Col. 1.18, 2.19). The head-body image is too firmly established in this late Pauline theology for it to be possible to sever the head from the body, as it were, in order to reconstitute the body as a distinct person, Christ's bride. The husband is head of the wife 'as' Christ is head of the body, but the analogy is set against the background of fundamental differences. In Ephesians 5.28–30 Paul attempts to make the analogy closer by comparing Christ's relation to the church to the husband's relation *to his own body*, which then in turn illustrates his relation to his wife. The stains and wrinkles that are removed by washing are therefore the marks that must be removed if the church is truly to be Christ's body, growing up into its heavenly head. There is no room here for a transcendent feminine other.[14]

'The husband is head of the wife as Christ is head of the church, and is himself saviour of the body' (v. 23). The point of similarity is confined to the relation indicated by the term 'head'. Otherwise the husband is unlike Christ. He is not head of the church, he is not saviour of the body; he is certainly not saviour of his wife's body. She may acknowledge him as her head, but not as her saviour. Husbands are to love their wives as Christ loved the church (v. 25), and here the point of similarity is confined to the term 'love'. Christ gave himself up for the church; but the husband does not give himself up for his wife. Christ sanctifies and washes the church, removing every impurity so that he may finally be united with it in glory; but the husband performs no such service for his wife. Far from being placed on a pedestal, the husband is helped down from the pedestal on which he may perhaps be standing, so as to stand instead with his feet on the ground, alongside his wife. In comparison with the exaltation of Christ to be our true head, 'far above every rule and authority and power and lordship' (1.21), the earthly pedestal looks ridiculous, and it is a relief to be rid of it and to live the truly human life of mutual agape and subjection rather than the imposing but inhuman life of the figure of marble or stone. In the new covenant, stony hearts are transformed into living human flesh (cf. Ez. 36.26, 2 Cor. 3.3).

---

[14] In opposition to the 'bridal' interpretation of vv. 26–7, E. F. Scott rightly states that 'it is doubtful whether Paul's language ought to be pressed in this somewhat artificial manner' (*The Epistles of Paul to the Colossians, to Philemon and to the Ephesians*, Moffatt's New Testament Commentary, London: Hodder and Stoughton, 1930, 240). E. Schüssler Fiorenza argues that the Ephesians passage takes up the 'Pauline bride-bridegroom notion found for the first time in 2 Cor. 11.2', where it is said: '. . . I betrothed you to Christ to present you [*parastesai*] as a pure bride to her one husband' (*In Memory of Her: A Feminist Theological Reconstruction of Christian Origins*, London: SCM Press, 1983, 269). But the Pauline bride-bridegroom notion is in fact found *only* in 2 Cor. 11.2. The fact that the word 'present' recurs in Eph. 5.27 (*hina parastēsē*) does not imply any transfer of the bridal imagery to this passage. Elsewhere the same verb is used of the body and its members (Rom. 6.13, 16, 19, 12.1); in the light of Eph. 5.23, 28–30, it is as his own body that Christ presents the church to himself (cf. also Col. 1.22).

THE HOMECOMING OF EROS (VERSES 28–33)

Thus husbands ought to love their wives as they do their own bodies. He who loves his wife loves himself. For no one ever hates his own flesh but nourishes and tends it, just as Christ does the church; for we are members of his body. (vv. 28–30) Man's love for his own body is a fleshly love, and to withhold this love – despising the body, regarding it as a corpse to which one's true self is chained – is to be guilty of inhumanity and self-deception. The body stands in constant need of shelter, clothing, food, drink, washing, exercise, relaxation and sleep. Being fragile, it needs to be protected from all that endangers it. From time to time, it will need medical attention (although one should accept with a good grace that the time bestowed on it by God is finite and not unlimited). The body is not to be pampered, but certain comforts are not to be denied it. The dividing-line between what it needs for its survival and what it demands for its comfort is not easy to draw, and to insist on this distinction – although this is often perhaps a necessary corrective – may be to imply the existence of a God other than the creator-God who 'gives generously and without reproach to all' (Jas. 1.5). It is human to love the human body because it is divine to love the human body, and because an alleged divinity that despises the human body and urges the human spirit to do likewise is a false god projected by human self-alienation. Of course, the despairing cry, 'Who will deliver me from this body of death?' has its own rationale and justification. Human self-alienation is real. Yet this cry is immediately followed by a thanksgiving – 'Thanks be to God through Jesus Christ our Lord!' – which arises from the knowledge that the body is not simply the place of death but that, through participation in the death and resurrection of Jesus' body, it finds again its own original life. The resurrection is the recovery of the natural, created life of the body – its securing in the face of all that threatens it.

But in Ephesians 5 the 'natural' love of the fleshly body is invoked in support of the exhortation to husbands to love their wives. It is as unnatural for a husband not to love his wife as it is for him not to love his own body. Since she is a being of flesh and blood as he is, his love for her is a fleshly love. Her flesh – the flesh created by God and declared to be good, not 'the flesh' in its parasitic fallen form – will be the object of his care and attentiveness just as his own flesh is; or rather, she herself in her fleshliness will be the object of his care and attentiveness. This relation is reciprocal, yet the emphasis is placed here not on this reciprocity but on the particular calling of the husband to cherish and tend his wife's flesh as his own – thus fulfilling the commandment to love his neighbour as himself. Within marriage, it seems, agape takes a peculiarly fleshly form. Human fleshliness is another constant factor of human existence which, in any given interaction with another, may stand closer to the background or to the foreground. (In the background during a telephone conversation, it is in the foreground during a medical consultation about a health problem.) Marriage is a mode of human interrelation in which the whole person stands in the foreground, including its fleshly aspect. In marriage, man and woman eat, drink, wash, dress, exercise, relax and sleep *together*, and these are all the affairs of the body. The body of the one is constantly present to the other, in the micro-events of daily life but also in the passage of the years, in which bodily life together moves through its various stages towards its eventual limit. The intimacy of husband and wife differs from other forms of intimacy in the extent to which it is a physical, bodily intimacy. Although agape is never purely bodily, any more than it is ever purely disembodied, it here reveals a marked bias towards the flesh. And, somewhere within this bodily intimacy, hidden yet manifestly permeating the entire relationship, is the factor of eros. If eros must elsewhere be limited in order to preserve the space of agape, at this point eros is to be found *within* the space of agape.

Eros is not the whole, and it would be meaningless to describe it as the most important element in the fleshly agape of marriage, or as at its centre. But it has its own unique importance. It is often said that eros is not only a means to an end (i.e. procreation) but also an end in itself, intrinsically good.[15] But

---

[15] Barth finds this point illustrated by Gen. 2, where 'the reference is to man and woman in their relationship as such, and therefore not to fatherhood and mother-

that is to divide something that is a single though complex phenomenon. Within marriage, there are not two sexual acts, one that intends procreation and another that intends only itself, in its intrinsic goodness. Where this distinction is made, the tendency is to regard 'procreation' as a predominantly biological phenomenon, a non-obligatory supplement to a sexual act whose intrinsic goodness lies in its capacity to spiritualize the flesh. In the 'household code' of Ephesians, however, there is no disjunction between the relation of husband and wife and the relation of parent and child (however limited the Pauline treatment of this latter relation may be). Rather than accepting a duality of mutuality and procreation, it is preferable to suppose that there is within marriage a *single* sexual act whose mutuality is intrinsic to it *as the precondition of the procreation that the act intends*. From a biological point of view, it is clear enough that the act intends procreation. But this 'biological point of view' is no more than a single strand within the complex, living continuum in which a third party comes into being and begins to participate in the shared bodily intimacy of those it will learn to address as its 'mother' and 'father'. Procreation is primarily a social event, and only as such is it also a biological event. But sexual union is also a social event, and it is as the *social* precondition for procreation that it is also its biological precondition. The immediate, 'normal', normative social context of the begetting, conceiving, bearing and rearing of children is the relation of physical intimacy between man and woman within which there is the special physical intimacy of sexual union.

Why, apart from biological considerations, is this particular act a necessary precondition of the physical intimacy into which there may enter a third, a fourth, a fifth . . . ? Husbands, we recall, are to love their wives 'as their own bodies' (Eph. 5.28). In marriage, agape takes a peculiarly fleshly form, disclosing

hood or the establishment of the family. . . The relationship of man and woman has its own reality and dignity' (*CD* III/2, 293; compare *CD* III/1, 312–15). But the eroticism of Gen. 2.23–5 and the call to procreation of Gen. 1.28 should not be separated from one another. In the exegesis of Gen. 1–2 that occupies most of *CD* III/1, the sharp distinction between the 'P' and 'J' creation accounts means that connections are sometimes overlooked.

here a bias towards the physical intimacy of bodily proximity. The bodies of husband and wife are near one another and constantly present to one another. Yet in cohabiting, eating, sleeping or ageing together, considered in themselves, they remain two. The body of the other is in close proximity to one's own body, but it is not *as* one's own body. The body continues to occupy its own space and its boundary remains intact, even where the two bodies establish physical contact with one another through touch. It is true that all physical intimacy involves a single, shared space. But that shared space (or shared space-time) is the external space *within which* the body exists, in proximity to the other; it is the social and physical space that *contains* one's own body and the body of the other. There is, so far, no sharing of *the space of the body itself* – the internal space marked out and enclosed by the boundary between body and world. Physical proximity to the other does not in itself cross this boundary. That crossing of the boundary into the bodily space of the other, at the same time an admission of the other into one's own bodily space, is what occurs in sexual union. In sexual union, the body continues to occupy its own space, but it does not do so alone. Its own space is now also the space of an other, a shared space. This shared space is a shared physical space, but it cannot be reduced to this any more than it can be reduced to a purely biological phenomenon. My body is (secondarily) a biological phenomenon and its space is a physical space, but it is in the first instance the possibility and the locus of my own life as lived among others. The mutual crossing of the bodily boundary is the social event that completes or 'consummates' the bodily intimacy of marriage, establishing the peculiar nature of marriage as that social relationship in which even the internal space of the body itself is not withheld. It is not the *telos* of that bodily intimacy; one does not live, eat, sleep with another *for the sake of* sexual union. It is more like the keystone of an arch, or the final piece in a jigsaw puzzle, without which the whole would be deficient, although once it is in place it need not continue to draw special attention to itself but exists only within a larger whole. Human arbitrariness or inventiveness can find new uses for the act of sexual union; the keystone of an arch or a piece of a jigsaw puzzle can no doubt be set within very different structures. But these will not be their natural habitat. And the natural habitat of sexual union is the physical intimacy of marriage, which it completes in the mutual opening-up even of the previously enclosed space of the body itself.

If the original and normative context for sexual union is marriage, then the original and normative context for eros is agape. Marriage is not necessarily characterized by agape. It is said to the woman that, in marriage outside paradise, 'Your desire shall be for your husband and he shall rule over you' (Gen. 3.16): the imbalance here between her desire and his rule suggests a disruption and distortion of the original goodness of the co-humanity of male and female. Agape is the proper *telos* of marriage, but it is disclosed as such only in Christ, the embodiment of the divine-human agape. Apart from this disclosure, how clear would it be that agape is the *telos* of marriage? The assumption that 'love' (or 'romantic love') is the primary basis for marriage is often said to be an innovation of the modern West. It is certainly a central preoccupation of the *novel*, the literary genre most characteristic of the modern West. The novel holds up a mirror to what is held to be the reality of 'love and marriage'; it is the image of a representation that arises from the reality and exercises an influence over it, although the reality is never reducible to the representation.[16] In the image of the novel, certain conventional assumptions about love become visible. One character 'falls in love' with another, and this is equivalent to his wanting to marry her. If she announces that she 'cannot love him', this is equivalent to a refusal of marriage. Outside the sphere of the modern West, the assumption that this love is the indispensable and sufficient condition

---

[16] The novel may be seen as a 'representation of reality', as in the subtitle of E. Auerbach's *Mimesis*, but it may also be seen as the 'image' of a 'representation of reality' given in discourse (or 'ideology'). I have in mind here a model analogous to Fredric Jameson's proposal that the literary text be seen 'as the rewriting or restructuration of a prior historical or ideological *subtext*, it being always understood that that "subtext" is not immediately present as such, . . . but rather must itself always be (re)constructed after the fact' (*The Political Unconscious: Narrative as a Socially Symbolic Act*, London and New York: Routledge, 1989, 81).

for marriage is, perhaps, much less 'natural'. But in the present context the more important question is how this modern western 'love' is related to agape. Even in the traditional novel, the link between love and marriage is in fact contingent. Marriage is often an end (the end of the novel), and not a transition to a new beginning. If marriage is the *goal* of love but not the context of its continuing development, is marriage tacitly presented as the *end* of love? Where, at the beginning of the novel, marriage has already occurred, love may well be sought outside marriage; the rendering of a love that both issues in marriage and develops and matures within it is much less usual (in spite of *Anna Karenina*, where this theme is rendered in counterpoint with the more traditional theme of extra-marital love). The more recent convention that 'love' is the pre-condition not of marriage but of 'sex' is a natural development of tradition rather than a reaction against it. 'Modern' and 'traditional' novels tend to display an ambivalence towards marriage combined with an unshaken faith in 'love' itself. (Where this faith in love is withheld, leaving behind only a loveless 'sex', the novel will be self-consciously cynical in tone.) These novels are familiar with the assumption that marriage is the proper context and home of love, but, in declining to make this assumption narratively *plausible*, their tendency is to induce scepticism towards it. They thereby hold up a mirror to the combination of faith in 'love' and ambivalence towards marriage that characterizes the representation of reality in discourse. If 'love' is seen as the blending of agape (a commitment to the whole person?) and eros (sexual attraction), then marriage is not its natural context or home in practice, even if it ought to be in theory; or so we are led to suspect, both by the novel and by the 'experience' that it reflects and shapes. If the novel holds up a true image, the modern West is the place where it is assumed both that love is the precondition and foundation of marriage and that this assumption is questionable or untrue. In this context, the claim that marriage is the home of a love that reflects the relationship of Christ and the church appears to belong only to the ethos of idealization, fragile aspiration and half-truth that pervades a wedding service. Only rarely does a novel (or the discourse that it reflects) show any knowledge of the divine-human agape that is the foundation of all things or of the possibility that marriage might be an expression of this reality.

The original and normative context for sexual union is marriage, just as the original and normative context for eros is agape: this is not a self-evident truth but a distinctively Christian insight (whatever analogies there may be elsewhere). It follows that extra-marital sexual relationships that claim to be based in 'love' are not in fact a true expression of agape. Agape is in the first instance 'the love of Christ'. In Ephesians 3.18–19, to 'know the love of Christ that surpasses knowledge' is equivalent to comprehending 'what is the breadth and length and height and depth'. The breadth and length and height and depth of the love of Christ surpass knowledge, but they may nevertheless be imperfectly but really known. They are known not by detached observers but by those whose entire lives are 'rooted and grounded in love' (*this* love, the love of Christ). The breadth of the love of Christ lies in its embrace not only of those who are near but also of those who are far off (2.17). There is no spatial limitation to the love of Christ on the horizontal plane. The length of the love of Christ is seen in the absence of temporal limitation. The love of Christ precedes the beginning – before the foundation of the world we were chosen in the beloved and for love (1.4–6) – and it outlasts the end, enduring for ever. The height and depth of the love of Christ indicate the absence of any vertical limit. We are not referred simply to an earthly event that would leave space for quite different events elsewhere, but to an event that expresses the divine plan 'to unite all things in Christ, things in heaven and things on earth' (1.10). The love of Christ is not marked off by any external limit. Is there an *internal* limit, set by the body of the beloved? But this body is Christ's own body; he is its head. The body cannot live without the head, nor can the head live without the body: to sever the head from the body is to destroy both head and body. Head and body occupy their own space, but they also share a single space. Just as there is no external limit to the love of Christ, whether spatial or temporal, so there is no internal limit.

Head and body are one. A man's care for his own body is an image of Christ's love for the church (5.29–30); but this image is merely a transition to the image of the love of Christ that is found in the love of man and woman.

If there is to be an inner-human image of the love of Christ within the eros of man and woman, there must be a counterpart here to the absence of limit. The agape of marriage must be marked by the absence of a *spatial* limit. Physical proximity is the norm here, but this agape is not destroyed by temporary physical separation. Separation is not to be seen as a welcome opportunity to behave for a while as though this agape did not exist. Nor is there any *temporal* limit to this agape, other than the limit of human existence itself. This agape is not a short-term or renewable contract, and divorce is fundamentally alien to it. To this absence of an *external* limit, spatial or temporal, there corresponds an absence of *internal* limit. The boundary that encloses the space of the body itself is no longer sacrosanct, but dissolves into the shared space of two bodies become one flesh. Agape here occupies the territory of eros.

'For that reason a man shall leave his father and mother and shall be joined to his wife, and the two shall become one flesh.' This is a great mystery; I speak of Christ and the church. However that may be, let each of you love his own wife as himself, and let the wife respect her husband. (vv. 31–3) The scriptural text (Gen. 2.24) speaks of marriage – not in the distorted forms it takes after the fall (Gen. 3.16) but in the original, created form that still subsists beneath the distortions and that becomes visible again when the existing institution of marriage is exposed to the light of Christ. 'When anything is exposed by the light it becomes visible, for anything that becomes visible is light. Therefore it is said: Awake, O sleeper, and arise from the dead, and Christ shall give you light' (Eph. 5.13–14). The daylight that Christ brings dispels the dreams and nightmares of the dark and discloses the world as it truly is. His disclosure of the original nature of marriage makes it possible for marriage, the relation of man and woman as husband and wife, to bear witness to him in his relation to the church. As we reflect on the nature of this belonging-together of man and

woman, we are also compelled to speak of the love of Christ for the church; and as we set these realities alongside one another, allowing the greater to illumine the lesser but also the lesser to illumine the greater, we learn to know the love of Christ and the love of man and woman in new and unforeseen ways. Rooted and grounded in the love of Christ for the *ekklēsia*, the love of man and woman becomes an acted parable of that love, and in pointing to the love that is its own comprehensive context it also uncovers its own true meaning. Thus it can be said of the love of man and woman as originally created by God: 'This is a great mystery.' *Sacramentum hoc magnum est.* It is not that this fleshly, material reality becomes transparent to a higher, spiritual reality, losing its own proper being in the process. There is no sacrifice here of the letter to the spirit. The correspondence of the lesser love to the greater love confirms and establishes the lesser love in setting it within its proper context, which is the mystery of God's will, his plan for the fullness of the times to gather up and reconcile all things in Christ (1.9–10).

If this plan is a reality, then we should expect to see correspondences, partial, frail, yet actual, between earthly phenomena (the *phaneroumena* illumined by the divine light (5.14)) and the peace and love of Christ. These phenomena will then become *parables*. Jesus' own parables are 'the prototype of the order in which there can be other true words alongside the one Word of God, created and determined by it, exactly corresponding to it, fully serving it and therefore enjoying its power and authority' (Barth, *CD* iv/3, 113).[17] As Jesus utters his parables, 'the material is everywhere transformed, and there is an equation of the kingdom with them, and of them with the kingdom, in which the being, words and activities of labourers, slave-owners, kings, fathers, sons, etc., become real testimony to the real presence of God on earth, and therefore to the events of this real presence' (113). Labourers, fathers, sons, yet not only men but also women: women bread-making or searching for a lost coin, bridesmaids awaiting the arrival of the bridegroom. If

---

[17] Barth's concept of 'parable' in this well-known section (§69.2, 'The Light of Life') is more appropriate to the male–female relation than an approach that elevates it into a uniquely privileged image of 'the sum of all truth and actuality' (*CD* iii/2, 297).

women as well as men inhabit these stories, the original belonging-together of man and woman might itself become a parable. Eve is present to Adam and Adam to Eve, for the first time, in unashamed nakedness; and this fleshly belonging-together finally dispels the possibility of a solitary male existence that the Creator himself has declared to be 'not good' (Gen. 2.18). This parable is acted out whenever 'a man leaves his father and his mother and is joined to his wife, and the two become one flesh'. But that common occurrence is not yet the meaning of the scriptural parable; in it, the parable becomes an *acted* parable, and the meaning of this acted parable is 'Christ and the church'. The correspondence between parable and meaning is anything but arbitrary, for both of them have their place within the single divine *oikonomia* (Eph. 1.10, 3.9). 'The order of reconciliation' is also 'the confirmation and restoration of the order of creation', and within it 'the eternal meaning and content of the order of creation is worked out in the one order of God . . .' (*CD*, iv/3, 43). It is perhaps not appropriate to describe the belonging-together of man and woman in agape and eros as the first or the greatest of the parables, but it must still be said: *sacramentum hoc magnum est.*

The parable is a mystery, and the divine *oikonomia* is a mystery of *reconciliation*. The crucified Christ reaches out to embrace Gentiles, formerly at enmity with the people of Israel but now a holy temple built upon the foundation of the Jewish apostles and prophets (Eph. 2.11–22). In Christ, the two become one as the enmity is dispelled (2.14). Is this also true of man and woman? 'No man hates his own flesh' (5.29); but it is unfortunately possible for a man to hate his own wife, and he must therefore repeatedly be exhorted to love her (5.25–33). It is also possible for a woman to despise her husband, and she is therefore exhorted to respect him (5.33). There is every possibility that this relationship of physical intimacy will degenerate into a vicious circle of hatred and contempt, within which age-old stereotypes and postures that divide man and woman will once again come to expression. Children too may be drawn into this abyss. They are subject to the divine command, 'Honour your father and mother', and to the promise of well-being that accompanies it (6.2–3). But how are they to honour a father who dishonours their mother, or a mother who dishonours their father? For them, there is no inclusive parental agape to serve as an earthly image of the love of Christ that surpasses knowledge. Where, on the other hand, there is mutual love and mutual subjection, the *oikonomia* of the home may become for them an image of the *oikonomia* of God. Within this parental order, there is an explicit 'instruction and discipline of the Lord' (6.4); but the inclusive agape of husband and wife also has its part to play in handing down to the next generation the knowledge of the divine agape embodied in Jesus. Where there is this agape, it may be said: 'He is our peace, who has made the two one, breaking down the dividing-wall of enmity in his flesh' (2.14).

This reconciliation of man and woman is also the reconciliation of agape and eros. Within the corporate life of the *ekklēsia*, the symbol of the veil marks a boundary that eros is not to transgress if agape is to be preserved. Forcibly separated from agape, eros is left out in the cold. We should not feel too sorry for him, however, for his exclusion is the result of his own shameless attempt to recreate the human person in his own image – not from without but from within, in the sinister form of *concupiscentia*, the law of sin that dwells within me. Like Milton's Satan, eros cannot bear to be merely a creature. He must be divine and wield a divine creative power. Yet as the eroticized human person is a distortion rather than a genuinely new creation, so this divinized eros is a distortion of a creaturely reality which continues to participate in the original divine affirmation. In the beginning, God saw everything that he had made, culminating in the human creature in its twofold existence as male and female – and behold, it was very good. In the agape of man and woman, eros sheds his pretensions, like the prodigal son in the far country, and returns home.

Index of subjects

abortion, 160–1
Acts of Paul and Thecla, 10
adultery, 133n, 215–17
agape, ix, 1–2, 41, 77–8, 92, 148–9, 151,
   155–6, 183–5, 187, 206–18, 243–6,
   249–59
analogy, 242–3
androcentrism, 58–9
angels, 217–18
Arianism, 43
Athanasian Creed, 10
authority, women's, 69–70

Birmingham, 25–7
bodiliness, 99–102, 250–3

canon, 130, 131n
castration, 23–4, 192
Congregation for the Doctrine of the Faith, 88
contraception, 99, 160–1, 193–4
creation, 55, 57–9, 62–5, 80–2, 115, 127,
   144–5, 186, 204, 213–17, 259
Cynics, 158–9

demythologizing, 71, 137
difference, 3–4, 189–90, 193, 204, 239–40
dress code, 13–14, 23

equality, 75, 80n
eros, 1–2, 41, 52–4, 56–7, 60–1, 63–4,
   66–9, 70, 78, 79–80, 92, 183–4,
   195–6, 206–18, 249–59
essentialism, 187n
eugenics, 123

Fascism, 17, 18–20
feminism, 5–6, 7, 15–16

guilt, 126

headship, 230–4, 248–9
hermeneutics of suspicion, 127, 222,
   229–30
hierarchy, 43, 55–6, 139n
historicism, 89
Holy Spirit, 148–52, 210, 217–18
homosexuality, 66–8, 81–2

image of God, 56
incarnation, 150–1
interdisciplinary work, vii–viii
intertextuality, 163

Judaism, 103, 118n, 136–8, 173

law, 103–4
London, 8–11, 13, 25–7

maleness of Christ, 230–2, 234–43
marriage, 98–9, 138–41, 157–9, 216, 229,
   249–59
misogyny, 81
Montanism, 48, 84–6

nature, 86–8
'new perspective', 134n, 137–8, 142–3
novel, 253–5

obedience, 219–22
Oedipus complex, 32, 79–80, 115–16,
   197–202
otherness, 238

pacifism, 17–28
parable, 186, 242–3, 257–8
parenthood, 194–6, 250–2, 258–9
patriarchy, 4–6, 11, 25, 27, 73–4, 80n, 141,
   188, 202n, 229
patriotism, 23

260

Index of names

Index of scriptural texts

CABRINI COLLEGE LIBRARY
610 KING OF PRUSSIA RD.
RADNOR, PA 19087-3699

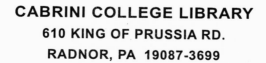

DEMCO